The Nobile Officium

*The Extraordinary Equitable Jurisdiction
of the Supreme Courts of Scotland*

To Eugenie

The Nobile Officium

The Extraordinary Equitable Jurisdiction of the Supreme Courts of Scotland

Stephen Thomson

LLB (Hons), LLM (Res) (by Thesis), PhD, Dip LP (Edin)
Assistant Professor, Faculty of Law,
The Chinese University of Hong Kong

Edinburgh
Avizandum Publishing Ltd
2015

Published by
Avizandum Publishing Ltd
25 Candlemaker Row
Edinburgh EH1 2QG

First published 2015

ISBN 978-1-904968-33-7

British Library Cataloguing in Publication Data
A catalogue entry for this book is available from the British Library

Typeset by Waverley Typesetting, Warham, Norfolk
Printed and bound by Martins the Printers, Berwick on Tweed

CONTENTS

FOREWORD

by LORD HOPE OF CRAIGHEAD KT

As Stephen Thomson has explained in his fascinating introduction to this book, it is far from easy to pin down exactly where the *nobile officium* that we are familiar with comes from and how exactly its jurisprudential basis can be explained. Moreover the words themselves, with their echo of the Praetorian power discussed by the Civilian commentators, make it sound a little more imposing, and perhaps rather more imperious, than in practice it really is. They suggest something that is elegant, notable, high-born or superior. But it would be more accurate to translate the noun "*officium*" by giving that word one of its ordinary meanings which is simply "function", and to translate the adjective "*nobile*" as meaning no more than "extraordinary". It is an extraordinary function because it gives the Supreme Courts of Scotland, within which it resides, the jurisdiction to do something out of the ordinary to prevent oppression or injustice where no other remedy or procedure is available. Because it is open-ended and there are no fixed rules or limits that govern its exercise, it is by its nature equitable. But it is not a licence to do whatever the court thinks fit. Its exercise is governed by principles, and it is those principles that give it its legitimacy.

The modern approach to the powers that courts can exercise is to define them as closely by statute as possible. As little as possible is left to judicial discretion, which governments are inclined to distrust. They tend to conclude that, because the judges are unelected, any decisions that stray outside what they have provided for themselves through legislation lack democratic legitimacy. So where powers are given they are usually set out in considerable detail, and more and more of what was formerly part of our common law is being redefined by statute. Devolution has assisted this process to an extent that was rarely possible when the only route for legislative reform was through Westminster.

These developments suggest that the opportunities for the exercise of the *nobile officium* today are much more limited than they once were. But, human nature being what it is, there is always room for error in the framing of statutory rules or for oversight in deciding what needs to be regulated by statute. The extraordinary and unexpected, for which no provision has been made and for which no other remedy is available, may suddenly appear in circumstances which show that the system has broken down and call out for something to be done by a court to prevent injustice. When these situations arise they will require an immediate solution which is crafted to the needs of each case, of a kind which a court can provide and which cannot await the attention of the legislature. It is to the credit of our legal system that it has created this highly unusual vehicle to enable challenges of that kind to be met. The author is surely right to conclude in his final chapter that it should not be assumed too readily from the fact that this jurisdiction is now not often exercised that it is in terminal decline.

But if the jurisdiction is to serve its purpose, it needs to be properly understood and to be applied in the right way. It needs to be invoked wherever it is needed to prevent injustice, and the courts need to be encouraged to use it. In the past this was often left to chance, as so little guidance as to its use was given in the textbooks. Nor had any attempt been made to conduct a systematic analysis of the subject. This book fills that gap. But the author is really being too modest when he says in his Preface that it is just a first step towards doing so. And this is more than just a textbook. What he has given us is a work of real scholarship, which makes a significant contribution to the literature on Scots law. We must all be grateful to him for having persisted with his impressive research to the point of bringing it to publication in this form.

DAVID HOPE
14 February 2015

PREFACE

The Court of Session and the High Court of Justiciary each have an extraordinary equitable jurisdiction known as the *nobile officium*. Notwithstanding centuries-long pedigree, the jurisdiction has evaded comprehensive scholarly scrutiny, discussed in a modest scattering of short articles, occasional paragraphs and encyclopaedic entries. It has, to the best of my knowledge, never been the subject of a dedicated study in its own right. Lord Kames described the *nobile officium* in his *Historical Law Tracts* as "so much talked of, and so little understood" and yet, over two centuries later, little progress has been made despite the jurisdiction's continued invocation in the supreme courts. There is uncertainty among Scots lawyers, of both a practitioner and academic persuasion, about the status and scope of the jurisdiction. There is, in short, a gap in the literature on the *nobile officium*, and this text aims to be a substantial first step towards filling it.

Being the first of its kind, this book has presented some significant challenges. The subject matter is fairly specialised, and yet the *nobile officium* is by its nature general; even vague. Holders of high judicial office have urged caution in treatment of the *nobile officium*. Lord Justice-Clerk Alness warned in *Gibson's Trustees, Petitioners* that it would be "inadvisable to attempt any definition of the circumstances" in which the *nobile officium* may or may not be exercised, whilst Lord Blackburn stated in the same case that it would be "idle to attempt to define precisely all that is included in the term *nobile officium*". More recently, Lord Justice-Clerk Ross declared in *The Royal Bank of Scotland plc v Gillies* that it is "neither possible nor desirable to define exhaustively or comprehensively all the circumstances in which resort may be had to the *nobile officium*", and similar notes of caution have sounded elsewhere in the case law. A systematic treatment of the subject is surely overdue, however, and as such this book aims to catalogue the *nobile officium* jurisprudence, draw out principles and patterns and systematise the subject.

The *nobile officium* may be applied to any issue which is justiciable in the supreme courts of Scotland, although it has made a more frequent appearance in particular subject areas. Among these are such diverse areas as trusts, bankruptcy and statutory omissions. The book is organised by the principal areas in which the *nobile officium* has seen activity, with a "miscellaneous procedure" chapter collecting a number of the remaining, multifarious applications of the jurisdiction.

The book must nevertheless resist any overstatement of a categorical framework of applications to the *nobile officium*, not least because of the general scope of the jurisdiction and its necessarily open-ended nature. The text seeks to bring together the many applications of the jurisdiction and to provide a commentary, analysis and rationalisation of the subject matter. The hope is that practitioners, teachers and students of Scots law are provided with a central resource which provides an overview of the jurisdiction past and present, and offers general guidance on how and when it might be appropriate for application. It also seeks to raise more general awareness of the jurisdiction and its potential for application.

The structure of the book has posed a particular challenge, primarily in the form of bringing shape to a discussion of what is in principle a catch-all jurisdiction for the transaction of miscellaneous cases across the whole sweep of Scots law. This presented the challenge of how best to present the themes which have emerged in the exercise of the *nobile officium*, whilst refraining from overstating or even claiming its systematic nature, and ensuring that themes and patterns are not presented as categorical or mutually exclusive. The range and structure of chapters is a trade-off between bringing an appropriate degree of structure to the text, and avoiding repetition where cases fall under more than one heading. For example, a number of bankruptcy cases involve a statutory omission, but these are primarily discussed in the bankruptcy chapter because that is one of the areas of substantive law where the *nobile officium* has been particularly active. Although a number of cases would legitimately fall to be discussed in more than one chapter, repetition is kept to a minimum.

A significant methodological challenge encountered at the research stage has been the intermittent lack of clarity in the law reports on whether the *nobile officium* or some other jurisdiction is being exercised in a given case. Whilst the jurisdiction is sometimes explicitly stated as exercised, at other times its exercise is a matter of inference, whether or not the term is mentioned in the rubric of the law report. There are several examples of cases in which no explicit reference was made to the *nobile officium* being described in later cases as exercises of that jurisdiction. There are far more cases in which the term "*nobile officium*" appears in the rubric of the case but not in the report itself. It may be too formalistic to regard only those cases that explicitly identify the *nobile officium* as the sole instances of its exercise, not least because the *nobile officium* has not always been a discrete jurisdiction governed by its own procedural rules. However, there are obstacles to the adoption of a purely functional approach.

First, the *nobile officium* is ill-defined and has been applied inconsistently in the case law. It almost certainly goes too far to regard all instances of equitable discretion as exercises of the *nobile officium*. One could point to many instances of an equitable discretion being exercised in the sheriff court, for example, and yet the *nobile officium* is reputed to be an exclusive jurisdiction of the Court of Session and the High Court. Likewise, not all petitions were made to the *nobile officium*, but could be made to other aspects of the courts' jurisdiction. Equitable discretion exists in many shades and forms, and the *nobile officium* is just one jurisdictional capacity in which the supreme courts act when transacting a "higher form" of equity. As such, the inclusion of all cases in which there has been an exercise of (inherent) equitable discretion would wrongly expand the scope and jurisprudence of the *nobile officium*, bringing many cases under that heading which ought not to be so regarded. This also has practical consequence, for an application which ought not to be properly regarded as made to the *nobile officium* should in general not be directed to the specialised procedure for invoking that jurisdiction. As the courts are cautious about exercising the *nobile officium*, and will tend only to intervene on this basis where no other remedy is available, one should not petition the *nobile officium* too freely. As discussed in the introduction, however, there is no bright line between the *nobile officium* and more generic equitable and common law powers, further complicating the task of classification.

The book has sought to strike a middle way between formalistic and purely functional positions, but has erred on the side of caution. Whilst attempt has been made not to adhere to a formalistic approach, I have been slow to infer an exercise of the *nobile officium* unless there has been good reason for doing so. A more adventurous position would have required a wider study of equity in Scots law, which would have exceeded the research parameters of this book.

I am very grateful for the generous support of the Clark Foundation for Legal Education on which the publication of this book has depended. I am also grateful to Margaret Cherry at Avizandum Publishing for her guidance and confidence in the project. I would like to express my sincere thanks to Professor James Chalmers of the University of Glasgow for his valuable comments on the High Court chapter, and to Christopher Wilson, Advocate, for evaluating the book as a whole. The final text remains, of course, my sole responsibility.

STEPHEN THOMSON
Hong Kong
April 2015

TABLE OF CASES

TABLE OF STATUTES

TABLE OF ORDERS, RULES
AND REGULATIONS

CHAPTER 1

INTRODUCTION

1.1 General introduction

The *nobile officium* is the extraordinary equitable jurisdiction of the supreme courts in Scotland. It is the jurisdiction by which the Court of Session and the High Court of Justiciary may perform such equitable actions as supplying a legal norm where an existing norm is deficient, unavailable or absent, and alleviating the rigour of the strict law where its application is unduly excessive, oppressive or burdensome. It is vested solely in the supreme courts, with inferior courts enjoying no *nobile officium*.[1]

The essence of the *nobile officium* is an equitable, rather than a strictly legal, jurisdiction. This means that the intending petitioner comes to the court not as a matter of legal right, but of equitable supplication.[2] He seeks not to vindicate a legal right, but to entreat the court to assist where it has no strict legal obligation to do so. It is an appeal made on the basis of justice, fairness and equity, one made in the spirit of the law, rather

---

[1] Viscount Stair, *The Institutions of the Law of Scotland* (5th edn, 1832, John Shank More (ed)) IV, 3, 1; W J Lewis, *Sheriff Court Practice* (6th edn, 1913, W Green) at 22; Thomas Alexander Fyfe, *The Law and Practice of the Sheriff Courts in Scotland* (1913, William Hodge) at 28; Viscount Dunedin et al (eds), *Encyclopaedia of the Laws of Scotland* (W Green, 1926–35) ("*Dunedin Encyclopaedia*") vol VI at 279–80; and James Avon Clyde, "Translator's Note" in Sir Thomas Craig of Riccarton, *The Jus Feudale* (1934, William Hodge) vol 1 at xxii. The Upper Tribunal does not have a *nobile officium*: *Eba v Advocate General* 2011 SC 70 at 89 per Lord President Hamilton.

[2] See, eg, *Burnett v St Andrew's Episcopal Church, Brechin* (1888) 15 R 723 at 731 per Lord President Inglis. See also *London and Clydeside Estates Ltd v Aberdeen District Council* 1980 SC (HL) 1 at 45 per Lord Keith of Kinkel and *Royal Bank of Scotland plc v Gillies* 1987 SLT 54 at 55 per Lord Justice-Clerk Ross. A student textbook from 1896 described applications to the *nobile officium* as "in cases for which there is no legal authority and requiring no *judicial* decision, but rather an equitable or *administrative* remedy": William Kinniburgh Morton, *Manual of the Law of Scotland* (1896, W Green) at 14.

than its letter. It has been said that the jurisdiction "involves the exercise of the court's discretion to provide a remedy where none would otherwise be available, in circumstances where the interests of justice clearly require it",[3] and that the "purpose of the *nobile officium* is to prevent injustice or oppression where the circumstances are extraordinary or unforeseen and where no other remedy or procedure is provided by the law".[4] The petitioner should "demonstrate that, unless a remedy is granted, he will suffer injustice or at least is at material risk of doing so".[5]

Although these principles have significant practical utility, the *nobile officium* is also symbolically important in recognition of the legal system as a vehicle for the attainment of justice, and not merely for what is legally due in the strict sense. It aims, in that regard, to fill a gap between imperfect law and justice. Lord Kames alluded to this idea when he wrote that "it is the province, one should imagine, of the sovereign, and supreme court, to redress wrongs of every kind, where a peculiar remedy is not provided", and that it would "probably in time produce a general maxim, [t]hat it is the province of this court, to redress all wrongs for which no other remedy is provided".[6] Although this would also filter into other equitable aspects of the courts' jurisdiction,[7] it finds its most quintessential expression in the *nobile officium*.

This is not a routinely invoked aspect of the courts' jurisdiction. On the contrary, there will be in the vast majority of cases an established legal basis on which the court will adjudicate, whether in vindication of a civil or criminal right, or in response to a civil or criminal wrong. In few cases will there be no existing or available legal avenue for redress, or a sufficiently onerous or oppressive provision requiring equitable

---

[3] *La Torre v Lord Advocate and Scottish Ministers* 2008 JC 72 at 74 per Lord Nimmo Smith.
[4] *Perrie, Petr* 1992 SLT 655 at 658 per Lord Justice-General Hope; see also *Cochrane v HM Advocate* 2006 JC 135 at 140 per Lord Justice-General Hamilton.
[5] *Henvey v HM Advocate* 2011 SCL 531 at 536.
[6] Kames, *Historical Law Tracts* at 228–29. Kames was referring to the Court of Session.
[7] See Section 1.3.

alleviation. Where another remedy or avenue of redress exists, the courts will usually require that such alternative channel is utilised. The *nobile officium* is a failsafe; it is, tersely put, a remedy of last resort.[8]

One of the essential features of the *nobile officium* is indeed its extraordinary nature. The jurisdiction is in most cases regarded as appropriate for invocation only where some exceptional, unusual or special circumstance has arisen which justifies and requires the equitable intervention of the court. This is not an easy threshold to satisfy, and the courts will not exercise the *nobile officium* lightly. There should usually be some pressing sense of need, injustice or oppression,[9] in addition to the unavailability of other avenues of redress, before the court will seriously entertain a petition to its *nobile officium*.

The jurisdiction is, by its nature, general and even vague. It attracts cases of miscellaneous substance, and is at the margins of judicial activity. It could hardly be otherwise. Its jurisprudence has, at its core, a shared feature of exceptional, unusual or special circumstances which, for some reason, give rise to a need or desire for equitable intervention. Those circumstances can arise and have arisen across the board, and potential for application can be found in almost every department of the law, from trusts and sequestration, to public office and criminal law.

The *nobile officium* is invoked by way of petition, under Chapter 14 of the Rules of the Court of Session 1994, or Chapter 29A of the Criminal Procedure Rules 1996 for an application to the High Court. In the Court of Session, the *nobile officium* resides by default in the Inner House, though certain petitions to the *nobile officium* must now be presented to the Outer House.[10]

---

[8] See Section 10.4.

[9] See, eg, *MacPherson, Petrs* 1990 JC 5 at 14 per Lord Justice-General Hope.

[10] Rules of the Court of Session 1994, r 14.2. Getting this wrong may result in the petition being rejected – even where the intending petitioner has acted on the advice of the court administration. See, eg, *Strock, Petr* 1996 JC 125 and *Institute of Chartered Accountants of Scotland, Petrs* 2002 SLT 921. Historically, petitions to the *nobile officium* had to be directed to the Inner House (see, eg, Lord Cooper of Culross, "The Central Courts after 1532" in

The *nobile officium* of each court is recognised in both primary[11] and secondary[12] legislation. There is no requirement to call a party as contradictor, such that many cases have proceeded with just a single party to proceedings. Nevertheless, a party might oppose the petition or lodge answers, and a number of cases have proceeded adversarially. Although the *nobile officium* may be invoked by way of petition, the courts also reserve the power to exercise the jurisdiction *ex proprio motu*, in the course of other proceedings.

Conform to the flexibility and versatility of the *nobile officium*, the court may award any remedy, do any thing or authorise or ordain any act it thinks fit in exercise of the jurisdiction. In the Court of Session, this includes the standard

---

An Introduction to Scottish Legal History (1958, Stair Society) at 345). For the historical context to the distribution of *nobile officium* business between the Inner and Outer House, see, eg, *Mitchell, Petrs* (1864) 2 M 1378; *Greig, Petrs* (1866) 4 M 1103; *Campbell, Petr* (1867) 5 M 1052; *Aberdeen University Court, Petrs* (1901) 4 F 122; *Snodgrass, Petr* 1922 SC 491; *Barton v London, Midland and Scottish Railway Co* 1932 SC 113 at 120 per Lord Ormidale; *Cockburn's Trs, Petrs* 1935 SC 670; *Brown, Petrs* 1936 SC 689; *Smith's Trs, Petrs* 1939 SC 489; *Laird's Trs* (12 May 1939, Court of Session, unreported); *Myles, Petr* 1951 SC 31; *Viscountess Ossington's Trs, Petrs* 1965 SC 410; *The Scots Style Book* (1905, W Green) vol 7 at 2; James Maclaren, *Bill Chamber Practice* (1915, William Hodge) at 4–5 and 253–54; Robert Berry (ed), *Balfour's Handbook of Court of Session Practice* (5th edn, 1922, W Green) at 206; and *Dunedin Encyclopaedia*, vol X at 330–32. Lord Nimmo Smith's recent statement that the *nobile officium* may, in a civil case, "only be exercised by the Inner House of the Court of Session" should be modified to take account of rule 14.2(c): *Helow v Advocate General* 2007 SC 303 at 305. It was suggested that there may have been some presumption in favour of the competency of the *nobile officium* when there was no "delegation of … authority" to the Lord Ordinary or the sheriff to be found in a statute: *Whyte v Northern Heritable Securities Investment Co Ltd* (1891) 18 R (HL) 37 at 40 per Lord Watson.

[11] See, eg, Civil Jurisdiction and Judgments Act 1982, s 22(3); Legal Aid (Scotland) Act 1986, s 25(6) (as amended by Criminal Procedure (Consequential Provisions) (Scotland) Act 1995) and s 30(3)(b); Criminal Procedure (Scotland) Act 1995, ss 298(1) and 298A (as amended by Criminal Proceedings etc (Reform) (Scotland) Act 2007); and Criminal Justice and Licensing (Scotland) Act 2010, ss 132, 134 and 162.

[12] See, eg, Act of Sederunt (Rules of the Court of Session 1994) SI 1994/1443, sch 2, paras 14.2 and 14.3 and Act of Adjournal (Criminal Procedure Rules Amendment No 2) (Contempt of Court) SSI 2009/243, r 2.

menu of remedies: declarator, reduction, suspension, interdict, implement, restitution, payment (including damages) and any interim order. In the High Court, it encompasses any order of the court including quashing a conviction or sentence. The *nobile officium* would, however, be unlikely to be used to impose or increase a sentence, as that would be an instance of aggravation rather than mitigation.[13] The court can dismiss a petition to the extent of one of several parties at whom it is directed.[14] In either court, an *ad hoc* remedy may be fashioned for application in the particular circumstances of the case. In addition, the court may award the remedy sought, award part of the prayer only,[15] or add one or more conditions as part of the award.[16]

The question has been posed of whether equitable jurisdiction might not also operate in the other direction to equitable mitigation, namely equitable aggravation.[17] It might, for example, be argued to be equitable for an unduly lenient sentence to be increased to render justice to the aggrieved parties and in the public interest. However, aside from objections to this from the perspective of legal certainty and predictability, equitable aggravation is not the character which has been assumed by the *nobile officium*. The jurisdiction has typically rendered "equity" to the petitioner to alleviate, mitigate or relieve his situation. Lord Ardmillan, for example, described the court's equitable function as one mitigating "the severity of the general rule by interposing in exceptional cases".[18] Although this may potentially have an adverse effect on some other party, it will rarely be calculated against the other party. As such, the *nobile officium* has been

---

[13] Though fines were imposed in *Atkins v London Weekend Television* 1978 JC 48. This was, however, an exceptional case in the context of contempt of court. See the following paragraph on equitable aggravation.

[14] See *Atkins v London Weekend Television* at 51.

[15] As, eg, in *Silverstone, Petr* 1935 SC 223.

[16] See, eg, *Grahame v Magistrates of Kirkcaldy* (1881) 8 R 395, discussed below at pp 170–71.

[17] See, eg, Martha C Nussbaum, "Equity and mercy" (1993) 22(2) Philosophy & Public Affairs 83–125; and John Tasioulas, "The paradox of equity" (1996) 55(3) CLJ 456–69.

[18] *Nicolson v Nicolson* (1869) 7 M 1118 at 1124 per Lord Ardmillan.

typified by equitable mitigation rather than equitable aggravation – its exercise tends towards a loosening, alleviation, amelioration and mollification; indeed, towards equitable relief.

The *nobile officium* has a more substantial historical pedigree in the Court of Session than in the High Court. Whereas the volume of petitions in the Court of Session has seen a general decline, there are now more petitions presented in the High Court. Notwithstanding a general decline in its exercise,[19] the *nobile officium* remains available for invocation in either court in cases of need. It was written in 1856 that the *nobile officium* was, even then, "seldom mentioned now except with a sneer",[20] yet many cases of its successful invocation would follow, and it continues to be exercised to the present day. The jurisdiction is there to be utilised in deserving cases.

The remainder of this chapter will give historical and conceptual context to the *nobile officium* prior to the book's exploration of the various areas of law in which the jurisdiction has seen activity.

1.2 Historical background

The *nobile officium* of the Court of Session is a legacy of its open-textured history. The Court was established in 1532 as the first centralised, characteristically judicial institution in Scotland. Although formally established by statute,[21] it inherited much of its jurisdiction from various manifestations of the king's council by which it was preceded. This included broad and indeterminate powers to interpose in disputes and to render equitable relief to persons in need. In short, it included aspects of equitable as well as more strictly legal jurisdiction, framed by only a generally expressed statutory framework.

Occasional references have been made to a more ancient source or comparator power for the *nobile officium* vested in the Roman praetor. Reference was made in a case before the House

---

[19] See Chapter 11.

[20] Henry Cockburn, *Memorials of his time* (1856, Adam and Charles Black) at 128.

[21] College of Justice Act 1532.

of Lords to the "praetorial power" of the First Division of the Court of Session.[22] Elsewhere, Lord President Clyde said that it:

> may not be easy to trace historically the connexion between what the commentators called the *nobile officium* of the praetor (Vulteius, De Judiciis, II. iv. 431; Bartolus, Ad Digestum, II. i. 12, *De jurisdictione omnium judicium*), and what we know as the *nobile officium* of the Court of Session.[23]

Regardless of whether a connection or analogy is made with the Roman praetor, the genesis and heritage of the Court of Session and its jurisdiction would lend foundation to the claim that the Court is one of law and equity.[24] In terms of historical pedigree, that is in sharp contrast to the separated legal and equitable judicatures in England, with equitable jurisdiction principally vested in the Court of Chancery until its consolidation with the High Court of Justice in the late nineteenth century.[25] This formal division was not impressed upon the Scottish legal system, where a much looser blend of legal and equitable powers was combined in a single court. Lord President Inglis said that:

---

[22] *Whyte v Northern Heritable Securities Investment Co Ltd* (1891) 18 R (HL) 37 at 39 per Lord Watson (referring to an argument advanced before the court).

[23] *Gibson's Trs, Petrs* 1933 SC 190 at 199. The praetorian connection was also made by Stair, IV, 3, 1–2; John Erskine, *An Institute of the Law of Scotland* (5th edn, 1824) I, VII, 54; Cockburn, *Memorials of his time* at 128; and Cooper of Culross, "The Central Courts after 1532" at 345.

[24] See Henry Home (Lord Kames), *Principles of Equity* (5th edn, 1825, Bell & Bradfute) at 32; Erskine, *Institute*, I, III, 22; Ilay Campbell, *Hints upon the Question of Jury Trial* (1809, Harding and Wright) at 22–23; Alexander Cockburn, *Our Judicial System* (1870, William Ridgway) at 15; Aeneas J G Mackay, *The Practice of the Court of Session* (1877, T & T Clark) vol 1 at 208; *Dunedin Encyclopaedia*, vol VI at 273 and 277–78; *Nicolson v Nicolson* (1869) 7 M 1118 at 1124 per Lord Ardmillan; and *Eba v Advocate General* 2011 SC 70 at 84 per Lord President Hamilton. See also *Grahame v Magistrates of Kirkcaldy* (1882) 9 R (HL) 91 at 97 per Lord Chancellor Selborne; and *Snodgrass, Petr* 1922 SC 491 at 495 per Lord Salvesen. The Court of Session has also been described as a "supreme court of equity": *Stevenson v Hamilton* (1838) 1 D 181 at 205 per Lord Meadowbank and *Hall's Trs v McArthur* 1918 SC 646 at 654–55 per Lord Skerrington.

[25] Supreme Court of Judicature Acts 1873 and 1875. Some reasons for the absence of a separate court of equity in Scotland were posited in *Dunedin Encyclopaedia*, vol VI at 275–76.

> We administer an equitable as well as a common law jurisdiction; and
> we are in the exercise of that mixed jurisdiction of law and equity. ...
> It is quite competent to a Judge presiding at a trial of issues in this
> Court to address to the jury principles of equity as well as rules of
> law.[26]

This long-standing compound of powers makes it difficult to
separate exercises of legal and equitable jurisdiction by the
Court of Session. From an early date, the Court has interposed
in cases without sharp distinction being drawn between different
jurisdictional capacities in which the Court might be acting. It
is difficult to disentangle aspects of common law jurisdiction,
supervisory jurisdiction, the *nobile officium* and broader equitable
jurisdiction, especially in the earlier jurisprudence. It may even
be anachronistic to distinguish these powers in the Court's earlier
period. One of the driving factors behind the institution of the
Court was an attempt to improve the standards of justice prevailing
in the Scottish legal order, and the Court assumed an important
role in the improvement and maintenance of those standards. The
idea of the Court as a guardian of civil justice, and an overseer
of standards prevailing in the wider legal order, was present from
an early stage. This basic sense of a supereminent authority and
jurisdiction vested in the Court was the normative wellspring
for what would and should now be separately identified as the
supervisory jurisdiction and the *nobile officium*.[27] It also serves as
the historical foundation for the Court's broader equitable remit,
discussed in Section 1.3.

Although these powers have an essentially shared heritage
and historical foundation, distinctions have emerged as the Court

---

[26] *Forrest and Barr v Henderson* (1869) 8 M 187 at 195 per Lord President Inglis.
It was stated by Lord Neaves at 203 that "equity will temper the strictness of the
law by its merciful interposition". Although the *nobile officium* is mentioned in
the rubric, it does not feature anywhere in the quite lengthy judgment, and might
not be an accurate classification of the case.

[27] Lord President Inglis' statement that it was "not of very much consequence" to
determine whether certain supervisory powers of the Court were aspects of its
nobile officium may be a product of the rather more amorphous view of both
its supervisory jurisdiction and *nobile officium* prevailing at that time: *Forbes v
Underwood* (1886) 13 R 465 at 468.

and its jurisprudence have developed. Indeed, as the Court's jurisprudence has evolved, it has become possible to distinguish between different jurisdictional capacities in which the Court has been adjudicating, a distinction made easier by the development of its procedural rules. So far as procedural access is concerned, the *nobile officium* has been channelled into Chapter 14 of the Rules of Court, and the supervisory jurisdiction into Chapter 58. As discussed below, however, there are remaining difficulties and ambiguities in distinguishing between the Court's various powers.

Viscount Stair described the *nobile officium* as arising from a Roman jurisdictional distinction between *officium mercenarium* and *judicium nobile*; or as the terms were applied in Scotland, *officium ordinarium* and *officium nobile*, respectively. He explained that the:

> Lords of Session have both the *officium ordinarium* and *nobile*; for it is only in some cases, that they may proceed, not according to the ordinary forms ... but in new cases, there is necessity of new cures, which must be supplied by the Lords, who are authorised for that effect by the institution of the College of Justice ... [I]n many cases, it is necessary wherein they may have recourse from strict law to equity, even in the matter of judgment.[28]

Unlike in England, Stair explained that "[o]ther nations do not divide the jurisdiction of their courts, but supply the cases of equity and conscience, by the noble office of their supreme ordinary courts, as we do".[29] John More, in his notes to the second volume of the 1832 edition of Stair's *Institutions*, observed that it was both difficult to define the limits of the *nobile officium* and to trace its origin, but the jurisdiction included a capacity to dispense with the strict rules of law.[30] Stair's view of equity was broader than what would fall under the scope of the modern *nobile officium*, for it included not only "that part of the law or

---

[28] Stair, IV, 3, 1. See also Campbell, *Hints upon the Question of Jury Trial* at 21–22.

[29] Stair, IV, 3, 1.

[30] Stair, ccclxxiv (notes by John More).

jurisprudence ... which supplies the omissions or corrects the excesses of pre-existing law", but also "the principle, spirit, or reason which underlies the whole law, its general rules or particular decisions".[31] This view of equity would not conflict with the doctrinal foundation of the *nobile officium*, however, which can be conceived as rationally connected to the same equity which underlies all law (if that view is adopted), but manifesting in a distinctive way when the "equity" of the law founders. John Erskine, for his part, described that the Court of Session, in its capacity as a court of law and equity, "may and ought to proceed by the rules of conscience, in abating the rigour of the law, and in giving aid, in the actions brought before them, to those who can have no remedy in a court of law".[32]

Not all of the commentary on the *nobile officium* has been endearing, particularly in the later eighteenth century. Notable is John Martin's indignant polemic, which denounced the *nobile officium* as a "legal monster".[33] It seems that the *nobile officium* complained of was somewhat more liberally applied than the narrower *nobile officium* of the modern day, but there remain familiar concerns expressed about the very concept of equitable jurisdiction. Martin described the *nobile officium* as the "arbitrium" or "will of the Judges" – uncertain and continually changing, "[w]hat is equity with one Judge, is iniquity with another".[34] He criticised Erskine for allowing to the Court of Session "a remedial power over positive law",[35] and variously described the jurisdiction as inconsistent, arbitrary, unlimited, illegal, unconstitutional, despotic and absurd.[36] These comments were reminiscent of John Selden's renowned view of equity:

---

[31] See *Dunedin Encyclopaedia*, vol VI at 258–59 and 274–75. These two meanings of equity have been regarded as contradictory, for in one law is equity, and in the other equity is opposed to law: *Dunedin Encyclopaedia*, vol VI at 259.

[32] Erskine, *Institute*, I, III, 22.

[33] John Martin, *An Inquiry into the State of the Legal and Judicial Polity of Scotland* (1792, W Creech) at 102.

[34] Martin, *State of the Legal and Judicial Polity* at 101–02.

[35] Martin, *State of the Legal and Judicial Polity* at 101.

[36] Martin, *State of the Legal and Judicial Polity* at 102–69.

> Equity is a roguish thing: for law we have a measure, know what to trust to; equity is according to the conscience of him that is chancellor, and as that is larger or narrower, so is equity. 'Tis all one as if they should make the standard for the measure we call a foot, a chancellor's foot; what an uncertain measure would this be? One chancellor has a long foot, another a short foot, a third an indifferent foot: 'tis the same thing in the chancellor's conscience.[37]

James Boswell described the *nobile officium* as a "kind of undefined arbitrary jurisdiction",[38] with Lord Cockburn calling it "dangerous".[39] Gilbert Stuart described it as a "supereminent ... boundless jurisdiction" which "carrying in its use and nature the precarious justice, and the unprincipled rudeness of a barbarous age, is not to be considered as a right, but as a deformity".[40] Stuart viewed the jurisdiction as a source of arbitrariness and despotism, in a "wild hostility with our constitution":[41]

> [To] urge that the *nobile officium* belongs to the court of session, as a court of equity, is to propagate a tenet in every respect frivolous. For equity has its rules as well as law, and depends not on what is called the moral sense or the conscience of particular men. It is to make a farce of all jurisprudence, and of all justice, to talk of equity as merely a deposit in the breast of a judge, and not as artificial, regular, and systematic. It is to exalt the dictates and the caprices of individuals about the wisdom and experience of ages, above evidence, authorities, and rules. It is to advance judges into despots.[42]

Of particular grievance to John Martin was the manner in which the Court is alleged to have purported to legislate by Acts of Sederunt, which were variously charged as a means of repealing

---

[37] Frederick Pollock (ed), *Table Talk of John Selden* (1927, Selden Society) at 43.

[38] James Boswell, *A Letter to the People of Scotland on the Alarming Attempt to Infringe the Articles of the Union* (1785, London) at 5. Stair also touched on the potential for arbitrariness: Stair, IV, 3, 1.

[39] Cockburn, *Memorials of his time* at 128.

[40] Gilbert Stuart, *Observations concerning the Public Law and the Constitutional History of Scotland* (1779, W Creech) at 268.

[41] Stuart, *Observations concerning the Public Law* at 275–77.

[42] Stuart, *Observations concerning the Public Law* at 272. In these references to the rule-based and systematic quality of equity, the author appears to have had the English system of equity in mind.

and extending statutory provisions, imposing taxes and penalties, and enacting penal laws.[43] In a similar vein, John More expressed concern that the Court of Session may have carried the *nobile officium* "beyond its just limits", as in the case of an Act of Sederunt from 1756 on leases.[44]

If the *nobile officium* was previously used in this manner, the present-day *nobile officium* is a far more disciplined and restrained jurisdiction. If it was ever a pretext for the performance of administrative or quasi-legislative functions, or the imposition of penalties when the statute was silent, it retreated some time ago from that adventurous position.[45] The jurisdiction will emerge in this book as a generally more moderate power which in modern times is exercised cautiously, exceptionally and infrequently.

Note should be taken of the potential role of the Scots Privy Council in the Court of Session's equitable powers. Lord Kames had written that the Court succeeded to the "noble office" of the Scots Privy Council on its abolition in 1708,[46] and it was contended by Lord President Hope that the Court's supervisory jurisdiction was essentially inherited from the Scots Privy Council upon and

---

[43] See, eg, Martin, *State of the Legal and Judicial Polity* at 107–26 and 134–37. See also Erskine, *Institute*, I, III, 22, who described the "ministerial powers" of the Court; and J D B Mitchell, *Constitutional Law* (2nd edn, 1968, W Green) at 33, who described various "administrative" acts of the Court, and noted Ilay Campbell's view that the *nobile officium* was an encroachment upon the executive power of government.

[44] John More, *Lectures on the Law of Scotland* (John McLaren ed) (1864, Bell & Bradfute) vol 2 at 250. Lord Cooper of Culross wrote that the Court's output of Acts of Sederunt was "prodigious", and that the Court "applied a very liberal interpretation to their powers as a subordinate legislature and enacted much new law": "The Central Courts after 1532" at 345.

[45] See *Dunedin Encyclopaedia*, vol X at 325. It is possible that some of this activity which took place under the guise of the *nobile officium* was inspired by similar activity under the *nobile officium* of the Scots Privy Council, which had since been abolished: see Peter G B McNeill, *"The Jurisdiction of the Scottish Privy Council, 1532–1708"* (PhD thesis, University of Glasgow, 1960) at 94.

[46] Kames, *Historical Law Tracts* at 228. See also More, *Lectures on the Law of Scotland* at 250; and Morton, *Manual of the Law of Scotland* at 14.

following its abolition.[47] However, Lord President Hamilton stated in *Eba v Advocate General* that Lord President Hope's claim "now appears to be doubtful",[48] referring to several cases by way of illustration and to the work of Mark Godfrey.[49]

It is submitted that the correct position is that the Court enjoyed a supervisory jurisdiction, coloured with equitable overtones, from an earlier period than the time of the abolition of the Scots Privy Council. The present writer has uncovered further substantial evidence for that view, to be presented in forthcoming work. The contention is therefore that any powers previously enjoyed by the Scots Privy Council, which passed to or were assumed by the Court upon or following the Privy Council's abolition,[50] joined an existing fund of equitable powers resident in the Court. This includes equitable powers which would in the present day be considered aspects of either the supervisory jurisdiction or the *nobile officium*. Nevertheless, caution should be exercised in describing the modern-day supervisory jurisdiction as an exercise, development or close comparator of the *nobile officium*.[51] It is respectfully submitted that the recent description of

---

[47] *West v Secretary of State for Scotland* 1992 SC 385 at 393–94 per Lord President Hope.

[48] *Eba v Advocate General* 2011 SC 70 at 84 per Lord President Hamilton. See also David M Walker, *A Legal History of Scotland: The Seventeenth Century*, vol IV (1996, T & T Clark) at 826–27.

[49] A M Godfrey, *Civil Justice in Renaissance Scotland: The Origins of a Central Court* (2009, Brill, Leiden and Boston).

[50] For just one indication of this, see the petition presented to the Court of Session in *Lynd and Sandilands, Petrs* 1744 Mor 7433, in which were cited authorities from the Scots Privy Council. On the *nobile officium* of the Scots Privy Council, see McNeill, *Jurisdiction of the Scottish Privy Council* at 92–99. On the Council's broader equitable jurisdiction, see McNeill at 68–108.

[51] As described in *City of Edinburgh District Council, Petrs* 1990 SCCR 511 at 518; *Helow v Advocate General* 2007 SC 303 at 305; *Eba v Advocate General* 2010 SLT 547 at 565–566; *Eba v Advocate General* 2011 SC 70 at 84; *G v Watson* [2014] CSIH 81 at para [21]; Lord Clyde & Denis Edwards, *Judicial Review* (2000, W Green) at paras 2.08 and 3.01–3.05. Lord Jones exercised caution in this regard in the recent case of *McCue v Glasgow City Council* 2014 SLT 891 at 899. It has been stated that the Court's "general power to review the proceedings of all inferior Courts" falls under the *nobile officium*, though it was conceded that this was "perhaps not strictly an equitable jurisdiction": *Dunedin*

the *nobile officium* as "the court's broad equitable jurisdiction"[52] is not sound, for reasons explained below.

In the criminal context, the office of Justiciar dates from at least the twelfth century.[53] The Justiciar had "supreme cognisance of all controversies of every kind"[54] acting in the name of the monarch and exercising a delegated jurisdiction of royal justice in matters civil and criminal.[55] He held the king's court, the *Curia Domini Regis vel Justiciarii*.[56] The monarch served the historical role of fount of justice (*fons aequitatis*), culminating in the criminal context in royal mercy and pardon.[57] The Justiciar's close association with royal justice may suggest an early capacity for equitable interposition and mitigation in this branch of jurisdiction. In addition, David Hume observed that the Scots Privy Council (which was vested with the prerogative of mercy[58]) was in use of naming assessors to the Justiciar and

---

Encyclopaedia, vol VI at 279. However, this is again viewed through the lens of an earlier period when there was less of a distinction between the Court's supervisory jurisdiction and its broader equitable powers.

[52] *Eba v Advocate General* 2011 SC 70 at 84.

[53] W C Dickinson, "The High Court of Justiciary" in *An Introduction to Scottish Legal History* (1958, Stair Society) at 408.

[54] David Hume, *Commentaries on the Law of Scotland respecting Crimes*, vol II (1844, Bell & Bradfute) at 1. See, however, *Stair Memorial Encyclopaedia*, Courts and Competency, vol 6 at para 854.

[55] A quite detailed overview of the Justiciar is given by Hume, *Commentaries*, vol II at 1–15. Civil and criminal jurisdiction have not always been sharply defined. Furthermore, the Scots Privy Council exercised civil and criminal jurisdiction, and this points to the shared heritage of general "judicial" power originally flowing from royal authority. Further discussion of this point is beyond the scope of the present work.

[56] *Stair Memorial Encyclopaedia*, vol 6 at para 850. See also A A M Duncan, "The Central Courts before 1532" at 324.

[57] Whether used or "abused" – *Stair Memorial Encyclopaedia*, vol 6 at para 854. It could of course be argued that, depending on the circumstances, mercy or pardon is inequitable.

[58] McNeill, *The Jurisdiction of the Scottish Privy Council* at 37. McNeill stated (at 66) that the Council had the power to "modify the pains inflicted by other courts". The Council's exercise of this power was "limited and personal" in its effect, and constituted "acts of grace which mitigated pains and punishments ... directly in the case of punishments and more formally in the case of suspensions and liberations". The King and Council also had the power to suspend the decree of any jurisdiction inflicting pains and punishment, and the Council had the

his deputies for advice in extraordinary cases,[59] indicating an early association with extraordinary business.

The holding of justiciary courts was attempted in the second half of the fifteenth century,[60] and over time the jurisdiction of the Justiciar became solely criminal. The Court of Justiciary was established by statute as the supreme criminal court in 1672.[61] This was a reconstitution of the court and a consolidation of its authority.[62] The Court of Justiciary was described by Hume as having almost universal jurisdiction in the trial of crimes,[63] and as the "Supreme Criminal Judicature" it had a "natural pretension to take cognisance of all offences".[64] The High Court of Justiciary is the direct descendant of that court,[65] and has been said to have, to a large extent, the power to "determine the limits of its own jurisdiction, so long as this does not conflict with what Parliament has provided".[66]

This broad, open-textured heritage of the High Court would serve as a foundation on which equitable powers could propagate. The *nobile officium* has historically been rather more identified with the Court of Session, and the powers of the High Court have sometimes been discussed by reference to their civil counterpart. Archibald Alison, for example, described the High Court's power as "[a]kin to the well known *nobile officium* of the Court of Session",[67] whilst *Renton and Brown* referred to the High Court's "exclusive power of providing a remedy for all extraordinary or

---

power to issue letters of supersedere giving a period of freedom from diligence to allow a debtor to clear up his accounts or attend court without molestation, and to grant equitable release from civil and criminal imprisonment (McNeill at 100–08).

[59] Hume, *Commentaries*, vol II at 15.
[60] Dickinson, *The High Court of Justiciary* at 408.
[61] Courts Act 1672.
[62] Hume, *Commentaries*, vol II at 59; Dickinson, *The High Court of Justiciary* at 411; *Stair Memorial Encyclopaedia*, vol 6 at paras 848 and 855.
[63] Hume, *Commentaries*, vol II at 31.
[64] Hume, *Commentaries*, vol II at 37.
[65] *Stair Memorial Encyclopaedia*, vol 6 at para 855.
[66] *Boyle, Petr (No 2)* 1993 SLT 1085 at 1090.
[67] Archibald Alison, *Practice of the Criminal Law of Scotland* (1833, William Blackwood) at 23.

unforeseen occurrences in criminal business" as "similar to the *nobile officium* of the Court of Session".[68]

Most recently, the Carloway Review described the *nobile officium* as "an ancient power of superintendence available to the High Court" and "very much a remnant from a bygone age before criminal procedures were regulated by the detailed statutory provisions which exist today".[69] As in the Court of Session, the *nobile officium* of the High Court seems to have grown out of a broader equitable remit, rather than having been demarcated as a distinct jurisdiction with unilinear development. As discussed below,[70] this may be bound up with such broader equitable capacity as the power to vindicate the fair and impartial administration of justice, and the declaratory power of the High Court, namely its inherent power to punish every act of a criminal nature.

However, the *nobile officium* of the High Court would increasingly acquire the character of dealing with extraordinary circumstances by providing a remedy where no other was available. Hume described the *nobile officium* as the High Court's "exclusive ... power of providing a remedy for all extraordinary occurrences in the course of criminal business".[71] Alison referred to the "general controlling power which the Justiciary Court possess, and the interference in mitigation of otherwise irremediable evils, which, in virtue of their *nobile officium*, they frequently exercise",[72] and Henry Moncreiff to the *nobile officium* as enabling the Court to "interfere in extraordinary circumstances

---

[68] Gerald H Gordon et al (eds), *Renton and Brown's Criminal Procedure* (6th edn, 1996, W Green) (electronic reproduction, Sweet & Maxwell Asia, Hong Kong, 2011) at para 2–09. See also T B Smith, *A Short Commentary on the Law of Scotland* (1962, W Green) at 44; *Stair Memorial Encyclopaedia*, vol 6 at para 870; *Milne v McNicol* 1944 JC 151 at 153 per Lord Justice-Clerk Cooper; and *Newland, Petr* 1994 JC 122 at 126 per Lord Justice-General Hope.

[69] *The Carloway Review: Report and Recommendations* (17 Nov 2011) at para 8.1.20.

[70] See Section 1.3.

[71] See Hume, *Commentaries*, vol II at 59.

[72] Alison, *Practice of the Criminal Law of Scotland* at 662.

to prevent injustice or oppression where there is no judgment or warrant to review".[73]

The *nobile officium* has therefore grown to serve a similar purpose in the Court of Session and the High Court, with regard to their respective spheres of jurisdiction. Whilst each court has exclusive possession of its own *nobile officium*, their principles are now generally analogous.

1.3 Conceptual location

Conceptually locating the *nobile officium* is not an easy task. This section shall address four conceptual questions: (i) to what extent are equitable powers unique to the supreme courts? (ii) is the *nobile officium* the name given to the equity exclusive to the supreme courts? (iii) to what extent should the *nobile officium* be regarded as an aspect of the common law? and (iv) is the *nobile officium* uniquely an inherent jurisdiction?

First, it is important to emphasise the distinction between the *nobile officium* and broader equitable power, a distinction that is neither unequivocal nor easily made. It is important, however, to insist on this distinction. In doing so, it follows that the *nobile officium* is neither synonymous with equitable power in general, nor with the specific equitable power of the supreme courts. It is instead a narrower aspect of equitable power unique to the supreme courts.

Equitable discretion manifests in many aspects of common law adjudication.[74] It may also materialise in statutory interpretation: a range of interpretive approaches and tools can be employed such as in the extent to which provisions are construed literally, or whether the court brings concepts of fairness and reasonableness to bear in statutory construction. There is scope for implicating equitable jurisdiction in this

---

[73] Henry J Moncreiff, *A Treatise on the Law of Review in Criminal Cases and on Procedure in Criminal Cases in Inferior Courts in Scotland* (1877, W Green) at 218. See further p 183.

[74] See generally *Dunedin Encyclopaedia*, vol VI at 258–81; and *Stair Memorial Encyclopaedia*, Sources of Law (Formal), vol 22 at paras 394–432.

interpretive activity. Equitable discretion manifests in a wider sense, however. Questions requiring discretionary judgment, which would typically be exercised with regard to justice and fairness, manifest in a much wider range of cases than those presented under the *nobile officium*: in the application of tests of reasonableness, in questions of what is fair or just, in questions of proportionality, in sentencing an accused, in fixing awards, fines and time periods, in questions of expenses and in the very regulation of court process where any discretion is permitted by the relevant procedural rules, to name just a few such areas.

Questions of this kind arise for consideration not only in the Court of Session and the High Court, but also in inferior courts. In other words, all courts have some measure of equitable discretion – indeed, of equitable jurisdiction.[75] This can also be seen in other contexts. For example, there has been discussion on the extent to which courts have an inherent power to vindicate the fair and impartial administration of justice, including the power to prevent vexatious conduct and abuse of process.[76] To the extent that courts (including inferior courts) have an inherent power to take steps towards securing these objectives, there is scope for arguing that this is also an aspect of equitable jurisdiction.

More generic common law powers also have the potential to be at least partly equitable in nature, for whilst the common law will serve to certify the "legality" of such powers, so that they take on an increasingly "legal" nature, those powers would have

---

[75] It was recently stated that the Inner House did "not dispute the petitioner's description of all Scottish courts as courts of equity as well as law": *Anderson v Shetland Islands Council* [2014] CSIH 73 at para [12] per Lord Brodie. See also *Dunedin Encyclopaedia*, vol VI at 279–80, which described the sheriff court as having a "general equitable jurisdiction in all actions as well as defences"; and Lord Cooper of Culross, "The Central Courts after 1532" at 345.

[76] See, eg, *Cordiner, Petr* 1973 JC 16 at 18 per Lord Justice-General Emslie; *Hall v Associated Newspapers Ltd* 1979 JC 1; *Esso Petroleum Co Ltd v Hall Russell & Co Ltd (No 2)* 1995 SLT 127; *Newman Shopfitters Ltd v M J Gleeson Group plc* 2003 SLT (Sh Ct) 83; *Tonner v Reiach & Hall* [2007] CSIH 48; *Global Santa Fe Drilling (North Sea) Ltd v Lord Advocate* [2009] CSIH 43; and *Hepburn v Royal Alexandra NHS Trust* [2010] CSIH 71.

to be examined to see whether and how they came into being in the first place. In addition to the more procedural powers already adverted to, substantive equitable concepts pervade a number of areas of law,[77] and to the extent that such areas are or have been shaped or transacted by inferior courts, this admits of the possibility of a basic equitable jurisdiction residing in those courts. T B Smith wrote that "[s]ince there is no separation of legal and equitable principles, as in England, remedies such as interdict (*anglice* – injunction) and specific implement (*anglice* – specific performance) are normal, and granted even by the sheriff".[78]

Furthermore, the sheriff court in particular has a long pedigree of broad jurisdictional powers which include administrative and quasi-administrative powers,[79] and although this is not the place to explore this subject, those powers and the manner in which they have been exercised may bear equitable aspects.

This overview indicates a range of grounds on which it may be contended that equity and equitable jurisdiction are not unique to the supreme courts. By contrast, they credibly support the argument that all courts have some measure of equitable jurisdiction. It therefore cannot be correct to equate the *nobile*

---

[77] Typically cited in this regard are trusts, unjustified enrichment and substantively equitable remedies. See generally David M Walker, "Equity in Scots law" (1954) 66 JR 103–47.

[78] Smith, *A Short Commentary* at 95. Smith complained that this fact had frequently been overlooked by both the House of Lords and the Court of Session when considering "whether an English precedent would be suitable for grafting onto Scots law".

[79] See *Stair Memorial Encyclopaedia*, Administrative Law Reissue at paras 12 and 154; Courts and Competency, vol 6 at paras 1022, 1059 and 1063; C M G Himsworth, "Scottish local authorities and the sheriff" (1984) JR 63; *The Sheriff Court: Report by the Committee appointed by the Secretary of State for Scotland* ("Grant Committee") (Cmnd 3248, 1967) at 17 and 80–110; *Allen & Sons Billposting Ltd v Corporation of Edinburgh* 1909 SC 70; *Ross–shire County Council v Macrae-Gilstrap* 1930 SC 808; *Glasgow Corporation v Glasgow Churches' Council* 1944 SC 97; *Arcari v Dumbartonshire County Council* 1948 SC 62; *Kaye v Hunter* 1958 SC 208; *F v Management Committee and Managers of Ravenscraig Hospital* 1988 SC 158; and *Rodenhurst v Chief Constable of Grampian Police* 1992 SC 1.

officium with the "equitable discretion of the Court",[80] nor can it be accurate to describe the *nobile officium* as the court's "equitable jurisdiction"[81] or even "the inherent equitable jurisdiction of the Court of Session",[82] for the other and wider aspects of equitable jurisdiction residing in that court are also "inherent" in the sense that they do not derive from some external source, but are often intrinsic to its function as a court engaging in common law adjudication.[83] Likewise, it is inaccurate to designate the *nobile officium* of the High Court as its "equitable jurisdiction".[84] A more accurate description of the *nobile officium* in either court would be its "extraordinary equitable jurisdiction",[85] as the *nobile officium* is just one type of equitable jurisdiction, but a special type which is resident only in the supreme courts. It is an "extraordinary process seeking an extraordinary remedy".[86] The use of the term *nobile officium* to refer to the broader equitable powers of the court should be discouraged, as the modern *nobile officium* is a narrower procedural mechanism for transacting particular types of equitable business.[87]

If inferior courts have equitable powers, however, the supreme courts must have greater or more extensive equitable powers. The *nobile officium* is a salient example of higher equitable powers

---

[80] John Erskine, *Principles of the Law of Scotland* (17th edn, 1886, Bell & Bradfute) at 620.

[81] James Paterson, *A Compendium of English and Scotch Law* (2nd edn, 1865, Adam and Charles Black) at 561; J W Brodie–Innes, *Comparative Principles of the Laws of England and Scotland* (1903, W Green) at 278.

[82] *Wright v Tennent Caledonian Breweries Ltd* 1991 SLT 823 at 826.

[83] The *nobile officium* was once described as a power used in the exercise of the Court of Session's "equitable sovereign jurisdiction": Berry (ed), *Balfour's Handbook* at 206.

[84] *Akram v HM Advocate* 2009 SLT 805 at 811–812.

[85] *Dunedin Encyclopaedia*, vol X at 325; *Jamieson, Petrs* 1997 SC 195 at 199.

[86] *Barns-Graham v City of Glasgow District Council* 1978 SLT (Notes) 50 at 51.

[87] It was stated in *London and Clydeside Estates Ltd v Aberdeen District Council* 1980 SC (HL) 1 at 45 per Lord Keith of Kinkel, that the "chief object" of the *nobile officium* is to "provide a means of rectifying obvious errors or omissions, principally of an administrative character, which cannot be dealt with in any other way"; and in *Cameron v Duke of Argyll's Trs* 1981 SLT (Land Ct) 2 at 8 that "the *nobile officium* of the Court of Session is nowadays confined to granting procedural relief in non-contentious cases".

vested in the supreme courts, which are not enjoyed by inferior courts. However, that does not mean that the *nobile officium* is simply the name given to those higher equitable powers which are vested in the supreme courts. Perhaps tellingly, a student textbook from the late nineteenth century described the Court of Session as a court of law and equity in "all matters coming before it"[88] – in other words, not solely in cases invoking the *nobile officium*.

Another example of a higher equitable power is the supervisory jurisdiction of the Court of Session. This appears to have grown out of the Court's broad equitable powers, and perhaps out of the same broad equitable powers as grew the *nobile officium*. Nevertheless, these are distinguishable and arguably quite distinct jurisdictions. They are, at a minimum, accessed via distinct procedural channels in the Rules of Court, but there are more substantive differences between the jurisdictions which cannot be explored here. The supervisory jurisdiction is a form of equitable jurisdiction which is not found in inferior courts, with equitable principles driving the Court's superintendence of bodies exercising jurisdiction, and yet it would be inaccurate to describe the supervisory jurisdiction as an aspect of the *nobile officium*. These are both, however, jurisdictions animated by equitable principles which are not possessed by inferior courts. It is therefore apparent that the supreme courts would exercise broader equitable jurisdiction than that encapsulated by the *nobile officium*. As Lord Hunter once said: "I do not understand that the Court is precluded from exercising an equitable jurisdiction altogether independent of an application to the *nobile officium*."[89]

---

[88] Although it was stated in the immediately preceding paragraph that when the Court adjudicates on an application to the *nobile officium*, it does not act as a court of law: Morton, *Manual of the Law of Scotland* at 14.

[89] *Snodgrass, Petr* 1922 SC 491 at 496. See also *Anderson v Hogg* 2000 SLT 634 at 643 per Lord Reed. It may be posed, as an open question, whether the High Court's "inherent power to punish every act which is obviously of a criminal nature", its so-called "declaratory power" (to the extent that it still exists), is an aspect of its *nobile officium* or other equitable powers – see *Renton and Brown's Criminal Procedure* at para 2-09. See also *Stair Memorial Encyclopaedia*, Courts and Competency, vol 6 at para 869 and Criminal Law Reissue at paras 6–15.

In this vein, T B Smith distinguished the "ordinary" and "extraordinary" equitable jurisdiction of the supreme courts, with the latter alone designated the *nobile officium*.[90] Among the powers under the Court's ordinary equitable jurisdiction, Smith included their intervention to modify exorbitant conventional penalties,[91] to permit irritancies to be purged at the Bar, and to grant redress by decree of interdict or specific implement. The *nobile officium* was distinct from these aspects of ordinary equitable jurisdiction.[92] Lord Bankton also adopted this view of the *nobile officium* as distinct from broader equitable jurisdiction, describing the *nobile officium* as "a supereminent power, founded in [the Court of Session's] high jurisdiction, in order to the discovery of truth, and cannot be said only to proceed upon their equitable powers".[93] Whereas "[e]quity is a favourable construction of the law, and may be prayed by either party", the *nobile officium* is distinctive because it allows the court to "interpose, otherwise than according to the ordinary rules or forms of law, and even contrary to the form of ordinary proceedings, when the case requires it, in order to bring out the truth, which could not otherwise be done".[94] That is neither within the general capacity of inferior courts, nor would it be an appropriate description of the supervisory jurisdiction, for example, and therefore not a faithful description of the entirety of the Court's equitable powers.

This insistence on the particularity of the *nobile officium*, distinguishable from broader equitable jurisdiction, has also been made in the courts:

---

[90] Smith, *A Short Commentary* at 44.
[91] On this, see *Forrest and Barr v Henderson* (1869) 8 M 187, which does not necessarily fall within the technical parameters of the *nobile officium* – see p 8, fn 26. Stair also described the modification of exorbitant penalties in bonds and contracts as an aspect of the *nobile officium*: Stair, IV, 3, 2. See also Mackay, *The Practice of the Court of Session*, vol 1 at 219.
[92] Smith, *A Short Commentary* at 44. See also Mackay, *The Practice of the Court of Session*, vol 1 at 208; and, eg, *Forrest and Barr v Henderson* (1869) 8 M 187.
[93] Andrew McDouall (Lord Bankton), *An Institute of the Laws of Scotland* (1752, rep 1994, Stair Society) IV, VII, 24.
[94] Bankton, IV, VII, 24.

Owing to its peculiar history, the law of Scotland has never known either distinction or conflict between common law and the principles of equity. It is often said, and truly said, that in the law of Scotland law is equity, and equity law; and when a Scots lawyer uses the expression common law, he uses it in contradistinction to laws made by Parliament. From this it at once appears that considerable reserve must be used in accepting too literally some of the descriptions of the *nobile officium* in the text-books, which might be read as suggesting that the *nobile officium* is only another name for our general jurisdiction, in as much as our whole jurisdiction is nothing unless equitable.[95]

The *nobile officium* is most accurately regarded as the purest or most quintessential form of equitable jurisdiction, in as much as it represents the courts' greatest departure from strictly legal adjudication. It is a mistake to regard it as the only form of equitable jurisdiction, and it is likewise a mistake to regard it as the equitable powers specific to the supreme courts.

A plausible, though partial, explanation for the relative narrowness with which the term *nobile officium* is used today, rather than how it appears to have been used historically, is that there appears to have been a metamorphosis of equitable to legal norms. As equitable norms (those which are not strictly legal in nature) were invoked with greater frequency, there may have been a growing sense of the invocation of a legal right. At some point there may have been a hardening or crystallisation of equitable into legal norms, as what were once remedies sought on an equitable basis acquired a common law foundation, becoming common law "rights". This would signify a shift from equitable supplication to the vindication of legal rights.

T B Smith appears to have had this kind of transformative process in mind when writing that instances which to the institutional writers were exercises of the *nobile officium* were "merged in the ordinary jurisdiction of the courts", and that "[t]his trend has misled some authorities into the belief that the term *nobile officium* (the extraordinary equitable jurisdiction

---

[95] *Gibson's Trs, Petrs* 1933 SC 190 at 198–99 per Lord President Clyde. See also *Anderson v Shetland Islands Council* [2014] CSIH 73 at para [12].

of the Court of Session) is applicable to the general equitable jurisdiction of the court".[96] Kames wrote that what was originally a rule of equity "loses its character when it is fully established in practice; and then it is considered as common law".[97] It was suggested in the *Dunedin Encyclopaedia* that much of what was formerly considered part of the *nobile officium* has become ordinary equity common to all courts, or has become regulated by statute and jurisdiction accordingly assigned to supreme or inferior courts.[98] It was also stated that some classes of petition:

> have become so much matter of course that, in a Court combining equity with common-law jurisdiction, it is not surprising they should be considered rather a branch of the *praxis curiae* than an exercise of extraordinary equitable jurisdiction, which is their real character.[99]

It is doctrinally significant that the *nobile officium* is accessed by way of petition. The Clyde Report of 1927 made the following distinction between the summons and the petition:

> The object of the summons is to enforce a pursuer's legal right against a defender who resists it, or to protect a legal right which the defender is infringing; the object of a petition, on the other hand, is to obtain from the administrative jurisdiction of the court power to do something or to require something to be done, which it is just and proper should be done, but which the petitioner has no legal right to do or to require apart from authority. The contentious character of the proceedings which follow a summons necessitates a higher degree of formality than is appropriate to an *ex parte* application such as a petition, even though opposed; hence the distinction between the "solemn" procedure in an action and the "summary" procedure in a petition.[100]

It was suggested in the *Stair Memorial Encyclopaedia* that this gave an unduly narrow description of the object of

---

[96] Smith, *A Short Commentary* at 44–45. See also Fyfe, *Law and Practice of the Sheriff Courts* at 28–29.

[97] Kames, *Principles of Equity* at 17.

[98] *Dunedin Encyclopaedia*, vol X at 325.

[99] *Dunedin Encyclopaedia*, vol X at 330.

[100] *Report of the Royal Commission on the Court of Session* (Cmd 2801, 1927) ("Clyde Report") at 50–51.

petitions, and that Lord Keith and the *Dunedin Encyclopaedia* were nearer the mark.[101] Lord Keith made the following distinction:

> The summons and the petition have different historical origins and the purpose of the summons is different from the purpose of the petition. A summons was a writ issued in the King's name, directed to messengers-at-arms, charging a defender to appear within a certain period, if he wished to resist decree passing against him, and the procedure in the event of his non-appearance was settled by a very long course of practice and regulation. A petition is an *ex parte* application addressed to the Lords of Council and Session and seeks their aid for some purpose or other, *e.g.*, by supplying some deficiency of power in the petitioner, in protecting pupils and minors, by exercising some statutory jurisdiction, or the *nobile officium*, in a variety of matters. We are entirely masters of the procedure in a petition, subject to any regulations thereanent made by Act of Sederunt.[102]

The *Dunedin Encyclopaedia* stated that:

> Historically the petition, or, as it was sometimes called supplication, was regarded in early times as purely an equitable proceeding, suitable whenever the ordinary forms of action were inapplicable or circumstances required a simple and summary form of procedure.... . Some traces of its origin survive in the rule that procedure by petition is incompetent whenever any other form of action can be used. The purely equitable jurisdiction of the Court known as the *Nobile Officium* has always been, and still is, invoked by petition.[103]

The heightened equitable nature of the *nobile officium* is therefore captured in its invocation by petition rather than by way of summons. Although the *nobile officium* is not the only object at which a petition may be presented,[104] it clearly involves addressing the court for assistance rather than initiating an action against a contradictor, with the court adjudicating over an adversarial dispute of right.

---

[101] *Stair Memorial Encyclopaedia*, Civil Procedure Reissue at para 26. See also para 31.

[102] *Tomkins v Cohen* 1951 SC 22 at 23 per Lord Keith.

[103] *Dunedin Encyclopaedia*, vol XI at 308.

[104] See Chapter 14 of the Rules of the Court of Session.

A conceptual puzzle lies in the question of whether the *nobile officium* should be regarded as an aspect of the common law. The question may depend on how the term "common law" is defined. Dicta can be sourced in support of either a positive or negative contention. On the one hand, it has been said that a petition to the *nobile officium* is a petition presented at common law.[105] That would be true if the term is used in the sense of non-statutory law, though the term "common law" can be used in a narrower sense, and one should bear in mind that in England the term was often used in historical contrast to equity.

It has elsewhere been said that resort was made to "the common law powers of the Court under its *nobile officium*".[106] For example, the power to appoint judicial factors was one "exercised in virtue of the *nobile officium*" and that "is not a statutory power; it is a common law power".[107] More recently, the Scottish Law Commission stated that there is "ample authority for the proposition that a judicial factor can be appointed to a company at common law, under the *nobile officium* of the Court of Session".[108] Furthermore, the perhaps surprising role of precedent[109] in *nobile officium* jurisprudence is redolent of the common law rather than what might be expected of a purely equitable jurisdiction, which should arguably use moral norms as its principal point of reference.

However, Lord Justice-Clerk Patton had this to say:

> The common law jurisdiction of this Court is ordinary jurisdiction, which is contentious; and extraordinary, in which the Court exercises its *nobile officium*. The present application is certainly not within

---

[105] *Leslie's Judicial Factor, Petr* 1925 SC 464 at 468.

[106] *Carmont, Petrs* 1922 SC 686 at 687 per Lord President Clyde. A similar statement was made in *Shariff v Hamid* 2000 SLT 294 at 294 per Lord Nimmo Smith. See also W A Wilson and A G M Duncan, *Trusts, Trustees and Executors* (2nd edn, 1995, W Green) at 329.

[107] *Innes, Chambers & Co v T D McNeill & Son* (1917) 1 SLT 89 at 91 per Lord Anderson.

[108] *Report on Judicial Factors* (Scot Law Com No 233, 2013) at 30.

[109] See Section 10.5.

the ordinary function of the Court, for we have no party called as contradictor, and no matter of right brought into contest as between litigants. The applicants call upon us to exercise our *nobile officium*. There is, confessedly, no precedent for such an application as the present, so that the exercise of the *nobile officium* cannot be called for as a thing recognised in practice. It must be rested upon alleged necessity, or such strong and clear expediency as to call for the special intervention of the Court to meet a case of exigency.[110]

This rather suggests that the *nobile officium* is other than a common law jurisdiction. In the same vein, in a case in which it was to be determined whether a process of division and sale was an Inner or Outer House cause, Lord Deas said that:

[the] whole question is solved when we come to be of opinion that the remedy of division and sale is a right at common law,–*i.e.*, at common law as distinguished not from statute law, but from an appeal to the *nobile officium* of the Court. If so, that right is to be vindicated by means of a summons, and it must be treated as an ordinary process in the Outer-House.[111]

Likewise, it was said of a case that "the Court used their *nobile officium* to do that which neither they nor the Sheriff had power under the statute or at common law to do",[112] and more recently, that the Court had no power "at common law or by virtue of the *nobile officium*" to allow late appeals in particular circumstances.[113] These again suggest that the *nobile officium* is distinctive from generic common law jurisdiction.[114] The

---

[110] *Dundas, Petrs* (1869) 7 M 670 at 671 per Lord Justice-Clerk Patton.

[111] *McBride v Paul* (1862) 24 D 546 at 547 per Lord Deas.

[112] *Liddall v Ballingry Parish Council* 1908 SC 1082 at 1088 (note) per Lord Johnston. A distinction between the *nobile officium* and the common law as the source for a legal principle has also been made in the sheriff court – see, eg, *AB v CD* (1910) 1 SLT 405 at 407 per Sheriff Lorimer.

[113] *GAS Construction Co Ltd v Schrader* 1992 SLT 505 at 506–07. See also Alexander Montgomerie Bell, *Lectures on Conveyancing* (3rd edn, 1882, Bell & Bradfute) vol 1 at 117 which, though not a strong example, seems to suggest that the *nobile officium* is a power distinct from the common law.

[114] The equitable power of the king was described as flowing "not from the common law", but being "*ex officio*": McNeill, *Jurisdiction of the Scottish Privy Council* at 68. The *nobile officium* has been described as arising by custom: Brodie-Innes, *Comparative Principles* at 278.

concept of the *nobile officium* would in its pure form require that there be no precedential requirement for equitable intervention, nor that individual cases would acquire precedential authority. However, even though precedent does feature in the *nobile officium* jurisprudence, the extent to which precedential authority is observed is at variance with, and less than, is found in ordinary process of the common law.[115]

These dicta and comments may or may not have been expressed with a view to taxonomically classifying the *nobile officium* as a jurisdiction, but they reveal different perspectives which may be adopted. The position of this text is that the *nobile officium* should not be regarded as an aspect of generic common law jurisdiction. If the *nobile officium* is at all regarded as an aspect of the common law, it should be regarded as a special category of common law jurisdiction. It would, in that case, be acceptable to speak of the *nobile officium* "or any other common law powers",[116] providing always that there is sufficient acknowledgement of the various differences from generic common law powers, such as in the extent to which precedential authority is observed (and required of intending petitioners), the exceptional and extraordinary nature of the jurisdiction, and the fact that it cannot be petitioned as of right. Better still, the *nobile officium* would be regarded as distinct from generic common law jurisdiction.

Caution might be urged in over-emphasising the extent to which the *nobile officium* is uniquely an inherent jurisdiction. A notable challenge to that presumption would be the existence of the supervisory jurisdiction as an inherent jurisdiction of the Court of Session. However, there are more subtle boundaries between the *nobile officium* and other aspects of the courts' inherent, even equitable, jurisdiction. Consider, for example, the courts' "inherent" power to vindicate the fair and impartial administration of justice, such as "the [High Court's] inherent common law power to adjourn where necessary in the interests

---

[115] See Section 10.5.
[116] *McLaughlin, Petr* 1965 SC 243 at 245 per Lord President Clyde.

of justice".[117] This is apparently regarded as intrinsic to the function of the High Court as a court of justice, and with that appeal to justice it may be regarded as an equitable function, but it would not be regarded as an aspect of the *nobile officium* as such. There is also the question of whether (to the extent that it still exists) the declaratory power of the High Court is inherent.[118]

A further complicating factor is the extent to which the *nobile officium* is capable of being procedurally channelled between the Inner and Outer House of the Court of Session. As noted, the jurisdiction was naturally vested in the Inner House, but certain petitions to the *nobile officium* (notably in relation to trusts) must now be directed to the Outer House, as per the Rules of Court. This indicates that the Rules of Court are a means of distributing *nobile officium* business between the Inner and Outer House, and suggests either that the Rules of Court are capable of apportioning the jurisdiction between either House, or that the *nobile officium* resides in the Court of Session as a whole, and it is merely the default position that it has been invoked by way of the Inner House.

A final observation should be made with regard to courts "superior" to the Court of Session and the High Court. The UK Supreme Court does not have a *nobile officium*, nor did the Judicial Committees of the House of Lords or the Privy Council. There is precedent for appealing in civil cases from the *nobile officium* to the House of Lords. A petition refused on its merits was competently appealed to the House of Lords,[119] and where a petition had been successfully granted, the respondents competently appealed.[120] It was also said that the Inner House could, in exercise of its *nobile officium*, consider whether to give

---

[117] *HM Advocate v Donnelly* 1997 SLT 1381 at 1381. See p 18.

[118] See fn 89 above.

[119] *Helow v Secretary of State for the Home Department* 2009 SC (HL) 1. The appeal was dismissed and the decision of the Inner House refusing the appellant's petition to the *nobile officium* affirmed.

[120] *Whyte v Northern Heritable Securities Investment Co Ltd* (1891) R (HL) 37; *Davidson v Scottish Ministers (No 2)* 2005 SC (HL) 7. Each appeal was dismissed.

leave to appeal to the House of Lords.[121] It has been stated that there is no appeal from the *nobile officium* of the High Court,[122] though elsewhere it was observed that it appears now to be accepted that the High Court can itself review an exercise of the *nobile officium*.[123] It has been indicated that the *nobile officium* could be regarded as an effective remedy for the purpose of Article 13 of the European Convention on Human Rights.[124]

---

[121] See *Davidson v Scottish Ministers (No 2)* at 28–31. See also *Grahame v Magistrates of Kirkcaldy* (1882) 9 R (HL) 91; and *Beggs v Scottish Ministers* 2006 SC 649.

[122] *Stair Memorial Encyclopaedia*, Courts and Competency, vol 6 at para 870.

[123] *Renton and Brown's Criminal Procedure* at para 34-07.

[124] See p 190.

CHAPTER 2

TRUSTS

One of the principal areas of activity for the *nobile officium* was the law on trusts. There has, however, been an erosion of the scope of the jurisdiction in this area, or at least the demand for intervention *ex nobile officio* has diminished. This has been effected primarily by various statutory reforms which have offset much of the activity of the *nobile officium* in the area of trusts, beginning with the Trusts (Scotland) Act 1861 and proceeding through such important statutes as the Trusts (Scotland) Act 1921, the Trusts (Scotland) Act 1961, and the Law Reform (Miscellaneous Provisions) (Scotland) Act 1990.

The Scottish Law Commission recently published a *Report on Trust Law* which included a draft Trusts (Scotland) Bill.[1] The contents of the draft Bill will not be scrutinised here, but it should be noted that significant change in the law of trusts may be afoot and may potentially further erode the utility of the *nobile officium* in this area. Nevertheless, it does not seem likely that the *nobile officium* would be rendered defunct by any such legislation, although the criteria on which trusts petitions are dealt with may be changed. The possibility of what are effectively gaps in the legislative framework secures an enduring function for the *nobile officium*, and although it is true that the scope of the jurisdiction is "uncertain", and of "limited utility" in, for example, dealing with administrative powers that prove inadequate,[2] that is entirely in keeping with the nature of the jurisdiction. Having moved from relatively frequent invocation in the field of trusts, the *nobile officium* has in a sense assumed its more natural role as

---

[1] *Report on Trust Law* (Scot Law Com No 239, 2014). The Report continues the work of the Commission on trusts including, *inter alia*, *Discussion Paper on Trustees and Trust Administration* (Scot Law Com DP No 126, December 2004).

[2] *Report on Trust Law* at 61.

a residual[3] and little used jurisdiction to be exercised only in exceptional cases. This goes to the nature, rather than the overall utility, of the jurisdiction. It has been:

> practically confined to cases where something administrative or executive is wanting in the constituting document to enable the trust purposes to be effectually carried out, and such cases are now largely met by the provisions of the modern Trusts Acts.[4]

This chapter traces the historical and present-day extent of the *nobile officium* in the area of trust law. It is not intended to be an overview of the law on trusts, examining instead the *nobile officium* as applied to trusts. The chapter begins with an overview of the *nobile officium* as it has applied to the appointment, resignation and removal of trustees, before examining its application to the powers of trustees and the variation of trust purposes. It concludes by considering the debate between a requirement for necessity, or a lower standard of expediency, for the Court's equitable intervention in this area.

By final way of introductory comment, the *nobile officium* has been said to be available for invocation in the area of trusts only by persons of whose title and powers as trustees, and over the funds in question, there is no doubt. The jurisdiction does not exist as a mechanism for transacting competing claims such as with regard to the powers and duties of trustees.[5] Under rule 14.2(c) of the Rules of the Court of Session, applications to the *nobile officium* which relate to the administration of a trust, the office of trustee or a public trust shall be presented to the Outer House. All other petitions to the *nobile officium* shall be presented to the Inner House.[6] However, where part of a petition may be competently dealt with by the Outer House, and

---

[3] See, eg, *Tod v Marshall* (1895) 23 R 36.

[4] *Hall's Trs v McArthur* 1918 SC 646 at 650 per Lord Johnston. It was said in *Anderson's Trs, Petrs* 1921 SC 315 at 322 per Lord Justice-Clerk Scott Dickson, that "it would be unfortunate if, through adhering to what may be regarded as the strict letter of the law, we were to prevent [the trustees] ... from carrying out what was clearly and distinctly stated by the truster as the purpose".

[5] *Barns-Graham v City of Glasgow District Council* 1978 SLT (Notes) 50.

[6] Rules of the Court of Session, r 14.3(d).

another part would require to be dealt with by the Inner House, it may be competent to present the whole petition to the Inner House.[7]

2.1 Trustees

(a) Appointment of trustees

The Trusts (Scotland) Act 1921 invests a statutory power in the Court to appoint trustees in specified circumstances, namely where (i) trustees cannot be appointed under the trust deed, (ii) a sole trustee acting under a trust deed is or has become insane or incapable of acting by reason of physical or mental disability, (iii) a sole trustee acting under a trust deed has been absent continuously from the United Kingdom for at least six months, or (iv) a sole trustee acting under a trust deed has disappeared for at least six months.[8]

The Court also has a residual, non-statutory power to appoint trustees by exercise of the *nobile officium*. This was often utilised prior to a statutory basis for the appointment and assumption of trustees, which has been traced back to the Trusts (Scotland) Acts 1861 and 1867,[9] but has continuing utility when it is sought to appoint trustees in situations not captured by the trust deed or legislation.

For example, where trustees under an antenuptial marriage contract had failed to agree on the investment of trust funds and on the assumption of new trustees, the Court appointed three new

---

[7] See *Prime Gilt Box Society, Petrs* 1920 SC 534; and *Anderson's Trs, Petrs* 1921 SC 315 at 319 per Lord Justice-Clerk Scott Dickson. See also Aeneas J G Mackay, *Manual of Practice in the Court of Session* (1893, W Green) at 529.

[8] Trusts (Scotland) Act 1921, s 22. This statutory power also pertains to the sheriff court since the enactment of the Law Reform (Miscellaneous Provisions) (Scotland) Act 1980, s 13. There is also a power in the Court under the Charities and Trustee Investment (Scotland) Act 2005 to appoint a trustee or suspend or remove any person concerned in the management or control of a charity, which may be comprised in the form of a trust (s 34(5)(d) and (e)). Under s 34(6), where the Court appoints a trustee under s 34(5)(d), s 22 of the Trusts (Scotland) Act 1921 applies as if the trustee had been appointed under that section.

[9] *Discussion Paper on Trustees and Trust Administration* at 30–31.

trustees in exercise of its *nobile officium*.[10] Likewise, where the administration of a trust had ceased to progress due to the refusal of one trustee (A) to co-operate with another (B), the Court exercised its *nobile officium* to appoint C as an additional trustee.[11] The petition had been presented by B, praying in addition for the removal of A; however the Court refused the petition inasmuch as it related to A's removal, noting that A was amenable to C's appointment. The *nobile officium* was also used to appoint new trustees contemporaneously with the removal of a sole trustee from office.[12]

Another application of the jurisdiction is where the offices of *ex officio* trustees have ceased to exist. This situation arose in *Mackay, Petrs*.[13] Two persons were *ex officio* trustees, by virtue of holding designated local administrative offices, for the administration of a charitable trust for the benefit of a district nurse's endowment fund. The two offices which were entitled to *ex officio* appointment as trustees were subsequently abolished by statute, and the trust lapsed. The former *ex officio* trustees petitioned the *nobile officium* for appointment of two new *ex officio* trustees. The Court granted the prayer of the petition, Lord President Clyde noting that as the application concerned a charitable trust and fell under the Rules of Court to be presented in the Inner House, the petition could "then invoke the wide equitable jurisdiction of the Court which is not available in a simple application under the Trusts (Scotland) Act, 1921".[14] The underlying rationale is to enable the trust to resume operation in such circumstances.

The Court has appointed trustees where a testator who established a trust in his settlement died shortly thereafter, prior to the execution of the declaration of trust or the naming of trustees. The trustees under the settlement petitioned the

---

[10] *Aikman, Petrs* (1881) 9 R 213. See also *Taylor, Petrs* 1932 SC 1.

[11] *Dick, Petrs* (1899) 2 F 316.

[12] *Lamont v Lamont* 1908 SC 1033.

[13] *Mackay, Petrs* 1955 SC 361; and see also *Thomson's Trs, Petrs* 1930 SC 767.

[14] *Mackay, Petrs* at 363. See also *Coal Industry Social Welfare Organisation, Petrs* 1959 SLT (Notes) 3.

Court for approval of a scheme for the administration of the bequest, with the next of kin being of the view that the bequest had failed. It was held that the bequest had not failed, but that trustees would be appointed by the Court to receive the bequest.[15]

The *nobile officium* has been used to appoint new trustees when trustees have died prior to the termination of the trust.[16] Petitions of this nature may be brought by persons having an interest in the trust estate, such as beneficiaries. Another situation where the *nobile officium* has been used is where an antenuptial marriage contract provided for trustees to appoint new trustees subject to the consent of the spouses. The wife having become insane, two trustees under the marriage contract petitioned the *nobile officium* for removal of the wife as a trustee and for authorisation for the trustees to assume new trustees without her consent. The Court, without delivering opinions, granted the prayer of the petition.[17] This case would not necessarily have fallen under section 22 of the Trusts (Scotland) Act 1921, had it occurred after the enactment of that statute, as it was not an instance of a sole trustee having become insane.

The *nobile officium* has had utility where there was a cross-border element to the case.[18] Where, for example, the sole trustee under an English trust (and under the estate of which were a

---

[15] *Lindsay's Trs v Lindsay* 1938 SC 44.

[16] *McAslan, Petrs* (1841) 3 D 1263; *Glasgow, Petrs* (1844) 7 D 178.

[17] *Adamson's Trs, Petrs* 1917 SC 440.

[18] This was not confined to the appointment of trustees, or even the broader field of trusts. The Court sometimes exercised an auxiliary jurisdiction by way of its *nobile officium* to facilitate, supplement or transact a decision or process relating to a foreign jurisdiction. Examples of this include *Allan's Trs, Petrs* (1897) 24 R 718; *Harris's Trs, Petrs* 1919 SC 432; *Campbell, Petrs* 1958 SC 275; and *Campbell-Wyndham-Long's Trs* 1962 SC 132. See also *Harris' Trs v Harris* (1904) 6 F 470. However, for a cross-border issue giving rise to what Lord President Robertson described as "overdriving" the *nobile officium*, see *Atherstone's Trs, Petrs* (1896) 24 R 39. Cross-border cases would now typically invoke rules of international private law. It is perhaps worth noting that the jurisdiction of the Scots Privy Council over conflict of laws has been classed as a branch of equity: McNeill, *Jurisdiction of the Scottish Privy Council* at vi and 89–91.

Scottish bank account and investments) became *incapax*, two new trustees had been appointed by the Chancery Division in England. Those trustees then petitioned the *nobile officium* for removal of the name of the *incapax* from the bank account and investments, and the substitution of their own names in its place. The Court granted the prayer of the petition.[19]

The circumstances in which the Court will appoint new trustees are not unlimited. At least two basic requirements must be demonstrated in such a petition. First, it must be the case that there is no existing mechanism in the trust deed (or the legislation) for the appointment of trustees. If there is, the petition may and probably will be refused on that basis.[20] This was the outcome in *Lindsay v Lindsay*,[21] where trustees under an antenuptial marriage contract had either died or resigned, and the trusters petitioned the *nobile officium* for the appointment of new trustees – even although they already had a power of appointment under the terms of the trust deed. As succinctly put by Lord Cockburn: "Assuming that we have power to nominate new trustees, it would require a strong case to make us exercise it; and a strong case cannot be said to exist where the parties can do it for themselves."[22] A distinction may be drawn in this regard between private and public trusts, for the Court more jealously guards public trusts and may require a petitioner to come before the Court when an analogous petition in respect of a private trust may not be required.[23]

Second, it should be demonstrated that appointment of the trustee(s) is necessary.[24] The tension between judgments which have imposed a standard of necessity, and those applying a lower

---

[19] *Evans–Freke's Trs, Petrs* 1945 SC 382.

[20] This conforms with the rule that the petitioner must use other remedies and procedural avenues prior to invoking the *nobile officium* – see Section 10.4.

[21] (1847) 9 D 1297.

[22] At 1299 per Lord Cockburn.

[23] *Glentanar v Scottish Industrial Musical Association* 1925 SC 226.

[24] *Melville v Preston* (1838) 16 S 457; *Preston v Preston's Trs* (1852) 14 D 1055. See also *Thomson's Trs, Petrs* 1930 SC 767 at 769–70 per Lord President Clyde; and *Stair Memorial Encyclopaedia*, Trusts, Trustees and Judicial Factors, vol 24 at para 158.

standard of expediency, is discussed later in this chapter.[25] It is undoubtedly the case, however, that the prospects of a petition will be enhanced if necessity can be demonstrated, for this would meet the required threshold regardless of which of the two standards is imposed by the Court.

(b) Resignation and removal of trustees

Since the Trusts (Scotland) Act 1861, there has been a statutory power for trustees to resign.[26] Section 3 of the Trusts (Scotland) Act 1921 provides that all trusts shall be held to include the power of any trustee to resign office.[27] If for some reason a trustee falls outside the statutory provisions, the Court may authorise resignation in exercise of its *nobile officium*.[28]

It may not be possible or appropriate for a trustee to resign, or he may refuse to do so. There is a statutory power to remove trustees in situations of their insanity, incapacity by reason of physical or mental disability, being absent from the United Kingdom continuously for a period of at least six months, or having disappeared for a like period.[29] However, the Court retains in its *nobile officium* a residual power to remove trustees,[30] though this has been described as rarely exercised,[31] and would typically be invoked by co-trustees or beneficiaries.

---

[25] See Section 2.3.

[26] *Discussion Paper on Trustees and Trust Administration* at 33.

[27] See, however, the exceptions identified in *Discussion Paper on Trustees and Trust Administration* at 34.

[28] *Orphoot, Petr* (1897) 24 R 871. There were, however, no opinions delivered by the Court, and the *nobile officium* is mentioned only in the rubric. In *Dick's Trs v Pridie* (1855) 17 D 835, the resignation of a trustee was authorised on the ground of ill health, although it is unclear whether this involved an exercise of the *nobile officium* or more general common law powers.

[29] Trusts (Scotland) Act 1921, s 23. The statutory power also pertains to the sheriff court, per the Law Reform (Miscellaneous Provisions) (Scotland) Act 1980, s 13.

[30] *Gibson's Trs, Petrs* 1933 SC 190 at 201 per Lord President Clyde; A J P Menzies, *The Law of Scotland affecting Trustees* (2nd edn, 1913, W Green) at 565; Mackay, *The Practice of the Court of Session*, vol 1 at 209. See, eg, *Shariff v Hamid* 2000 SLT 294, in which a petition for the removal of trustees was refused, but not on point of competency.

[31] *Shariff v Hamid* at 296 per Lord Nimmo Smith.

In *Cherry v Patrick*,[32] for example, one of four trustees (A) had brought an action against the trust estate on an essential allegation of fraud against the deceased truster. A refused to resign from office, and two of the other trustees petitioned the *nobile officium* for A's removal. The Court, noting that it was incompatible for a person to both pursue an action against a trust estate, and act as a trustee of that estate, removed A from office. Likewise, in *Fleming v Craig*,[33] there had been a conflict between the trustee's duty as a trustee and his interests as an individual, and this resulted in the trustee's removal and the appointment of a judicial factor. In *Maclean, Petr*,[34] however, a petition to confirm the resignation of a trustee where a conflict of interests had arisen was dismissed as incompetent.

The *nobile officium* may also be invoked to remove a trustee who obstructs the administration of a trust,[35] or who shows a complete and persistent disregard for his duty as a trustee,[36] or who is guilty of malversation of office or has shown by his conduct in his capacity as trustee that he is unfit to discharge the duties of that office.[37] Obstruction should comprise something more than mere disharmony among trustees.[38] A trustee could not be removed on the basis that the beneficiaries were dissatisfied with his performance, assuming that he had executed the purposes of the trust.[39] Lord Blackburn drew on a principle expressed by himself in an appeal before the Privy Council from the Cape of Good Hope:

> [I]f satisfied that the continuance of the trustee would prevent the trusts being properly executed, the trustee might be removed. It must

---

[32] 1910 SC 32.

[33] (1863) 1 M 850.

[34] (1895) 3 SLT 74.

[35] *Hope v Hope* (1884) 12 R 27 at 30 per Lord President Inglis.

[36] *MacGilchrist's Trs v MacGilchrist* 1930 SC 635; see also *Walker, Petrs* (1868) 6 M 973; *McWhirter v Latta* (1889) 17 R 68; and *Waugh's Tr, Petrs* (1892) 20 R 57 at 58 per Lord McLaren.

[37] *Russo v Russo* 1998 SLT (Sh Ct) 32 at 35–36 per Sheriff Principal Cox. These comments were made in the context of an executor in his capacity as trustee.

[38] See *Shariff v Hamid* 2000 SLT 294 at 296.

[39] *McWhirter v Latta* (1889) 17 R 68 at 70 per Lord Lee.

always be borne in mind that trustees exist for the benefit of those to whom the creator of the trust has given the trust-estate.[40]

It is possible, of course, that the grounds for seeking to remove a trustee from office are less contentious. In any event, the power of the Court to remove trustees by virtue of its *nobile officium* is complemented by a statutory power of removal, and it of course remains possible for a trustee to be removed as specified in the trust deed.

2.2 Powers of trustees and variation of trust purposes

Trustees have the powers lawfully conferred upon them by the trust deed and those conferred by statute. Where neither of these sources confer the required power, petition may be made to the *nobile officium* for additional powers or for authority to perform certain acts. In such questions, the Court has been described as a "Court of Equity".[41] This may also include, for example, the *nobile officium* being used to "turn nonsense into sense", to omit from a trust deed a word "obviously inserted by mistake".[42]

A number of petitions have been presented for additional powers or for authority to perform certain acts, with varying success. It must be emphasised that the rationale behind the Court's willingness to grant additional powers is an eagerness to facilitate the administration of the trust in line with the intention of the truster. The circumstances in which it will be justified to petition the *nobile officium* for such powers will tend to be limited in view of the usually wide powers conferred on trustees by the trust deed and the additional powers conferred by statute. The scope for granting additional powers in this way is further limited by a requirement to properly justify the enlargement of powers sought.

---

[40] *Orr Ewing's Trs v Ewing* (1885) 13 R (HL) 1 at 23 per Lord Blackburn; quoting himself in *Letterstedt v Broers* (1884) 9 App Cas 371 at 386.

[41] Charles Forsyth, *The Principles and Practice of the Law of Trusts and Trustees in Scotland* (1844, W Blackwood) at 168; see also, eg, *Young v Rose* (1839) 1 D 1242 at 1244 per Lord Mackenzie.

[42] *Fowler's Trs v Fowler* (1898) 25 R 1034 at 1037 per Lord Young.

(a) Enlargement of powers of trustees and authority to perform acts

In general, the Court is reluctant to enlarge the powers of trustees or to authorise acts which are not permitted by the trust deed. This is because it is a central function of trustees to achieve the trust purposes as expressed in the trust deed, and as their powers principally derive from the trust deed, the idea is that their powers are generally circumscribed to those already conferred. In other words, it may be regarded as contrary to the trust deed, or an extension of the trust deed, to grant powers which were not granted by the deed itself.

Nevertheless, the *nobile officium* may be exercised to grant additional powers to trustees or to authorise certain acts beyond what is expressly provided by the trust deed. This power is apart from any statutory provisions for the extension of the powers of trustees, or where for some reason the statutory provision cannot be actuated. The power is exercised carefully to ensure that the trust purposes are being upheld. It may be, for example, that changing circumstances which had not been foreseen by the truster require the grant of additional powers for realisation of the trust purposes. In these circumstances, it may unnecessarily defeat the trust purposes if the required powers do not already reside in the trustees and the Court declines to confer them. It has been said that the Court "in the exercise of its *nobile officium*, has jurisdiction at common law to supervise the administration of trusts and to take such steps as may be appropriate to see that they are properly executed".[43]

The Court has attempted to strike a balance between facilitating the administration of trusts and becoming overtly involved in their administration. Indeed, the Court has regarded its capacity to involve itself in the actual administration of trusts as less than that of the Chancery Division in England.[44] Lord

---

[43] *Shariff v Hamid* 2000 SLT 294 at 294 per Lord Nimmo Smith.

[44] *Dundas, Petrs* (1869) 7 M 670 at 671–72 per Lord Deas; *Hall's Trs v McArthur* 1918 SC 646 at 650 per Lord Johnston, and at 652 per Lord Mackenzie. See also Forsyth, *Law of Trusts and Trustees* at 168.

McLaren viewed this as a matter of jurisdiction.[45] It has been made clear that trustees are not entitled to come to the Court for advice,[46] as this would implicate the Court in an advisory, or even administrative role.[47] As Lord President Inglis said in *Berwick, Petrs*:

> The powers of trustees are defined by the trust-deed, and the Court will give no higher power. The trustees are not entitled to come to the Court for advice. If they have not the power given them by the deed it is not competent for us to give it them.[48]

The matter was similarly put by Lord Kinnear in *Edinburgh Young Women's Christian Institute, Petrs*:

> If the petitioners have power to do what they ask us to authorise, there is no necessity for our authority; if they have no such power, I am unable to see that by anything we can do we can give it to them.[49]

Trustees "cannot come here to ask us to back them up by saying that their discretion has been exercised wisely".[50] Instead, the Court "can only give relief from technical difficulties or useless restrictions where a situation has arisen which has not been contemplated by the truster or which has emerged through supervening changes".[51] Of course, it is possible that petitions that are substantively for directions may be technically styled otherwise, and therefore be competent, though the circumstances in which directions would be given must surely be limited.

The Court has declined to confer additional powers on trustees in a number of cases on the basis that such powers were not conferred by the trust deed, either by construction or

---

[45] See *Edinburgh Young Women's Christian Institute, Petrs* (1893) 20 R 894 at 896 per Lord McLaren.

[46] *Gibson's Trs, Petrs* 1933 SC 190 at 197 per Lord President Clyde and at 220 Lord Morison, though, on some interpretations, *Neech's Executors, Petrs* 1947 SC 119 might be construed as involving advice-giving.

[47] See *Noble's Trs, Petrs* 1912 SC 1230 at 1234 per Lord Mackenzie.

[48] (1874) 2 R 90 at 92.

[49] At 896 per Lord Kinnear.

[50] *Noble's Trs, Petrs* at 1234 per Lord Johnston.

[51] *Gibson's Trs, Petrs* 1933 SC 190 at 220 per Lord Morison.

implication.[52] This has included petitions for such authority as the power to borrow,[53] and the power to allocate part of the capital to a different purpose.[54] The Court has also declined to exercise the *nobile officium* to relax or set aside the direction of the truster as expressed in the trust deed, even where it would be "expedient" to do so. This would result in the Court authorising contrary to the directions of the trust deed, and it may be incompetent for the Court to do so.[55] Authority was refused for part of a bequest to be paid to the inheritor institution of a redesignated charitable organisation, with the Court instead suggesting the pursuit of some other common law process, such as multiplepoinding.[56]

In an apparent measure to protect itself against involvement in the actual administration of trusts, the Court has declined to authorise powers where these may already have been granted by the trust deed. Where, for example, trustees petitioned the *nobile officium* for authority to take a farm into their own hands and manage it for a trust, having been unable to secure an offer of tenancy at an adequate rent, the Court dismissed the petition as unnecessary on the ground that what was proposed was an ordinary act of trust administration which did not require the authority of the Court.[57] The practical utility of such a finding is, however, that trustees have a certain amount of protection in doing the thing for which they sought authority. If trustees purport to exercise powers they do not have, the Court cannot grant them those powers; whilst if they seek to exercise powers that they do have, it is for them as trustees to exercise those powers at their discretion.[58] Not all have been satisfied with this position:

> It has been said—and the saying correctly represents the law of Scotland—that the Court will not advise trustees. If trustees possess

[52] *Kinloch, Petrs* (1859) 22 D 174 at 177 per Lord President McNeill.

[53] *Ker, Petrs* (1855) 17 D 565; *Kinloch, Petr.*

[54] *Noble's Trs, Petrs* 1912 SC 1230.

[55] *Scott's Hospital Trs, Petrs* 1913 SC 289 at 291 per Lord Salvesen.

[56] *McLevy's Trs, Petrs* 1947 SLT (Notes) 38.

[57] *Dunbar's Trs, Petrs* 1915 SC 860.

[58] *Noble's Trs, Petrs*. See also *Edinburgh Young Women's Christian Institute, Petrs* at 896, above.

a power, however difficult and delicate may be its exercise, and however serious the responsibility which they may incur either by exercising it or refusing to exercise it, the Court will not lift a finger to help them; it declines to advise them. I should have thought that a primary purpose of a Supreme Court of Equity was to assist trustees and beneficiaries in circumstances of difficulty by aiding them in the exercise of powers which already belonged to them in circumstances where such assistance was desirable. I should further have thought that a Supreme Court of Equity should have jurisdiction to confer upon trustees powers which the testator had not conferred upon them, if the circumstances made that course desirable. The only reason which I have ever heard stated in justification of the legal theory on which our Courts proceed is that of expense, that it is undesirable that the Court in Scotland should undertake the administration of trusts because that course may lead to expense. Cheapness may be too dearly bought.[59]

Nevertheless, the position taken in the case law is that it is for trustees to exercise their discretion within the parameters of the trust deed (and statute), and if there is doubt on their part about whether they can or cannot exercise a particular power, the Court will not act in an advisory capacity to set them right. That is the general position, although the Court has not always adopted a consistent approach to the question of when it would be prepared to intervene.

In addition to cases in which the Court has refused to grant additional powers to those conferred by the trust deed, it has also refused to authorise certain acts where other ways existed of dealing with the matter. In *Waugh's Tr, Petrs*,[60] for example, a petition was made to the *nobile officium* by a trustee and beneficiaries for authority for that trustee to grant conveyances of trust property and wind up the trust, in the absence of another trustee who had left for the United States without leaving an address. The Court refused the prayer of the petition, noting that the matter could be dealt with by, for example, removing the absent trustee. Meanwhile, in *Sutherland, Petrs*,[61] a petition was made

---

[59] *Hall's Trs v McArthur* 1918 SC 646 at 654–55 per Lord Skerrington.
[60] (1892) 20 R 57.
[61] (1903) 10 SLT 600.

to the *nobile officium* for authority to convey school buildings gratuitously to a school board on the basis that no funds were available for building additional accommodation in satisfaction of a requirement for continuing to receive government grants. The Court refused the prayer of the petition, but extended to the petitioners an opportunity to propose an amended scheme. Lord McLaren explained that although the Court could authorise the gratuitous transfer of the school buildings to the school board if the choice were between that and allowing the school to go to ruin, the present circumstances did not disclose that such a stark choice had to be made.[62]

There have, of course, been successful petitions seeking additional powers or authority to perform certain acts. The Court has demonstrated its willingness to assist trustees in carrying out the intention of the truster in a number of cases. It has authorised a power to sell,[63] a power to sell and bid for sale items,[64] a power to borrow,[65] a power to purchase heritage,[66] a power to purchase heritage and borrow on the security of the estate,[67] a power to sell heritage and reinvest the proceeds,[68] a power to grant a mineral lease and feu heritage,[69] a power to apply the future income of a fund to revenue purposes instead of accumulating it,[70] an increase in the scope of food and materials provided under a charitable trust,[71] and the relocation of gravestones.[72]

---

[62] At 602 per Lord McLaren.

[63] *Erskine's Trs v Wemyss* (1829) 7 S 594; *Henderson v Somerville* (1841) 3 D 1049. See also *Campbell's Trs v Campbell* (1838) 1 D 153.

[64] *Coats's Trs, Petrs* 1914 SC 723.

[65] *Glasgow and West of Scotland Technical College, Petrs* (1902) 4 F 982.

[66] *Fletcher's Trs, Petrs* 1949 SC 330. See also *Wardlaw's Trs* (1902) 10 SLT 349.

[67] *Anderson's Trs, Petrs* 1921 SC 315.

[68] *Chalmers Hospital (Banff) Trs, Petrs* 1923 SC 220.

[69] *Pender's Trs, Petrs* (1903) 5 F 504.

[70] *Glasgow Young Men's Christian Association, Petrs* 1934 SC 452.

[71] *Guardian of Thomson's Mortification, Petr* 1908 SC 1078. This was authorised without the approval of a formal scheme.

[72] *Christie, Petrs* 1926 SC 750. Lords Ormidale and Hunter expressed reservations on the competency of the petition in this case, even though they considered it meritorious.

An example of changing circumstances leading to a successful petition may be taken from *Harrison, Petrs*.[73] *Ex officio* trustees were determined with regard to the diocese in which a church was situated. A particular church was originally in the Diocese of Glasgow, but was later designated as within the Diocese of Edinburgh. Trustees of the church (under its original designation) petitioned the *nobile officium* for authority to convey property held by them to trustees under the church's new designation. The Court authorised and ordained the trustees to convey the property.

In *Dowden, Petrs*,[74] attendance at a religious trust school had considerably declined due to an increase in free education, and the school served no continuing purpose. The trustees petitioned for authority to give up the school and to devote the school funds to the purpose of the religious mission alone. The Court granted these heads of the prayer, but refused a third, which was to consolidate the separate trusts into a single mission trust.

Another example of a successful petition in changing circumstances was in the case of *Clark Bursary Fund (Mile End) Trs, Petrs*.[75] At the time of the constitution of a trust deed for awarding scholarships, bursaries and fellowships at the University of Glasgow, all ordinary classes were closed to female students. The university regulations had since been amended to allow females to be admitted to most classes, and the scholarship in modern languages had only one purported candidate, who was a female, and who subsequently obtained first class honours in her examination. The Court authorised the trustees to appoint the female concerned to the scholarship, it having been averred by the petitioners that if she was not so appointed, the modern languages scholarship would lapse.

In *Anderson's Trs, Petrs*,[76] a trust deed provided no power for the trustees to purchase heritage or to borrow on the security of the estate. Developments in the circumstances of the case made

---

[73] (1893) 20 R 827.
[74] (1899) 7 SLT 219.
[75] (1903) 10 SLT 580.
[76] 1921 SC 315.

it impossible to secure the object of the trust without purchasing heritage and borrowing on the security of the estate. The trustees therefore petitioned the *nobile officium* to authorise those acts. Lord Justice-Clerk Scott Dickson opined that the circumstances were so exceptional that the Court should undertake the "duty" of exercising the *nobile officium*. If it did not do so in order to grant the powers requested, the main purpose of the trust deed would be completely frustrated. It would be "almost pedantic" if the Court laid down difficulties in the way of the trustees' securing the main purpose of the trust.[77] The Court would simply be supplying a want of machinery,[78] the case being one of a *casus improvisus* in the trust deed.[79] Accordingly, the Court granted the prayer of the petition.

Similarly, it was stated in another case that:

> If the trustees of a charitable trust can satisfy the Court that the circumstances of the trust are such that the carrying out of the trust will be seriously hampered unless the powers craved are granted, then it is within the power of the Court to intervene. In other words, to save a charitable trust from wreckage it is not necessary for the Court to hesitate until the trust is actually upon the rocks.[80]

As a final example, trustees petitioned the Inner House, under both the Trusts (Scotland) Act 1921 and the *nobile officium*, for authority to sell heritage and reinvest the proceeds, and to admit to a trust hospital paying patients from any area (rather than just Banff) in order to raise income. The revenue received had become insufficient to maintain the hospital. The Court granted the prayer of the petition, Lord Justice-Clerk Alness noting that if the Court did not do so, the object of the trust would be defeated.[81]

---

[77] At 319–21 per Lord Justice-Clerk Scott Dickson.
[78] At 322 per Lord Dundas.
[79] At 323 per Lord Ormidale.
[80] *Glasgow Young Men's Christian Association, Petrs* 1934 SC 452 at 458 per Lord Blackburn.
[81] *Chalmers Hospital (Banff) Trs, Petrs* 1923 SC 220 at 226–27 per Lord Justice-Clerk Alness.

(b) Authority for advances to beneficiaries

The *nobile officium* has been used to authorise advances from trust funds to beneficiaries. A statutory power of advancement is found in section 16 of the Trusts (Scotland) Act 1921; however, a residual power to authorise advancement subsists in the *nobile officium*. Where it was open to the Court to authorise advances under section 16 of the 1921 Act, it was held unnecessary to address the question of whether the same could have been achieved in exercise of the *nobile officium*.[82]

The typical exercise of the *nobile officium* in this category of case has regarded the authorisation of advances to minor beneficiaries for their maintenance and education.[83] Advances have also been made to major beneficiaries,[84] and even to offspring who have reached old age.[85] Whilst a petition was refused on the basis that a right had not yet vested in the beneficiaries,[86] vesting has not always been deemed vital for advances to be authorised.[87] The Court cautioned against setting any precedent in the latter situation, for the circumstances were "very special" and a *casus improvisus* had arisen.[88] Whilst actual advances have been sought in their own right, there may be some other form of advance sought such as the increase of an allowance[89] or an additional annuity.[90]

---

[82] *Macfarlane v Macfarlane's Trs* 1931 SC 95. See also *Anderson's Trs, Petrs* 1936 SC 460.

[83] *Hamilton, Petrs* (1860) 22 D 1095; *Latta, Petr* (1880) 7 R 881; *Websters v Miller's Trs* (1887) 14 R 501; *Muir v Muir's Trs* (1887) 15 R 170; *Colquhoun, Petrs* (1894) 21 R 671; *Bett's Trs, Petrs* 1922 SC 21. Such petitions have been brought by various parties including trustees, judicial factors, beneficiaries and liferenters. See also *Taylor, Petr* (1851) 13 D 948.

[84] *Robertson, Petrs* 1909 SC 236; *Sinclair's Trs, Petrs* 1921 SC 484; *Frew's Trs, Petrs* 1932 SC 501; *Craig's Trs, Petrs* 1934 SC 34 (see, in particular, the comments of Lord Hunter at 38). See also A Mackenzie Stuart, "The nobile officium and trust administration" 1935 SLT (News) 1 at 4–5; and Smith, *A Short Commentary* at 566.

[85] *Allan, Petr* (1869) 8 M 139.

[86] *Mundell, Petrs* (1862) 24 D 327.

[87] *Christie's Trs, Petrs* 1932 SC 189; *Stewart v Brown's Trs* 1941 SC 300.

[88] *Stewart v Brown's Trs* at 308 per Lord Mackay.

[89] *Baird v Baird's Trs* (1872) 10 M 482.

[90] *Allan, Petr* (1869) 8 M 139.

The Court not only has the power to authorise the increase of an allowance, but to fix that allowance at a particular sum. This was done in *Baird v Baird's Trs*,[91] in which Lord Ardmillan regarded this as "within the power of the Court, in the exercise of a sound judicial discretion ... if your Lordships think it just and right to do so".[92] It should be noted, however, that Lord Deas dissented, opining that this was a matter for the discretion of the trustees, and that the Court should not interfere in that unless something had gone "extravagantly wrong" and there was a case of "necessity or of clamant expediency".[93] In a case in which a widow unsuccessfully petitioned the *nobile officium* for increased allowances from her deceased husband's trust for her children on account of their "very delicate health", Lord President Inglis explained that "[i]t is almost unnecessary to observe that the Court is not wont to interpose in cases of this kind except upon very strong grounds".[94]

The Court has refused to authorise certain advances to be made to beneficiaries where those advances were prohibited by the terms of the trust deed, it also being noted that even if the Court had the power to authorise the advances, it would not be a fair and reasonable exercise of that power.[95] It has also refused to authorise the payment of trust funds where a direct action against the trustees would be a more proper mode of recourse than petition to the *nobile officium*.[96] In the particular circumstances of that case, Lord Ormidale added that the *nobile officium* may only have been exercisable had there been "circumstances of distress" or something "making the administration of the trustees difficult".[97]

---

[91] (1872) 10 M 482. The case is artfully mocked in James Balfour Paul, *Ballads of the Bench and Bar or Idle Lays of the Parliament House* (privately printed, Edinburgh, 1882) at 110–13.

[92] At 491 per Lord Ardmillan.

[93] At 490 per Lord Deas.

[94] *Douglas v Douglas's Trs* (1872) 10 M 943 at 945 per Lord President Inglis.

[95] *Thomson v Miller's Trs* (1883) 11 R 401 at 404 per Lord Young.

[96] *Snodgrass, Petr* 1922 SC 491.

[97] *Snodgrass, Petr* at 496 per Lord Ormidale.

The Court has held that it could not competently exercise its *nobile officium* to alter the terms of a bequest for the purpose of insuring a larger income for a liferentrix.[98] Lord President Clyde explained that:

> [t]he *nobile officium* does not entitle the Court to make a will for a testator which he has not made for himself; although it does enable the Court to exercise wide powers for the rescue of a plan of testamentary disposal from inherent conditions which make it unworkable or which tend to defeat its own purpose. ... [T]he *nobile officium* never has been invoked, and I do not think it could be used, for the simple purpose of enabling a beneficiary to enjoy a larger interest in the testator's estate than the testator has seen fit to give. The only exercise of the *nobile officium* which approaches anything of this sort is that by which trustees are given power to make necessary advances for the maintenance and education of the truster's children out of that part of his estate which is already vested in them. ... But this power is exercised only when the maintenance and education of the children is unprovided for in the settlement, or hampered by a direction to accumulate, or the like. The situation is really in the nature of a *casus improvisus*, in which the legal right of the testator's children to be maintained out of his estate has been unintentionally defeated or left unprovided for.[99]

Likewise, the Court did not authorise a wife's assignation of part of her alimentary liferent to an insurance company in exchange for a capital payment, with regard to an antenuptial marriage contract.[100] It would have been unjust to give the insurance company an absolute right to that sum in preference to the wife's potential future creditors, and would not have been *res judicata* against those creditors. Lord Justice-Clerk Thomson explained that the Court was in effect being asked to "vary the terms of a trust deed in order that a beneficiary may enjoy more advantageous terms than the trust deed itself confers", to be achieved by an act which was not permitted by the marriage contract. He concluded:

---

[98] *Anderson's Trs, Petrs* 1932 SC 226.
[99] *Anderson's Trs, Petrs* at 231 per Lord President Clyde.
[100] *Coles, Petr* 1951 SC 608.

> I would be slow to think that it would be a proper exercise of the *nobile officium* so to interfere with the trust purposes, at any rate in a case where interference is not required to prevent the trust from becoming unworkable or to protect the trust estate from loss or the beneficiary from hardship.[101]

(c) Retrospective authorisation of acts

In *Christie's Trs, Petrs*,[102] trustees under a marriage contract sought authorisation for certain advances out of the capital of the estate, and to sanction advances already made, under section 16 of the Trusts (Scotland) Act 1921 or, alternatively, in exercise of the *nobile officium*. The Court granted the prayer of the petition in exercise of its *nobile officium*.

However, the view was taken in *Dow's Trs, Petrs*,[103] that what was essentially being prayed for was retrospective validation of *ultra vires* acts, and that the course adopted in *Christie's Trs* was to be used only exceptionally:

> I do not doubt that a retrospective validation is not beyond the powers of this Court in the exercise of the *nobile officium*. I consider, however, that such an order should only be made in exceptional circumstances and for very compelling reasons.[104]

That was essentially an affirmation that the Court possessed the power of retrospective validation. Lord Keith added that in *Dow's Trs* he would have preferred to grant authority under section 16 of the Trusts (Scotland) Act 1921.[105]

Dow's Trs was followed in *East Kilbride District Nursing Association, Petrs*,[106] in which the Association petitioned the *nobile officium* for authorisation of a *cy-près* scheme. That would, by necessary implication, involve the Court giving retrospective

---

[101] *Coles, Petr* at 617.
[102] 1932 SC 189.
[103] 1947 SC 524. The Court had declined to retrospectively authorise the sale of part of a trust estate in *Clyne, Petr* (1894) 21 R 849.
[104] *Dow's Trs, Petrs* at 527 per Lord President Cooper.
[105] At 527 per Lord Keith.
[106] 1951 SC 64.

validity to certain acts of the Association's executive committee. Lord President Cooper confirmed that his statement of principle, quoted above, applied "with at least equal force to a charitable trust". The circumstances in the present case were neither "exceptional" nor "very compelling" to justify retrospective validation by the Court.[107]

Dow's Trs was also followed in the case of *Horne's Trs, Petrs*.[108] Authority was sought by petition to the *nobile officium* by English trustees for the sale of heritable property in Scotland,[109] and to retrospectively authorise a sale which had already been effected on the basis that the trustees believed they had the requisite authority. The Court was not prepared to grant that aspect of the petition relating to retrospective authorisation. Lord President Cooper explained that it had been made plain in *Dow's Trs* that such authorisation should only be given in exceptional circumstances and for "very compelling reasons". He added that:

> If this had been a Scottish trust I have no doubt that the remedy would not be granted, for, if trustees have as a result of an *ultra vires* act given a bad title to heritage, the *nobile officium* could not in any ordinary case be used for the purpose of relieving the trustees from the possible consequences of a breach of trust, least of all when these consequences are future and hypothetical. To use the *nobile officium* in such circumstances and for such an object would create a dangerous precedent with alarming possibilities.[110]

(d) Cy-près schemes and the administration of public trusts

A *cy-près* scheme is an arrangement with a view to rescuing a public trust from failure.[111] It involves an application for

---

[107] At 66 per Lord President Cooper.

[108] 1952 SC 70.

[109] See also p 35, fn 18.

[110] *Horne's Trs, Petrs* at 72.

[111] A good overview of the Court's *cy–près* jurisdiction is given in Wilson and Duncan, *Trusts, Trustees and Executors* at 238–58. See also Menzies, *The Law of Scotland affecting Trustees* at 235.

administrative machinery to carry out the trust purposes where the machinery has not been provided by the truster, or for variance of the trust purposes where the truster's directions cannot be carried out but there is a general charitable intention, or where the trust fails after a period of operation.[112] Although the *cy-près* doctrine embraces charitable trusts in addition to public trusts more broadly, the essence of the Court's involvement in this area was captured by Lord President Clyde in the notable case of *Gibson's Trs, Petrs*:

> [T]he Court will not allow a charitable bequest or trust to be held void from uncertainty, or to fail, if that can possibly be avoided. Pious intentions, in short, are more favoured than the claims of the heir-at-law or of the Crown; which is an equitable principle or nothing. If *(in the first place)* a settlor has clearly manifested an intention to establish some specific kind of charitable institution, but has failed to provide his trustees with the powers and machinery to establish and work it, the endowment will not only not be allowed to fail, but the Court will take it upon itself to carry out the establishment of the specific institution by creating the powers and machinery. ... [If] a charitable endowment, which its founder has – no matter how clearly and specifically – prescribed and equipped with powers and machinery sufficient to effectuate it, should cease to operate owing to changed circumstances, the Court will intervene to prevent such failure ... by what may well seem the extreme course of taking upon itself to vary the founder's settlement, so as to preserve the underlying charitable purpose consistently with making the least possible departure from the founder's directions.[113]

In approving a *cy-près* scheme, it is often said that the Court is exercising its *cy-près* jurisdiction. Lord President Hope said that "[i]t is a matter for the Inner House of the Court of Session to define the limits of its *cy-près* jurisdiction in the exercise of its

---

[112] *Discussion Paper on Trustees and Trust Administration* at 61.

[113] *Gibson's Trs, Petrs* 1933 SC 190 at 199 per Lord President Clyde. See also *Clephane v Magistrates of Edinburgh* (1869) 7 M (HL) 7, still regarded as a leading case in *RS Macdonald Charitable Trust Trs v Scottish Society for the Prevention of Cruelty to Animals* 2009 SC 6 at 17 per Lord Drummond Young.

nobile officium",[114] and elsewhere it has been said that invocation of the *cy-près* jurisdiction involves an application to the *nobile officium*.[115]

It is uncertain whether this should properly be regarded as an aspect of the *nobile officium*;[116] however, the *nobile officium* may at least be used in fulfilling *cy-près* objectives.[117] It may be helpful to conceive of *cy-près* jurisdiction as a common law jurisdiction which sometimes draws on the *nobile officium* for its efficacy, or as a blend of common law and *nobile officium* powers. Indeed, the character of *cy-près* jurisdiction may become less associated with the *nobile officium* if proposals to delegate certain *cy-près* work to the sheriff court are implemented.[118] The *nobile officium* has been used to approve schemes whether or not they carry the designation "*cy-près*", and the courts have broader jurisdiction to approve schemes in relation to public and charitable trusts.[119] Distinctions in this area of law cannot be overstated, particularly as trusts are now governed by a mélange of statutory, common law and *nobile officium* powers. Applications "to the *nobile officium*" for approval of a *cy-près* scheme are now made to the Outer House.[120]

---

[114] *Mining Institute of Scotland Benevolent Fund Trs, Petrs* 1994 SLT 785 at 786 per Lord President Hope.

[115] *Discussion Paper on Trustees and Trust Administration* at para 61.

[116] See *Stair Memorial Encyclopaedia*, Trusts, Trustees and Judicial Factors, vol 24, para 106.

[117] Kenneth McK Norrie & Eilidh M Scobbie, *Trusts* (1991, W Green) at 173–74.

[118] *Discussion Paper on Trustees and Trust Administration* at 62–64.

[119] Law Reform (Miscellaneous Provisions) (Scotland) Act 1990, s 9. This provision is "without prejudice to the power of the Court of Session to approve a cy pres scheme in relation to any public trust" (s 9(7)). See also the Trusts (Scotland) Act 1921, s 26; the Charities and Trustee Investment (Scotland) Act 2005; and *Forrest's Trs v Forrest* 1960 SLT 88.

[120] Rules of the Court of Session, rr 14.2(c), 14.3(d) and 63.7–63.15. It is also provided therein that applications for the reorganisation of endowments under Part VI of the Education (Scotland) Act 1980, and Part I of the Law Reform (Miscellaneous Provisions) (Scotland) Act 1990 in relation to charities and the reorganisation of public trusts, shall be made to the Outer House. See also Part III of Chapter 63 of the Rules of Court generally.

Approved schemes have typically featured such proposals as for funds to be applied to a different purpose,[121] or the purchase[122] or transfer[123] of property.[124]

A scheme has been approved for the application of funds and the constitution of a trust where a charitable association in whose hands assets were held was being wound up.[125] A scheme has also been approved for the payment to trustees of a hospital bequest.[126] Where an art collection had been bequeathed in trust to a university, and that university had subsequently obtained the approval of a statutory scheme without having served the petition on the nominated trustees, the *nobile officium* was exercised to approve the statutory scheme of new with the trustees having become involved in the process.[127] Another example of a successful application of this power has been to wind up two regimental benevolent associations and to transfer their assets to a new association, where there had been an amalgamation of the two infantry regiments to which the original benevolent associations related.[128]

---

[121] *McDougall, Petr* (1878) 5 R 1014 (in which regard, see also *Grant v Macqueen* (1877) 4 R 734); *Glasgow Royal Infirmary, Petrs* (1887) 14 R 680; *Glasgow Royal Infirmary v Magistrates of Glasgow* (1888) 15 R 264. For a scheme approved for a division of funds, see *Kirk Session of Old Monkland v School Board of the Parish of Old Monkland* (1893) 1 SLT 304.

[122] *Robertson's Trs, Petrs* 1948 SC 1.

[123] *Stranraer Original Secession Congregation, Petrs* 1923 SC 722.

[124] For other successful petitions for the approval of a scheme, see *Magistrates & Nine Incorporated Trades of Dundee v Morris* (1861) 23 D 493; *Kirk Session of Prestonpans v School Board of Prestonpans* (1891) 19 R 193; *Governors of John Watt's Hospital* (1893) 20 R 729; *Old Monkland School Board v Bargeddie Kirk Session* (1893) 21 R 122; *Trustees of Portobello Female School, Petrs* (1900) 2 F 418; *Goodman, Petrs* 1958 SC 377; and *Parsons, Petrs* 1976 SC 245.

[125] *Clyde Industrial Training Ship Association, Petrs* 1925 SLT 446. In *Burnett v St Andrew's Episcopal Church, Brechin* (1888) 15 R 723, two congregations each claimed a whole trust fund "not as a matter of legal right, but because they each consider that they have the best claim in equity to the remaining balance of the property of this lapsed trust". The Court held one of the congregations entitled to the funds in equity.

[126] *Robertson, Petrs* 1938 SLT 145.

[127] *University of Edinburgh v The Torrie Trs* 1997 SLT 1009.

[128] *Clutterbuck, Petrs* 1961 SLT 427.

There is a small cluster of cases in which the *nobile officium* was used to approve a scheme proposing to enlarge or extend a class of potential beneficiaries.[129] In one case, the scheme sought to enlarge the pool of potential candidates for a research prize by relaxing the requirements for its satisfaction, due to the existing criteria having – in the trustees' view – failed to attain the truster's stated object.[130] In another case, the scheme proposed an enlargement of the permitted provenance of candidates for a bursary offered under a bequest, the original bequest having required that candidates be from Dunbar, but with no application ever having been made.[131] Likewise, where a bursary comprised of bequest funds was to be given to a young man from the Presbytery of Ayr for studying divinity at the University of Edinburgh, but where difficulties had been encountered in finding qualified candidates with most from the presbytery preferring to study at the University of Glasgow, the Court authorised the alteration of the conditions to extend to qualified persons studying divinity at any university in Scotland where no qualified candidate could be found for Edinburgh.[132] A scheme also sought to widen the scope of potential recipients of funds for dependants of crew lost aboard the *SS Celerity* some years after its establishment.[133] In each of these cases, the proposed scheme was approved by exercise of the *nobile officium*.[134]

---

[129] As, eg, in *Governors of Mitchell's Hospital, Petrs* (1902) 4 F 582.

[130] *Trustees of the "John Reid Prize", Petrs* (1893) 20 R 938.

[131] *Kirk Session of Dunbar, Petrs* 1908 SC 852.

[132] *Pollock, Petrs* 1948 SLT (Notes) 11.

[133] *Gibson, Petr* (1900) 2 F 1195.

[134] It appeared, however, that extending the eligibility for a bursary to include women was a step too far. Where a scheme sought to open a bequeathed medical bursary to young women from Nairnshire, the trustees having experienced difficulty in attracting male candidates for the bursary, the Court refused to approve the scheme. Lord President Balfour described the proposed change as "drastic", whilst Lord McLaren noted that it was being proposed to "admit women to the benefit of an endowment expressly given to men, and given by a member of a profession not very friendly to the admission of women within its ranks": *Grigor Medical Bursary Fund Trs, Petrs* (1903) 5 F 1143 at 1145 per Lord President Balfour and at 1145 per Lord McLaren.

The *nobile officium* has been exercised to approve a scheme with regard to a body incorporated by royal charter, being a situation in which the Court would not normally exercise the jurisdiction, but in which there was no other remedy available for approval of the scheme.[135] The Court has also held that where a previous scheme had become wholly inoperative, and the enlargement of powers of investment was necessary as part of a new scheme, the *nobile officium* could be used to authorise that enlargement.[136] Although, as noted above, the Court will not enter into the administration of a trust, in some cases views have been expressed on the merits (or otherwise) of the proposed scheme, rather than merely its legal credentials. For example, the Court has adverted to the "expediency" of schemes.[137]

Where it is alleged that a scheme should be approved due to a failure of trust purposes, it may indeed have to be demonstrated that the trust purposes have failed.[138] In addition, a petition to the *nobile officium* for approval of a *cy-près* scheme would not usually be an appropriate context in which to determine a claim on funds under a lapsed trust.[139] The Court has refused to approve a scheme on the basis that the petitioners had been nominated as trustees, but had neither accepted nor declined office.[140]

The emphasis in the approval of schemes has been on the extrication of public trusts from failure and, related to this, facilitating the realisation of the intention of the truster.[141] On

---

[135] *Glasgow Magdalene Institution, Petrs* 1964 SC 227.

[136] *McCrie's Trs, Petrs* 1927 SC 556.

[137] *Caird, Petrs* (1874) 1 R 529 at 531–32 per Lord President Inglis; *Trustees of Carnegie Park Orphanage, Petrs* (1892) 19 R 605 at 608 per Lord Kinnear.

[138] *Thomson v Anderson* (1887) 14 R 1026. See also *Scotstown Moor Children's Camp, Petrs* 1948 SLT 531.

[139] See *Church of Scotland Trust v O'Donoghue* 1951 SC 85. See also, on a more general note, *Barns-Graham v City of Glasgow District Council* 1978 SLT (Notes) 50.

[140] *Watt, Petrs* (1895) 23 R 33.

[141] See, eg, the comments of Lord McLaren in *Trustees of Carnegie Park Orphanage, Petrs* at 608.

occasion, preventing a trust from failure has required acting against the letter of the trust deed. This occurred in *Stranraer Original Secession Congregation, Petrs*,[142] in which trustees for a congregation which had been dissolved petitioned the *nobile officium* for approval of a scheme which included transferring certain uninhabitable properties. The bequest under which the properties were originally obtained expressly prohibited their alienation. The Court granted the prayer of the petition, noting that if it failed to do so, the scheme would prove abortive. Lord President Clyde observed that the trustees could ordinarily have obtained a power of sale under the Trusts (Scotland) Act 1921, but in the present case there were special circumstances, as the power to vary related to the only permanent asset of the trust.[143] Although the authorisation of a scheme against the letter of the trust deed may be exceptionally justified, a scheme against an implied statutory prohibition may not.[144] Lord President Clyde said that any such power would have to be obtained "not from the Court but from Parliament".[145]

It is worth highlighting the case of *Galloway v Magistrates of Elgin*[146] as an instance of the Court refusing to approve a scheme. Trustees had petitioned the *nobile officium* for approval of a scheme whereby they would have discretion to reduce certain payments. Lord President Cooper explained that the petitioners had failed to satisfy two criteria:

> In a case of this class it is a prerequisite of the exercise of the *nobile officium* that it should be shown (i) that the intentions of the truster cannot be carried into effect by obedience to his explicit instructions, and (ii) that it is possible to find in the settlement an overriding charitable purpose of which the truster's explicit instructions are only the machinery. These generalised propositions were not disputed, and they are amply vouched by the authorities to

---

[142] 1923 SC 722.

[143] At 726 per Lord President Clyde.

[144] See Section 10.3.

[145] *Mitchell Bequest Trs, Petrs* 1959 SC 395 at 398 per Lord President Clyde.

[146] 1946 SC 353.

which we were referred. In my view, the petitioners fail to satisfy both these requirements.[147]

2.3   The necessity/expediency debate

There is a tension in the law as to the required threshold for the Court to exercise its *nobile officium* in the area of trusts. That is a tension between the standards of necessity and expediency. It came to a head in *Gibson's Trs* where the matter was the subject of open disagreement; however an outline of the pre-*Gibson* case law shall first be given.

A number of the earlier cases imposed a standard of necessity. Views were expressed that the Court had the power to appoint a trustee "where a necessity exists for it",[148] and "only in cases of necessity, where danger is to be apprehended if the Court do not interpose".[149] The granting of a power of sale to trustees was one which should be exercised cautiously and "under the deepest necessity only",[150] whilst in another case Lord Deas opined that if such a power could be granted in exercise of the *nobile officium*, it "must be on the ground of necessity, and not of expediency or discretion".[151] Where an increased allowance was sought for children, Lord Ardmillan said that "nothing but a very urgent necessity can justify the interference of the Court in a case of this kind",[152] whilst Lord President Inglis opined that there were "no sufficient reasons ... to necessitate our interference".[153] With regard to the Court's power to fix the amount of an allowance from trust funds, Lord Deas dissented from the majority position with the view that this was a matter for the discretion of the trustees, and that the Court should not interfere unless something had gone

---

[147] At 364 per Lord Justice-Clerk Cooper. See also *Davidson's Trs v Arnott* 1951 SC 42 at 55 per Lord Mackay.

[148] *Melville v Preston* (1838) 16 S 457 at 470 per Lord Gillies.

[149] *Preston v Preston's Trs* (1852) 14 D 1055 at 1056 per Lord President McNeill.

[150] *Graham v Graham's Trs* (1850) 13 D 420 at 428 per Lord Medwyn; and see also at 424 per Lord Justice-Clerk Hope.

[151] *Farquharson v Farquharson's Tr* (1866) 4 M 831 at 840 per Lord Deas.

[152] *Douglas v Douglas's Trs* (1872) 10 M 943 at 946 per Lord Ardmillan.

[153] *Douglas v Douglas's Trs* at 945 per Lord President Inglis.

"extravagantly wrong" and there was a case of "necessity or of clamant expediency".[154] The Court declined to exercise the *nobile officium* to relax or set aside the direction of a truster as expressed in the trust deed, even where it would be "expedient" to do so.[155] Lord President Clyde stated that the case law had shown that the "equitable powers" of the Court with regard to charitable trusts had never been held to extend beyond what is necessary.[156]

Necessity was not adopted across the board in cases pre-*Gibson*. Where advances were sought from trust funds, Lord President Inglis noted that, so far as the children were concerned, there was a "pressing necessity" for money.[157] However, in another case involving advances from trust funds, Lord Kinnear stated that the case was not one of "pressing necessity", but one in which the mother would be able to provide for her daughters' maintenance and education "much more conveniently and advantageously for them … a ground which the Court will always take into consideration in dealing with applications of this kind".[158] This appears to have been a nod towards expediency.

On a petition for approval of a scheme for the management of a charitable school, Lord President Inglis expressed views on the content of the scheme, including views on what would be expedient.[159] That is notwithstanding the position that the Court will not involve itself in the administration of trusts. On a petition for authority to relocate gravestones, the Court reporter deemed the relocation "expedient".[160] The Court granted the prayer of the petition, though Lords Ormidale and Hunter – who found the petition meritorious – expressed reservations over its competency.

---

[154] *Baird v Baird's Trs* (1872) 10 M 482 at 490 per Lord Deas.

[155] *Scott's Hospital Trs, Petrs* 1913 SC 289 at 290 per Lord Justice-Clerk Macdonald.

[156] *Thomson's Trs, Petrs* 1930 SC 767 at 770 per Lord President Clyde. Necessity was also the general standard related to the *nobile officium* in Berry (ed), *Balfour's Handbook* at 206.

[157] *Latta, Petr* (1880) 7 R 881 at 883 per Lord President Inglis.

[158] *Colquhoun, Petrs* (1894) 21 R 671 at 673 per Lord Kinnear.

[159] *Caird, Petrs* (1874) 1 R 529 at 531–32 per Lord President Inglis.

[160] *Christie, Petrs* 1926 SC 750.

Elsewhere, the standard adopted has been a variation on necessity. Lord Deas said the following in a petition for the Court's effective audit of trust accounts in accordance with the trust deed:

> I have only to add that the observation is new to me, that the exercise of our *nobile officium* in reference to charitable trusts is limited to cases of necessity. The will of the founder is, according to my understanding, all the necessity that is required. In short, I should have had no difficulty whatever in entertaining and acting on this petition, had it not been that the majority of your Lordships take a different view of it.[161]

In a case in which application was made under both the *nobile officium* and section 7 of the Trusts (Scotland) Act 1867, but in which the Court appeared to grant the application under the Act, Lord Justice-Clerk Macdonald stated:

> The only remaining question is whether we can hold under this clause of the Act, that the advances are necessary for the maintenance and education of such beneficiaries. Now, that is always a question of degree according to circumstances. Absolute necessity is not in question in the case; it is necessity in regard to the condition of the parties on whose behalf the application is made.[162]

It nevertheless seems that necessity was the preferred test in this earlier period.

Gibson's Trs, Petrs[163] brought the issue of whether necessity or expediency should be the test for the Court's intervention under sharp scrutiny before a court of seven judges. The case concerned a petition for approval of a scheme for the administration of an endowment, including a crave for a power to sell and invest. It was held, on point of the *nobile officium*, that the strong expediency of granting the enlarged powers of investment was sufficient to warrant the granting of those powers by exercise of the *nobile*

---

[161] *Dundas, Petrs* (1869) 7 M 670 at 673 per Lord Deas.

[162] *Clark's Trs, Petrs* (1895) 22 R 706 at 710. Absolute necessity was cited for the appointment of new trustees and interference with the constitution of the trust by Forsyth, *Law of Trusts and Trustees* at 434.

[163] 1933 SC 190.

officium. The case is notable both for this apparent shift from a test of necessity to one of expediency, and for the dissent of Lord President Clyde in that regard.[164]

Lord President Clyde regarded *Scott's Hospital Trs, Petrs*[165] as authority for the principle that the *nobile officium* could not competently be exercised to vary the powers or directions of a charitable trust merely because the Court considered that such a variation would be expedient. Instead, it had to be shown that the variation was "necessary in order to prevent a failure or breakdown in the operation of the charity". This was a "sound principle" which had "never been disputed until now". Moreover, "a change from necessity to expediency as a test of competency of using the *nobile officium* for the purpose of varying the powers and directions of a charitable settlement may involve far-reaching consequences".[166]

He went on to explain that necessity and expediency had different existing modes of application with regard to charitable trusts. Where the *nobile officium* was sought to enable the specific object of the founder's imperfect directions to be realised, the rule was one of the "highest expediency", with the Court granting all of the powers that it could for that purpose. However, where the *nobile officium* was sought to vary the settler's specific and unambiguous directions, the rule was one of necessity. In the latter case, the Court was restricted to those variations "necessary to preserve the underlying charitable intention of the founder from failure. This is precisely what is meant by approximation or *cy pres*".[167]

Lord President Clyde also pointed out that necessity was, in his view, the standard in other areas in which the *nobile officium* was in use, such as the appointment of judicial factors, the appointment of public officers and the supply of defects in

---

[164] This may have been a period of a more general change in the Court's attitude to the *nobile officium* as applied to trusts: see Mackenzie Stuart, *The Nobile Officium and Trust Administration.*

[165] 1913 SC 289.

[166] *Gibson's Trs, Petrs* at 198 per Lord President Clyde.

[167] *Gibson's Trs, Petrs* at 200 per Lord President Clyde.

statutory machinery. If the test of expediency was to be substituted for that of necessity in the present case, it would be:

> difficult to prevent the *nobile officium* (as applying to the doctrine of approximation or *cy pres*) from transforming itself into a sort of cornucopia of judicial favours for distribution as may seem expedient among deserving applicants, especially trustees of charitable endowments, who think ... that the founder's directions could be improved upon, or that a variation ... would make their duties less irksome.[168]

Lord Justice-Clerk Alness drew on John More, in his notes on Stair, as stating that the fixed principle of the *nobile officium* was that "it will never be exercised except in cases of necessity, or very strong expediency". If the change that was sought neither injuriously affected the interests of the beneficiaries nor was inconsistent with the main trust purpose, the Court was entitled to sanction the change on the basis of strong expediency. He continued:

> I am not disposed to draw a hard-and-fast line between the categories of necessity and expediency. ... I am not aware of any authority, in principle or in decision, for treating the categories of expediency and necessity as being in water-tight compartments, and mutually exclusive the one of the other. The truth is that necessity and expediency cannot be compartmented. The ideas underlying these concepts shade into one another. What to one man seems desirable to another man appears essential.[169]

However, Lord Justice-Clerk Alness did not only pursue a descriptive approach. He also made a normative case for expediency:

> If, however, it be suggested that the intervention of the Court in virtue of its *nobile officium*, is limited to a case of necessity in the sense that the trust machinery has broken down and that the enterprise threatens in consequence to become derelict, then I respectfully protest against that doctrine. I think that there is not the smallest justification for the suggested limitation.[170]

---

[168] *Gibson's Trs, Petrs* at 201–02 per Lord President Clyde.
[169] *Gibson's Trs, Petrs* at 205 per Lord Justice-Clerk Alness.
[170] *Gibson's Trs, Petrs* at 205–06 per Lord Justice-Clerk Alness.

Lord Sands was also prepared to add a normative dimension to his opinion:

> We may be humble flies, but, such as we are, [i]s our function limited to ascertaining what was determined two hundred years ago or what may have been provided by a modern statute? Have we no function in the moulding of jurisprudence such as our predecessors exercised? ... Immense changes, however, have taken place within the last hundred years in countless ways. Is it unreasonable to suggest that this may be allowed to react upon the *nobile officium* and to sanction a somewhat freer exercise of it? Or must we say: "This is not within the *nobile officium* as contemplated by Kames and Hailes, and by this consideration we are bound." Respect for the pious founder does not discourage the more liberal view. If the pious founder could be reincarnated and offered the choice between the *nobile officium* and a Parliamentary Commission, can there be any doubt as to what would be his choice?[171]

Lord Morison added that the principle was really that the exercise of the *nobile officium* depended on "equitable considerations abating the rigour of the law where, in a matter of mere trust administration, it may appear to operate harshly". There were cases in which expediency in carrying out the trust purposes was enough. Each petition should be gauged on its own merits, but there seemed to be no reason against the Court assisting trustees in charities when it might not assist other public or private trustees.[172]

This blend of descriptive and normative reasoning supported a finding in favour of strong expediency by a majority in the seven-judge court. If the law was not already that expediency could on occasion be enough for intervention in trusts *ex nobile officio*, it was modified to include that possibility.[173]

---

[171] *Gibson's Trs, Petrs* at 215 per Lord Sands.

[172] *Gibson's Trs, Petrs* at 220 per Lord Morison.

[173] Strong expediency was applied as the relevant standard in *Glasgow Young Men's Christian Association, Petrs* 1934 SC 452; and it was more recently suggested to be the standard for enlarging the powers available under a trust deed relating to a public trust: *Pringle, Petr* 1991 SLT 330 at 332 per Lord President Hope.

Post-*Gibson*, the standard of necessity had not altogether disappeared. Lord Jamieson stated in the following decade that the Court would authorise advances for the maintenance or education of a beneficiary only where this was necessary.[174] However, more recent cases have come down on the side of expediency. In *Mining Institute of Scotland Benevolent Fund Trs, Petrs*, Lord President Hope stated:

> [W]hile at one time a strict approach was taken to this matter, the court is now willing to exercise its power in cases of strong expediency falling short of impossibility of performance. The flexibility of approach which is inherent in the *nobile officium* enables the Inner House to take full account of the circumstances of each case and to act in accordance with principle as each case requires.[175]

In *RS Macdonald Charitable Trust Trs v Scottish Society for the Prevention of Cruelty to Animals*,[176] the Court granted a petition presented by trustees of a charitable trust for approval of a *cy-près* scheme. In doing so, Lord Drummond Young explained that although recent cases which had tended to show a less restrictive construction of the Court's powers generally involved statutory powers, he was prepared to take that general approach as equally applicable to the *nobile officium*.[177] He regarded the standard of strong expediency as representing the current state of the law and added that, in a compelling case, expediency would also be a sufficient ground for varying trust purposes.[178] "[S]trong or compelling expediency is sufficient to justify the exercise of the *cy-près* jurisdiction."[179]

---

[174] *Stewart v Brown's Trs* 1941 SC 300 at 308 per Lord Jamieson.

[175] 1994 SLT 785 at 786 per Lord President Hope. As noted, the *nobile officium* relating to trusts is now accessed via the Outer House, per the Rules of Court of Session, r 14.2(c).

[176] 2009 SC 6.

[177] At 21 per Lord Drummond Young. See also *Mining Institute of Scotland Benevolent Fund Trs, Petrs* at 786 per Lord President Hope.

[178] At 22 per Lord Drummond Young.

[179] At 24 per Lord Drummond Young. See, however, *Mining Institute of Scotland Benevolent Fund Trs, Petrs* at 787–88 per Lord President Hope, which suggested that basic expediency might be sufficient.

It is not entirely clear whether the standard of expediency applies across the board, or whether there are variable standards depending both on the nature of the prayer in the petition, and on whether it concerns a public or private trust. For example, the *Stair Memorial Encyclopaedia* suggests that necessity is the standard for the appointment,[180] resignation[181] and removal[182] of trustees.

Indeed, there are variable thresholds in the statutory framework. Necessity is the standard set out in the Trusts (Scotland) Act 1921 for the Court's statutory power to authorise advances for the maintenance or education of minor beneficiaries,[183] though as noted above, a standard of expediency had previously been indicated by the Court.[184] Expediency is the standard for the Court's statutory power to authorise the acts of trustees even where these are at variance with the terms or purposes of the trust.[185] Expediency is also the effective standard for the Court's statutory power to approve schemes relating to public trusts.[186]

The Court's statutory power to appoint a trustee to the trust of a charitable body must, on an application by the Office of the Scottish Charity Regulator and where there has been no misconduct in administration, pass a test of necessity or desirability.[187] A test of necessity or desirability also applies to the Court's power to approve schemes relating to charities.[188] The Court's power to approve reorganisation schemes for charities is subject to what is essentially a test of expediency or effectiveness.[189]

---

[180] Trusts, Trustees and Judicial Factors, vol 24 at para 158; Forsyth, *Law of Trusts and Trustees* at 434.

[181] See Trusts, Trustees and Judicial Factors at para 165; Menzies, *The Law of Scotland affecting Trustees* at 548.

[182] Trusts, Trustees and Judicial Factors at para 167.

[183] Trusts (Scotland) Act 1921, s 16.

[184] *Colquhoun, Petrs* (1894) 21 R 671 at 673 per Lord Kinnear.

[185] Trusts (Scotland) Act 1921, s 5.

[186] Law Reform (Miscellaneous Provisions) (Scotland) Act 1990, s 9(2).

[187] Charities and Trustee Investment (Scotland) Act 2005, s 34(1)(b).

[188] Charities and Trustee Investment (Scotland) Act 2005, s 35(2)(b) and (3)(b).

[189] Charities and Trustee Investment (Scotland) Act 2005, s 40(1)(b).

The Court's statutory power to approve, on behalf of certain persons, arrangements varying or revoking trust purposes, or enlarging the powers of trustees, is subject to a standard of non-prejudice to the person on whose behalf they are approving the arrangements.[190] Where, in relation to such a trust, there is a trust purpose entitling any of the beneficiaries to an alimentary liferent of, or any alimentary income from, the trust estate or any part thereof, the Court has the power to authorise arrangements varying or revoking that trust purpose and making new provision in lieu thereof, subject to a test of reasonableness.[191]

Meanwhile, some other statutory powers, such as the power of the Court to appoint new trustees,[192] and to remove existing trustees,[193] carries no designated standard.[194]

Whilst *Gibson's Trs* signalled a shift towards expediency as the standard for the Court's intervention by way of the *nobile officium*, with more modern cases endorsing that standard, the patchwork of standards in this area of law does not point to a conclusive standard of expediency across the board. Indeed if, as is the case, the statutory power for the Court to authorise advances for the maintenance or education of minor beneficiaries is subject to the standard of necessity,[195] how would it be justified for the Court to adopt the lower standard of expediency if, for some reason, a case arises under the *nobile officium* praying for such an advance to be authorised? It may therefore be concluded that whilst expediency seems the preferred standard in the area

---

[190] Trusts (Scotland) Act 1961, s 1(1).

[191] Trusts (Scotland) Act 1961, s 1(4)(a).

[192] Trusts (Scotland) Act 1921, s 22.

[193] Trusts (Scotland) Act 1921, s 23.

[194] The Scottish Law Commission's draft Trusts (Scotland) Bill would impose standards of expediency (cll 1(1)(a) and 61(1)(a)) and of what would be beneficial (cl 14(1)). Curiously, a standard of expediency is adopted in cl 60(9) on the Court's power to alter trust purposes to offset or counter the effect of a material change in circumstances, yet a standard of necessity is discussed in the explanatory note: see Scottish Law Commission, *Report on Trust Law*.

[195] Trusts (Scotland) Act 1921, s 16.

of trusts, necessity and other standards linger on in the legal framework. Of course, if necessity can be demonstrated, the strength of a petition will be greatly enhanced as this would clear the thresholds of each of the various standards that has been applied.

CHAPTER 3

JUDICIAL FACTORS, CURATORS, TUTORS AND GUARDIANS

The Scottish Law Commission described a judicial factor as "a person appointed by the court to hold, manage, administer and protect property in cases where it is not possible, practicable or sensible for those responsible for the property to do so".[1] A judicial factor is an officer of the court and has a fiduciary duty towards the estate over which he is appointed. The office is appointed by the Court of Session or, in some cases, the sheriff court.[2] As this chapter deals with the *nobile officium* as it relates to judicial factors, and as the *nobile officium* is a feature of the Court of Session, the powers of the sheriff court are not discussed.

The chapter includes discussion of what are effectively sub-categories or special types of factor, such as curators *bonis*, curators *ad litem*, factors *loco tutoris* and factors *loco absentis*. It also includes tutors and guardians whom, although not factors in the strict sense, may be (but are not always) appointed by the court to fulfil an essential, custodial function which is similar to factory.[3] When the latter offices are not appointed by the court, as for example in the case of tutors-nominate, it must be remembered that such persons would not be officers of the court.[4]

---

[1] *Report on Judicial Factors* (Scot Law Com No 233, 2013) at 1.

[2] Power was initially conferred on sheriffs for the appointment of certain factors *loco tutoris* and curators *bonis* by the Judicial Factors (Scotland) Act 1880. See also the Judicial Factors (Scotland) Act 1889, s 11A and the Law Reform (Miscellaneous Provisions) (Scotland) Act 1980, s 14.

[3] It may be noted, for example, that Chapter 61 of the Rules of the Court of Session defines a judicial factor as including a curator *bonis*, a factor *loco absentis*, a factor on trust or other estates, and a guardian.

[4] See *Morison's Tutors, Petrs* (1857) 19 D 493 at 495 per Lord Deas.

Factory has been a feature of Scots law since at least 1581,[5] and the Court of Session may have had the power to appoint judicial factors by the first half of the seventeenth century.[6] It has been said that the Court's power over curators *bonis* expanded with the abolition of the Scots Privy Council in 1707, and that, prior to 1730, applications for the appointment of curators *bonis* "had become so frequent, that the Court, in that year, found it necessary to pass an Act of Sederunt for regulating the duties and ascertaining the powers of these curators *bonis*".[7]

Lord President Clyde enumerated, though non-exhaustively, eight categories of judicial factory:

   (i)   factories on trust estates (including charities);

  (ii)   factories on the estates of *incapaces* (pupils, minors, absentees and lunatics);

 (iii)   factories on intestate estates;

 (iv)   factories on partnership estates;

  (v)   factories on estates actually sequestrated or threatened with sequestration (pending confirmation of a trustee);

 (vi)   factories on company estates under the Companies Clauses Consolidation Act 1845 and the Railway Companies Act 1867;

 (vii)   factories pending litigation (*pendente lite*); and

(viii)   factories on *pro indiviso* estates.[8]

This gives a flavour of the broad scope of judicial factory.

The Court derives its jurisdiction over judicial factors from a blend of statutory and non-statutory sources. Examples of statutes which have been relevant to judicial factors include the Judicial Factors Act 1849, the Court of Session Act 1857, the Trusts (Scotland) Act 1921 and the Charities and Trustee Investment (Scotland) Act 2005. It should be noted in this regard that judicial

---

[5] *Report on Judicial Factors* at 9.

[6] See N M L Walker, *Judicial Factors* (1974, W Green) at 3. See also Walker, *Legal History of Scotland* at 826–27.

[7] *Bryce v Grahame* (1828) 6 S 425 at 430.

[8] *Leslie's Judicial Factor, Petr* 1925 SC 464 at 469.

factors have been included within the definition of "trustee" in a number of statutory provisions, such as in the Trusts (Scotland) Act 1921.[9] The Scottish Law Commission has recommended, however, that the link between trustees and judicial factors be cut.[10]

The Court has the power to appoint and regulate judicial factors in exercise of its *nobile officium*. It has been said that the remedy of appointing a judicial factor may be the only way of protecting an estate for behoof of those entitled to it, and that in each case the idea is one of preservation and management of the estate and not some other purpose which could be achieved using the ordinary remedies of the court.[11] It has also been said to be "unquestionable" that the Court has the power, in the exercise of its *nobile officium*, to take from persons the management of their own affairs, or to prevent them from resuming the management of their own affairs, but that this power should be used carefully and cautiously.[12]

Whilst the Scottish Law Commission had, at the time of writing, recently published a *Report on Judicial Factors* together with a draft Judicial Factors (Scotland) Bill, the Commission recommended that the power of the Court to appoint judicial factors in exercise of the *nobile officium* would continue, and be recognised as such in the draft Bill.[13]

3.1 Appointment

There are numerous instances of the Court appointing a judicial factor in exercise of its *nobile officium*.[14] This was said to

---

[9] Trusts (Scotland) Act 1921, s 2.

[10] *Report on Judicial Factors* at 7.

[11] *Institute of Chartered Accountants in Scotland v Kay* 2001 SLT 1449 at 1451 per Lord Carloway.

[12] *Forsyth, Petr* (1862) 24 D 1435 at 1439 per Lord Curriehill.

[13] *Report on Judicial Factors* at 22; and draft Judicial Factors (Scotland) Bill, cl 5(1)(a).

[14] See *Wife and Children of John Anderson, Supplicants* 1743 Mor 7439; *Campbell, Petrs* 1755 Mor 7445 (on which see also *Earl of Galloway, Petrs* 1747 Mor 7438); *Cairns, Petrs* (1838) 16 S 335; *Campbell v Grant* (1869)

have once been the entire basis on which judicial factors were appointed.[15] Although there is a statutory basis for the appointment of a judicial factor in certain circumstances,[16] appointment by way of the *nobile officium* is a mechanism of last resort where ordinary legal remedies are either unavailable or would not provide appropriate protection.[17]

The scope of the Court's power of appointment is fairly wide, as confirmed by Lord President Clyde:[18]

> Now, there is no limit to the circumstances under which the Court, in the exercise of its *nobile officium*, may appoint a judicial factor, provided the appointment is necessary to protect against loss or injustice which cannot in the circumstances be prevented by allowing the ordinary legal remedies to take their course.

For example, the Court exercised its *nobile officium* to appoint a judicial factor on sequestrated estates where the trustee of the deceased debtor had died, and a meeting of creditors proved abortive due to the non-attendance of creditors.[19] A judicial factor was appointed to distribute funds in a sequestration on the strength of the argument that an attempt to revive the sequestration by appointing a meeting of creditors for the

---

8 M 227 at 232 per Lord Deas; *Campbell v Grant* (1870) 8 M 988 at 989 per Lord Deas. See also *Thurso Building Society's Judicial Factor v Robertson* 2000 SC 547 at 553–54 per Lady Paton; *Rosserlane Consultants Ltd, Petrs* [2008] CSOH 120 at para [20] per Lord Hodge; More, *Lectures on the Law of Scotland* at 250; and Mackay, *The Practice of the Court of Session*, vol 1 at 209–10. Chapter 61 of the Rules of the Court of Session applies to the appointment of a judicial factor.

[15] *Browning's Judicial Factor, Petr* (1905) 7 F 1037 at 1041 (note) per Lord Johnston. See also *Innes, Chambers & Co v T D McNeill & Son* (1917) 1 SLT 89 at 91 per Lord Anderson, who also outlined the historical distribution of this business across the Court.

[16] See, eg, the Judicial Factors (Scotland) Act 1880, s 4; Judicial Factors (Scotland) Act 1889, s 11A; Local Government (Scotland) Act 1975, sch 3, para 20; Law Reform (Miscellaneous Provisions) (Scotland) Act 1980, s 14; and Charities and Trustee Investment (Scotland) Act 2005, s 34.

[17] *Rosserlane Consultants Ltd, Petrs* [2008] CSOH 120 at para [20] per Lord Hodge.

[18] *Leslie's Judicial Factor, Petr* 1925 SC 464 at 469.

[19] *Moncrieff's Trs v Halley* (1899) 1 F 696.

election of a trustee would prove abortive.[20] The Court appointed a factor on the petition of a sole trustee who was resigning due to his taking up permanent residence abroad.[21] A judicial factor was also appointed where trustees were unable to act in terms of the trust deed,[22] and to administer a fund where no trustees had been specified in an antenuptial contract of marriage, and the father of one of the parties who had assumed obligations had died.[23]

With regard to the appointment of judicial factors on partnership estates, Lord President Inglis set out three general principles. First, the Court would appoint a factor to wind up a partnership estate where all of the partners were deceased.[24] Second, the Court would not intervene where there were surviving partners and there was no fault or incapacity preventing them from carrying on their business.[25] Third, where surviving partners were unfitted to carrying on or winding up the partnership, the Court would appoint a factor in a case of necessity.[26]

In a more general context, the appointment of a judicial factor should be competent, appropriate and reasonable.[27] As for other offices, a curator *bonis* was appointed where a manufacturer had become mentally deranged to the extent that he was incapable of carrying on the business,[28] and a curator *ad litem* was appointed so that a wife may have advice on her election between different

---

[20] *Cheyne's Trs, Petrs* 1933 SLT 184.

[21] *Shand v Macdonald* (1862) 24 D 829.

[22] *Paterson, Petr* (1890) 17 R 1059. It was held that the petition was properly presented to the Inner House. See also *Hedderwick's Trs v Hedderwick's Executor* 1910 SC 333 at 336.

[23] *Melville, Petr* (1856) 18 D 788; see also *Leslie's Judicial Factor, Petr* at 470 per Lord President Clyde.

[24] *Dickie v Mitchell* (1874) 1 R 1030 at 1033 per Lord President Inglis.

[25] *Dickie v Mitchell* at 1033 per Lord President Inglis.

[26] *Dickie v Mitchell* at 1033 per Lord President Inglis.

[27] *Institute of Chartered Accountants in Scotland v Kay* 2001 SLT 1449.

[28] *Thomas, Petr* (1827) 6 S 103. On the appointment of a curator *bonis*, see also *Grant, Petrs* 1790 Mor 7454; *Young v Rose* (1839) 1 D 1242; *Irving v Swan* (1868) 7 M 86; *The Public Trustee of New Zealand, Petrs* (1921) 2 SLT 240; and Berry (ed), *Balfour's Handbook* at 206.

succession options.[29] The Court has also appointed factors *loco tutoris*[30] and *loco absentis*.[31]

There have been instances in which petitions to the *nobile officium* for the appointment of a judicial factor have proved unsuccessful. The Court has held that a creditor cannot petition the *nobile officium* for the appointment of a judicial factor simply because he requires assistance in pursuing a debtor.[32] The Court declined to appoint a judicial factor on petition of the truster alone where the sole trustee had become insolvent, but did so with the agreement of a beneficiary under the estate.[33] A petition for the appointment of a factor was refused as unnecessary where a trust deed provided that the beneficiary had the power to nominate new trustees on the failure of all those appointed by the deed.[34] The Court refused a petition from a factrix *loco tutoris* to grant an absolute feu right of certain ground,[35] and refused in exercise of its discretion to appoint a factor *loco absentis*.[36]

It was held that, by statute, a petition for recall of the appointment of a curator *bonis* and the appointment of a new curator *bonis* was incompetent in the Inner House, and had to be presented to the Lord Ordinary.[37] In addition, where members of a building society petitioned the Inner House for the appointment of a judicial factor in circumstances in which it was impossible to wind up the society under the Building Societies Act 1874, the Court refused the petition on the basis that it should have been presented to the Outer House.[38]

---

[29] *Sillars v Sillars* 1911 SC 1207.

[30] *Wotherspoon, Petrs* 1775 Mor 7450 and 16372; *Collins v Eglinton Iron Co* (1882) 9 R 500. See also *Cochrane, Petr* (1891) 18 R 456 at 458 per Lord Young; and Berry (ed), *Balfour's Handbook* at 206. Though see the early case of *Cowan, Petrs* 1788 Mor 7452; and also *Wardrop v Gossling* (1869) 7 M 532.

[31] Mackay, *The Practice of the Court of Session*, vol 1 at 209.

[32] *Paterson v Best* (1900) 2 F 1088 at 1092–93 per Lord Justice-Clerk Macdonald.

[33] *Christie, Petr* (1827) 5 S 272.

[34] *Dunlop, Petr* (1835) 13 S 681.

[35] *Thomson, Petr* (1837) 15 S 807.

[36] *Watson, Petr* (1864) 2 M 1333.

[37] *Souter v Finlay* (1890) 18 R 86.

[38] *Gaff, Petrs* (1893) 20 R 825.

Section 3 of the Trusts (Scotland) Act 1921 provides that a judicial factor shall not, by virtue of that Act, have the power of assumption or resignation without judicial authority. The *nobile officium* has been used to remove a co-executor from office on the ground that she had persistently and unjustifiably failed to co-operate in the executry.[39]

3.2 Powers

The *nobile officium* has been used to regulate the powers of judicial factors, including the authorisation of particular acts. It has, for example, authorised a judicial factor to pay an additional annuity out of an estate,[40] and to pay the income of the residue of an estate to a beneficiary.[41] It confirmed that it may authorise a curator *bonis* to continue payment of a voluntary annuity to a third party which the ward himself had paid prior to incapacity.[42] A petition was competently presented for the Court to warrant that a judicial factor pay over part of certain funds where a trust deed had been set aside.[43] The Court has also conferred a power of sale on a factor.[44] It was said that the question of whether a factor was entitled to pay over the balance of an estate to parties having a right thereto was a question for the Court in exercise of its *nobile officium*.[45]

The Court authorised a curator *bonis* to make up a lunatic's titles to a bond and disposition in security,[46] and to make from the proceeds of a lunatic's estate payments for the maintenance of the lunatic and his wife and child, in addition to travelling expenses for the lunatic's brother when visiting him.[47]

---

[39] *Wilson v Gibson* 1948 SC 52.

[40] *Allan, Petr* (1869) 8 M 139.

[41] *Walker, Noter* (1905) 13 SLT 141.

[42] Though it would not authorise an increase in the amount of that annuity: *Bowers v Pringle Pattison's Curator Bonis* (1892) 19 R 941. See also *Dunbar, Petr* (1876) 3 R 554.

[43] *Couper, Petrs* (1863) 1 M 286.

[44] *Morison, Petr* (1855) 18 D 132.

[45] *Campbell v Grant* (1870) 8 M 988 at 988 per Lord President Inglis.

[46] *Cuthbertson, Petr* (1841) 4 D 58. See also *Campbell, Petr* (1841) 4 D 136.

[47] *Hamilton, Petr* (1842) 4 D 627.

A nine-judge court granted authority to a factor *loco tutoris* to borrow money and grant heritable security over a pupil's estate, setting out the historical pedigree of the Court's powers as follows:

> The power of the Court to appoint persons, under the name of factors *loco tutoris*, to manage the estates of persons who, from various causes, are not capable to manage their own affairs, and have no proper tutors or mandatories for that purpose, seems to rest on consuetudinary law, now of very considerable standing. There is a case in the books as far back as the 30th June, 1708, Lin, in which such factor had applied to the Court for extraordinary powers, which, however, in that case, was refused, apparently from the nature of the application, because the authority prayed for fell under his ordinary powers. And the Act of Sederunt, 1730, proceeds on the narrative—"That the Lords have been often applied to for appointing factors on the estates of different persons," not capable of managing their own affairs, so that the power of the Court to name such tutors is now firmly established; and the Act of Sederunt, 1730, was passed to regulate the ordinary duty and responsibility of such factors.[48]

Authority was granted to a factor *loco tutoris* for the completion of the erection of buildings which were unfinished on the death of the pupils' father, and to burden the pupils' heritage to defray the cost of the buildings.[49] Authority was also granted to a factor *loco tutoris* to renounce a lease,[50] and the jurisdiction was also used to commit a child to the custody of a factor *loco tutoris*.[51]

The Court authorised a tutor-dative to let out family property of the pupil's estate for a period not exceeding three years,[52] and authorised the guardian of a pupil outside the jurisdiction to complete title to certain property in the pupil's name, and to sell

---

[48] *Somervilles' Factor, Petr* (1836) 14 S 451 at 452.

[49] *Tweedie, Petr* (1841) 3 D 369. It was said that the Court had occasionally granted higher powers to tutors-nominate than they would have granted to trustees: *Berwick, Petrs* (1874) 2 R 90 at 92 per Lord President Inglis.

[50] *Meikle v Meikle* (1823) 2 S 274; *Carrick v Warden* (1829) 8 S 208, following *Carrick, Petr* (1829) 7 S 848.

[51] *Muir v Milligan* (1868) 6 M 1125.

[52] *Speirs, Petr* (1854) 17 D 289.

that property.[53] Authority was granted to a father, as tutor and administrator-in-law for his son, to feu part of the son's estate,[54] as it was to a father as administrator-in-law of his pupil son to sell that son's property,[55] and to a father as tutor and administrator-in-law to sell property in which his pupil daughter had a joint right.[56] The Court authorised a tutrix-at-law to grant a conveyance of her pupil son's property to trustees under a marriage contract,[57] tutors-nominate to accept a reconveyance of subjects which had been feued out by the father of a ward,[58] and tutors-nominate to grant bonds and dispositions in security of a pupil's estate, in order to pay off provisions to the pupil's siblings.[59] It authorised a tutor to repay to herself out of capital a sum expended by her on her pupil children's maintenance and education, and for her to expend out of capital further sums for the aliment, maintenance and education of the children.[60] It also granted authority for tutors to raise a second loan on behalf of a "destitute" pupil,[61] and for tutors-nominate to grant a lease of a farm.[62]

The Court has also rendered assistance in the context of judicial factories in exercise of its *nobile officium*. For example, it assisted a judicial factor when a trustee would not deliver certain writs to the factor, and when the factor's successful action for delivery of the writs and for count, reckoning and payment was ignored by the trustee in question. The Court granted warrant for messengers-at-arms to search for, recover and take possession of the writs for delivery to the factor.[63] Likewise, it granted warrant for messengers-at-arms to search for, recover and take possession

---

[53] *McFadzean, Petr* 1917 SC 142.
[54] *Lord Clinton, Petr* (1875) 3 R 62.
[55] *Logan, Petr* (1897) 25 R 51.
[56] *Shearer's Tutor, Petr* 1924 SC 445, disapproving *Forbes, Petr* 1922 SLT 294.
[57] *Ferrier's Tutrix-at-law, Petrs* 1925 SC 571.
[58] *Campbell, Petrs* (1881) 8 R 543.
[59] *Grant, Petrs* (1889) 16 R 365.
[60] *Milne, Petr* (1888) 15 R 437.
[61] *Earl of Buchan, Petrs* (1839) 1 D 637.
[62] *Morison's Tutors, Petrs* (1857) 19 D 493.
[63] *McAlley's Judicial Factor, Petr* (1900) 2 F 1198. See also *Orr Ewing's Judicial Factor, Petr* (1884) 11 R 682.

of an assurance policy for delivery to a curator *bonis*.[64] In another case, the Court ordained an insane woman to be delivered up to a curator *bonis*, on the petition of the curator and the woman's brother, for removal from a private dwellinghouse to an asylum.[65]

So far as unsuccessful applications are concerned, the Court has refused authority to a judicial factor to sell heritable property on the ground that there was no urgent necessity of administration.[66] It has also refused to approve a sale by a judicial factor where he took it upon himself to exercise powers which had not been granted to him.[67] The Court refused to allow the surplus income of a lunatic beyond what was required for his comfortable maintenance,[68] and doubted the competency of a request to ordain a factor to make payments to annuitants out of the income of a factory estate.[69] Authority was refused for a curator *bonis* to pay an alimentary allowance out of surplus income on the ward's estate to a third party, on the basis that this would interfere with the curator's discretion.[70] The Court has also declined advice to a factor on a burdened estate.[71]

It is also useful to note that it may not be competent for a judicial factor who derived his powers from the *nobile officium* to seek to put an end to them by way of ordinary action.[72]

3.3   Necessity and expediency

The question of whether the threshold for the Court's intervention *ex nobile officio* in the area of trusts was one of necessity or expediency was discussed in Section 2.3. It was seen that, whilst the standard largely shifted from one of necessity to one of expediency, necessity was not altogether removed from the picture,

---

[64] *Ferguson, Petr* (1905) 13 SLT 222.

[65] *Gardiner, Petrs* (1869) 7 M 1130.

[66] *Watson, Petr* (1856) 19 D 98.

[67] *Drummond's Judicial Factor, Petr* (1894) 21 R 932.

[68] *Stewart, Petr* (1852) 15 D 37.

[69] *Sharp v Society of Sailors of the Port of Dunbar* (1903) 10 SLT 572 at 575.

[70] *Dunbar, Petr* (1876) 3 R 554. See also *Bowers v Pringle Pattison's Curator Bonis* (1892) 19 R 941. On the regulation and limitation of the authority of a curator *bonis*, see *The Public Trustee of New Zealand, Petrs* (1921) 2 SLT 240.

[71] *Wright, Petr* 1701 Mor 7429.

[72] See *Campbell v Grant* (1870) 8 M 988 at 989–90 per Lord Ardmillan.

and the current legal framework exhibits a patchwork of standards including, but not limited to, both necessity and expediency.

The standard of necessity has perhaps featured more consistently in the area of judicial factors. Necessity was the standard applied with regard to the Court's appointing a factor where surviving partners were unfitted to carrying on or winding up a partnership.[73] It was also the standard imposed on the curator *bonis* of a lunatic, and the tutor of a pupil, applying for a power of sale in exercise of the *nobile officium*.[74] In a case in which the standard of expediency was rejected, it was said by Lord President Inglis that the Court would not sanction the alienation by a tutor of a pupil's heritage except in a case of necessity.[75] Lord Ardmillan stated in the same case that "[m]ere expediency, however high, will not be sufficient".[76] A standard of necessity was also articulated by Lord Justice-Clerk Alness, who added that the necessity in question was in order to avoid loss.[77]

A standard of "urgent necessity" was applied with regard to whether a judicial factor should be granted a power to sell heritable property,[78] and James Campbell Irons also attributed the standard of urgent necessity to the appointment of an interim factor.[79] Necessity was cited in *Bryce v Grahame*:

> As the interference of the Court, however, has arisen, more especially in [particular cases], solely from the necessity of the measure, and can be justified only by this necessity, the appointment made by the Court is of a temporary nature; and being meant to supply the want of a regular tutor, it is at an end the moment a tutor is served.[80]

---

[73] *Dickie v Mitchell* (1874) 1 R 1030 at 1033 per Lord President Inglis.

[74] *Lawson v Lawson* (1863) 1 M 424, and in particular at 429 per Lord Justice-Clerk Inglis. See also *Meikle v Meikle* (1823) 2 S 274; and *Cuthbertson, Petr* (1841) 4 D 58.

[75] *Lord Clinton, Petr* (1875) 3 R 62 at 66.

[76] *Lord Clinton, Petr* at 67.

[77] *Shearer's Tutor, Petr* 1924 SC 445 at 448.

[78] *Watson, Petr* (1856) 19 D 98.

[79] James Campbell Irons, *Law and Practice in Scotland Relative to Judicial Factors* (1908, W Green) at 441.

[80] *Bryce v Grahame* (1828) 6 S 425 at 431, and see also the same case at 432 and 438. See also *Report on Judicial Factors* at 9, though note the Report at 19 where necessity or desirability are both cited as standards.

The standard of necessity also featured in the following dictum of Lord President Clyde which is well known in the law of judicial factors:

> Now, there is no limit to the circumstances under which the Court, in the exercise of its *nobile officium*, may appoint a judicial factor, provided the appointment is necessary to protect against loss or injustice which cannot in the circumstances be prevented by allowing the ordinary legal remedies to take their course.[81]

Moreover, it has been said that interference by the Court in the area of judicial factors was based on legal necessity, and that when the necessity ceased, so did the office.[82]

The Scottish Law Commission referred to a standard of necessity in its *Report on Judicial Factors*, especially (but not exclusively) with regard to the appointment of judicial factors,[83] although the Commission has recommended that its proposed statutory framework should require only the lesser standard of high desirability.[84] The explanatory note to the proposed section relating to those standards sets out that a judicial factor can be appointed "where, strictly speaking, it is not necessary but would be advantageous".[85] The Commission recommended a variable standard of necessity or expediency in the appointment of an interim factor.[86]

A variable standard of necessity or expediency has also made an appearance in the case law. It was set out by a nine-judge court with regard to the grant of powers to factors,[87] and more recently with regard to the appointment of factors.[88] The

---

[81] *Leslie's Judicial Factor, Petr* 1925 SC 464 at 469.

[82] George Hunter Thoms, *Treatise on Judicial Factors, Curators Bonis and Managers of Burghs* (1859, Bell & Bradfute) at 4.

[83] See *Report on Judicial Factors* at 11, 14–15, 23, 55 and 121.

[84] *Report on Judicial Factors* at 29.

[85] Draft Judicial Factors (Scotland) Bill, cl 4 (explanatory note): see *Report on Judicial Factors* at 102.

[86] Draft Judicial Factors (Scotland) Bill, cl 2(1): see *Report on Judicial Factors* at 101.

[87] *Somervilles' Factor, Petr* (1836) 14 S 451 at 453.

[88] *Rosserlane Consultants Ltd, Petrs* [2008] CSOH 120 at para [20] per Lord Hodge.

standard has occasionally been one not of simple expediency, but of "high expediency" (either on its own or coupled with necessity) which has sometimes been regarded as little short of necessity itself.[89] Whilst it was said that the Court would not sanction the alienation of a pupil's heritage merely to procure future advantage for the minor,[90] a petition was successful where there was "some chance of advantage" to a pupil's estate from a proposed sale.[91] A petition for the granting of powers to tutors-nominate was successful where it was merely in the interests of the pupil to grant them, and where an alternative course would constitute "maladministration of the property, according to sound principles of rural economy"[92] – a standard which surely falls short of necessity.

Whilst, therefore, the standard of necessity seems to have held in the area of judicial factors more firmly than it has in relation to trusts, there is a scattering of cases in which a standard of expediency has been applied. This has tended to be a standard of high expediency, rather than simple expediency, but on occasion the Court has applied a standard of simple expediency. In addition, it has been seen that a variable standard of necessity or expediency has been applied. The Scottish Law Commission, in its *Report on Judicial Factors*, has not proposed a consistent standard across the board.

---

[89] *Campbell, Petrs* (1881) 8 R 543. See also *Lord Clinton, Petr* (1875) 3 R 62; *Grant, Petrs* (1889) 16 R 365; and *Shearer's Tutor, Petr* 1924 SC 445 at 450 per Lord Anderson.

[90] *Lord Clinton, Petr; Shearer's Tutor, Petr* at 448 per Lord Justice-Clerk Alness.

[91] *Logan, Petr* (1897) 25 R 51, and see the same case at 52, per Lord President Robertson.

[92] *Morison's Tutors, Petrs* (1857) 19 D 493 at 495.

CHAPTER 4

BANKRUPTCY, INSOLVENCY AND SEQUESTRATION

Bankruptcy, insolvency and sequestration has, after trusts, been one of the main focal areas of the *nobile officium*. A number of cases in this area arose due to omissions or deficiencies in bankruptcy statutes, especially the Bankruptcy (Scotland) Acts of 1856 and 1913.[1] These are, however, flanked by a few examples from the Bankruptcy (Scotland) Acts of 1839, 1853 and 1985. One of the most common areas of activity was in providing for failure to meet the statutory requirements on the publication of sequestration notices in the Edinburgh and London Gazettes, the official public newspapers of record. We find the *nobile officium* being used in such areas as the appointment of trustees in sequestrations, discharge from sequestration and recall of sequestration. As Lord President Clyde described in *Maitland, Petr*, the *nobile officium* was "often invoked in connexion with the omission of some procedural, technical, step in bankruptcy or in the liquidation of companies".[2] There is no separate treatment given in this chapter to sequestration as applied to individuals and companies, for some applications of the *nobile officium* – such as those relating to Gazette notices – are found with regard to both individuals and companies. Some specifically company-oriented uses of the jurisdiction are also found, however, such as in the invalidation of company dissolution.

A number of cases in this area arose due to statutory omissions or deficiencies that have since been remedied, and

---

[1] The Bankruptcy (Scotland) Act 1913 was repealed by the Bankruptcy (Scotland) Act 1985, s 75(2) and sch 8.

[2] 1961 SC 291 at 293.

the statutory framework is changing.[3] A major reform in recent years was to move much of the bankruptcy work of the Court of Session to the sheriff court, it no longer being competent to petition for sequestration or recall in the Court of Session. The Accountant in Bankruptcy also determines debtor applications for sequestration on an administrative basis, rather than these being determined by the court.[4] It nevertheless remains useful to give a broad overview of the *nobile officium* as applied in cases of bankruptcy, insolvency and sequestration. First and foremost, as this was one of the focal areas for the *nobile officium*, it is an important part of the story in the development of the jurisdiction. However, it also demonstrates the potential scope and utility of the jurisdiction in this area of law, and may offer ideas and prior examples for the practitioner in this area who finds himself at a procedural impasse or where the statutory machinery has not operated as anticipated. Indeed, although the Court of Session is less involved in bankruptcy proceedings than previously, the *nobile officium* remains available for invocation where there is a breakdown in the statutory machinery.

4.1 Gazette notices

We find cases in the records from at least the 1840s in which the *nobile officium* has been used with regard to bankruptcy, insolvency and sequestration notices in the Gazettes. The relevant case law extends to *The Law Society of Scotland, Petrs*[5] in 1974 as the most recent at the time of writing. There is no longer a requirement to insert notice of a statutory meeting of creditors in the Edinburgh Gazette,[6] and publication

---

[3] The current statutory framework is essentially the Bankruptcy (Scotland) Act 1985 as amended by the Bankruptcy (Scotland) Act 1993, the Bankruptcy and Diligence etc (Scotland) Act 2007, and the Bankruptcy and Debt Advice (Scotland) Act 2014.

[4] The principal reforming statute is the Bankruptcy and Diligence etc (Scotland) Act 2007. See Donna McKenzie-Skene, "The reform of bankruptcy law in Scotland" (2009) 22(2) Insolvency Intelligence 17–25, particularly at 20.

[5] *The Law Society of Scotland, Petrs* 1974 SLT (Notes) 66.

[6] *Stair Memorial Encyclopaedia*, Bankruptcy Reissue at para 45.

requirements in the Edinburgh Gazette are in the process of being wound down.[7]

(a) Failure to (timeously) insert statutory notice

One of the most common reasons for petitioning the *nobile officium* in this area was failure to insert a statutory notice in the Gazette, either at all, or within the time period specified by statute. Cases of no insertion include *Tolmie, Petrs*,[8] in which there had been inadvertent non-compliance with a number of statutory requirements including a failure to insert notices in both the Edinburgh and London Gazettes. The Court authorised the insertion of the required notices in the Gazettes of new, in addition to postponing the meeting of creditors for the election of a trustee and commissioners.

The Court in *Somerville & Co Ltd, Petrs*,[9] exercised its *nobile officium* to appoint a date for a new meeting of creditors upon failure by the creditors to insert the requisite statutory notice of meeting in the London Gazette. In *Robertson, Petr*,[10] a clerk had failed to dispatch notices of a statutory meeting of trustees to the Edinburgh and London Gazettes. The petitioner sought authority to insert a notice in the Gazettes calling the meeting of trustees, in addition to authority for the sheriff to proceed as though the statutory notices had been inserted in the Gazettes and the meetings held on their due dates. The Court granted the prayer of the petition.

Another case in which statutory notices had failed to be inserted at all is *Liquidator of Nairn Public Hall, Petrs*.[11] Three petitions were respectively presented to the Court by liquidators of various companies. The petitions were heard together, each petitioner having inadvertently omitted to insert notice in the

---

[7] See Bankruptcy Reissue at para 40, noting in particular the updates. See, eg, the Bankruptcy and Debt Advice (Scotland) Act 2014, s 24.

[8] (1853) 16 D 105.

[9] (1905) 7 F 651.

[10] 1909 SC 444.

[11] 1946 SC 395.

Edinburgh Gazette of special resolutions passed for the voluntary winding-up of those companies. They prayed for exercise of the *nobile officium* to authorise them to insert the notices belatedly. Lord Justice-Clerk Cooper stated that there was no reported case in which such applications had been granted, but that the Court was "informed that one or two similar cases have in fact slipped through". He went on to say:

> I do not share the view that this Court possesses in the *nobile officium* a general discretionary power to dispense on demand with the imperative requirements of an Act of Parliament passed so recently as 1928 and fenced with a penalty, or that we have unlimited power to amend the Act of Parliament by allowing such extension of time as the circumstances of any case may in our judgment require.[12]

However, Lord Justice-Clerk Cooper recommended granting the respective prayers of the petitions in this case, adding that it should not be assumed that similar treatment would be given in future applications of that kind, and that each case must be dealt with on its own facts.

In other cases there have been notices inserted in either or both of the Gazettes, but not in conformity with the statutory requirements on timing. The notices could be inserted either too early or too late. For example, the Bankruptcy (Scotland) Act 1913 provided that:

> [t]he Lord Ordinary ... by the deliverance which awards the sequestration, shall appoint a meeting of creditors, to be held at a specified hour on a specified day, being not earlier than six nor later than twelve days from the date of the appearance in the Gazette of the notice of the award of sequestration ... to elect a trustee.[13]

In *Car Mart Ltd, Petrs*,[14] notices of a meeting of creditors appeared in the Gazette just five days before the date of the meeting. An

---

[12] At 397 per Lord Justice-Clerk Cooper.
[13] Bankruptcy (Scotland) Act 1913, s 63. This closely tracks the wording of the Bankruptcy (Scotland) Act 1856, s 67. See now the Bankruptcy (Scotland) Act 1985, s 21A; and the Bankruptcy and Diligence etc (Scotland) Act 2007, ss 11 and 28, and sch 1.
[14] 1924 SC 269.

objection was made at the meeting on point of competency, as the Gazette notices had not given six days' notice as required by statute; however, the meeting proceeded and a trustee was elected. The Court exercised its *nobile officium* to appoint a further meeting of creditors, with warrant granted for intimation of new in the Edinburgh and London Gazettes in conformity with statute.

Failure to timeously insert notices in the Gazettes could be due to a range of factors. For example, the failure could be due to an error on the part of a creditor, but it could equally be due to an error on the part of the bankrupt himself,[15] a trustee-in-sequestration,[16] commissioners on sequestrated estates,[17] the sheriff awarding sequestration,[18] a bankrupt's agent,[19] a newspaper agent,[20] or even an industrial dispute.[21] Whomever or whatever has been the cause of the failure to insert a statutory notice, either timeously or at all, a common theme in successful petitions has been that the omission was inadvertent or "*per incuriam*".

Petitions have been successfully presented by a range of parties including the bankrupt,[22] creditor,[23] commissioner on the sequestrated estate,[24] and some combination of these such as the bankrupt and concurring creditors.[25]

There have been two outcomes most commonly sought in petitions in this area. First, the appointment of a new meeting of creditors, possibly accompanied by a request for intimation of new in the Gazette(s) (though sometimes the Court might require intimation in any event). Second, that the Court finds an already-inserted, though untimely, Gazette notice to be equivalent to a statutorily-compliant notice.

---

[15] *Morrison, Petr* (1874) 1 R 392.
[16] *Lipman & Co's Tr, Petr* (1893) 20 R 818; also known as *Myles, Petr*.
[17] *Naismith, Petrs* (1910) 1 SLT 305.
[18] *Watt, Philp & Co, Petrs* (1877) 4 R 641.
[19] *Taylor, Petr* (1900) 2 F 1139.
[20] *Garden, Petrs* (1848) 10 D 1509.
[21] *The Law Society of Scotland, Petrs* 1974 SLT (Notes) 66.
[22] *Taylor, Petr* (1900) 2 F 1139.
[23] *Foubister, Petr* (1869) 8 M 31; *Car Mart Ltd, Petrs* 1924 SC 269.
[24] *Naismith, Petrs* (1910) 1 SLT 305.
[25] *Garden, Petrs* (1848) 10 D 1509; *Watt, Philp & Co, Petrs* (1877) 4 R 641.

The Court has been willing to appoint a new meeting of creditors following an untimely Gazette notice, assuming of course that various other requirements (such as inadvertence in the failure to timeously insert the notice) are met.[26] However, we also find petitioners seeking the Court's declaration that a notice which had been inserted in the Gazette, though not in compliance with the statutory time periods, is equivalent to a statutorily-compliant Gazette notice. The Court has shown varying enthusiasm for this prayer. In *Naismith, Petrs*,[27] and *The Law Society of Scotland, Petrs*,[28] the Court granted the prayer. In *Taylor, Petr*,[29] the Court was strict with the wording of the prayer – the petitioner had sought declaration that the untimely Gazette notice was a due and sufficient compliance with the statutory requirements, but the Court required amendment of the wording of the prayer to the untimely notice being held equivalent to a timeous notice, the Court thereafter granting the prayer of the petition. However, in *Car Mart Ltd, Petrs*,[30] the petitioners prayed for the Court to hold the already-published (untimely) notices as equivalent to statutorily-compliant notices, or alternatively to order a further meeting of creditors to be held. The Court preferred that a further meeting of creditors be held.

The Court has typically been keen to ensure that the expenses of the petition and associated procedure are not charged against the sequestrated estates where some party associated with the sequestration (other than the bankrupt) is essentially at fault for failing to ensure (timeous) insertion of a notice in the Gazette. Where the cause is attributable to some external event such as an industrial dispute at the press of one of the Gazettes, the Court may be persuaded to charge the expenses against the sequestrated estates.[31]

---

[26] *Garden, Petrs*; *Foubister, Petr*; *Watt, Philp & Co, Petrs*.

[27] (1910) 1 SLT 305.

[28] 1974 SLT (Notes) 66.

[29] (1900) 2 F 1139.

[30] 1924 SC 269.

[31] As, eg, in *The Law Society of Scotland, Petrs* 1974 SLT (Notes) 66.

(b) Error in statutory notice

Some cases have seen a statutory notice published in one or both Gazettes, but with errors. These have included inserting an erroneous name for the bankrupt,[32] inserting an erroneous name for an agent,[33] omitting the time of a meeting of creditors,[34] inserting an incorrect date for a meeting of creditors,[35] and failing to comply with the wording of a statutory form of notice.[36] As in other cases, the error should typically have been inadvertent before the Court will consider exercising its *nobile officium*.

The prayer of the petition in such cases has typically been for the Court to appoint a (new) meeting of creditors, often combined with authority for new statutory notices to be inserted.[37] Sometimes the prayer has simply been for the insertion of new statutory notices,[38] and sometimes in addition to authorisation for the sequestration to proceed.[39]

The rationale for the Court's intervention in such cases is not necessarily to come to the assistance of the party who committed the error, but to ensure that notice is properly given to interested creditors. As Lord President Robertson explained in *McCosh, Petr*, where notices of sequestration contained errors on the part of the printers:

> This case seems to fall within the class of cases of which *Von Rotberg* is the clearest type, where the Court do exercise their *nobile officium* to correct an error of this description, and I understand that the Court in so doing do not come to the rescue of an applicant who has made a blunder in the proceeding for his own sake, but rather exercise their power in order that the interests of creditors who may have been lying by should not be affected by a mistake for which they are not responsible.[40]

---

[32] *Fife, Petr* (1844) 6 D 686; *McCosh, Petr* (1898) 25 R 1019.
[33] *McCosh, Petr* (1898) 25 R 1019.
[34] *Von Rotberg, Petr* (1876) 4 R 263.
[35] *Murray, Petr* (1906) 8 F 957.
[36] *Morgan, Petr* 1922 SC 589.
[37] *Fife, Petr*; *Von Rotberg, Petr*; *McCosh, Petr*.
[38] *Morgan, Petr* 1922 SC 589.
[39] *Murray, Petr* (1906) 8 F 957.
[40] At 1020 per Lord President Robertson.

The expenses in such a petition and its associated procedure may not, however, be chargeable against the sequestrated estates.[41]

(c) Other

There are two other cases worth mentioning which do not fall neatly under the above headings. One is the case of *AB, Petr*,[42] in which a petition had been presented in a sequestration case in the name of a particular creditor. However, that creditor disclaimed the petition as unauthorised by him. The Lord Ordinary reported the case to the Inner House, suggesting that intimation of this fact should be made in the Gazette before recalling the sequestration, as other creditors might have been relying on the validity of the petition in question. The Inner House instructed the Lord Ordinary to order accordingly.

In another case, *West of Scotland Refractories Ltd, Petrs*,[43] the creditors on a bankrupt's estate presented a petition to the *nobile officium* for authority to insert a notice in the Edinburgh Gazette. An award of sequestration had been regularly achieved, and notice timeously made in the Edinburgh and London Gazettes. In the circumstances of the case, the petitioners were under the impression that section 17 of the Bankruptcy (Scotland) Act 1913 required them to insert a notice in the Gazette intimating remit of the sequestration to the sheriff court. However, the Court viewed this as unnecessary on a construction of the relevant statutory provisions. The prayer of the petition was therefore not granted.

4.2 Reporting, recording and registration requirements

A number of cases arose in which there had been a failure to transmit to a statutory keeper the abbreviate of a petition for the award of sequestration and the deliverance thereon, in a manner compliant with statute. This could either be a complete failure to transmit those documents, or a failure to transmit them

---

[41] *Morgan, Petr* 1922 SC 589.
[42] (1842) 5 D 74.
[43] 1969 SC 43.

timeously within the statutory framework. The keeper in question has typically been the Keeper of the Register of Inhibitions (and variations thereon[44]). As in the case of other omissions, inadvertence would typically be a prerequisite to the Court's exercise of the *nobile officium*. Wilful non-compliance with statute is not conducive to securing the equitable intervention of the Court.

The prayer in such cases has often been for the Court to warrant the transmission to the relevant statutory keeper of the documents in question, and for the Court to authorise the keeper to receive and record those documents. Such petitions have often been successful.[45] In some cases, attempt had been made to transmit the documents to the keeper out of time, but the keeper had refused to receive and record them.[46] In one case, the keeper did receive and record the abbreviate and deliverance thereon out of time, but the Court took the view that this was probably ineffectual in law.[47] The petition in that case sought for the Court to ratify, approve and confirm the recording of the abbreviate or, alternatively, to authorise recording by the keeper of new. The Court's position was that the appropriate course would be to authorise recording of new, and it granted the prayer of the petition on that basis and to that extent.

The Court might not permit the expenses in such petitions to be charged against the estate in question.[48]

---

[44] At the time of writing, the Register of Inhibitions and Adjudications was being redesignated the Register of Inhibitions: Bankruptcy and Diligence etc (Scotland) Act 2007, s 80, not yet in force.

[45] *Munro v Dickson* (1851) 13 D 1209; *Martin, Petr* (1857) 20 D 55; *AB, Petr* (1858) 21 D 24; *Allan, Petr* (1861) 23 D 972; *Stark and Hogg, Petrs* (1886) 23 SLR 507; *Train & McIntyre Ltd, Petrs*, 1923 SC 291; *Kippen's Tr, Petr* 1966 SC 3 (this case rather concerned a memorandum for the renewal of an abbreviate in the sequestration, and the statutory keeper in this case was the Keeper of the Registers of Scotland). See also *Morrison, Petr* (1874) 1 R 392.

[46] As, eg, in *Martin, Petr* (1857) 20 D 55; and *AB, Petr* (1858) 21 D 24.

[47] *White Cross Insurance Association, Petrs* 1924 SC 372.

[48] As, eg, in *Stark and Hogg, Petrs* (1886) 23 SLR 507; and *Train & McIntyre Ltd, Petrs* 1923 SC 291.

4.3 Revival of sequestration/appointment of trustee

As discussed in Section 2.1(a), the *nobile officium* has been used to appoint trustees. Petitions have also been successfully presented for the appointment of trustees in sequestrations, including for the revival of sequestrations which had for some reason come to a standstill or which had ceased to proceed. This would typically be effected by the Court's appointment of a meeting of creditors. Depending on the circumstances of the individual case, petitions have been successfully brought by such persons as creditors,[49] a former trustee,[50] representatives of commissioners on an estate,[51] and the trustees and executors of a creditor's successor.[52] There is even precedent for the bankrupt bringing a successful petition.[53]

There have been varying situations in which it was desired to appoint a new trustee on a sequestrated estate, though typically the trustee had been discharged or died.

In *Thomson, Petr*,[54] the estates of a company and its individual partners had been sequestrated. The estates were divided in the normal manner, and the trustee was discharged some four years after appointment. Thereafter, a further sum became available, with the bankrupt having not yet obtained discharge. A former trustee on the estate petitioned the Court to appoint a meeting of creditors for the purpose of electing a new trustee. Lord Justice-Clerk Inglis had the following to say:

> This petition is presented under extraordinary circumstances ... There seems no reason to doubt that the application is unprecedented. It becomes us, therefore, to walk warily in dealing with it. It presents a case of great practical embarrassment in the working of the Bankrupt

---

[49] *Struthers, Petr* (1861) 23 D 702; *Steuart v Chalmers* (1864) 2 M 1216; *Northern Heritable Securities Investment Co Ltd v Whyte* (1888) 16 R 100; *Philip Woolfson Ltd, Petrs* 1962 SLT 252; *W & A Gilbey Ltd v Franchitti* 1969 SLT (Notes) 18.

[50] *Thomson, Petr* (1863) 2 M 325.

[51] *Young, Petrs* (1888) 16 R 92.

[52] *Cheyne's Trs, Petrs* 1933 SLT 184.

[53] *Macdonald, Petrs* (1861) 23 D 719; *MacDuff v Baird* (1892) 20 R 101.

[54] (1863) 2 M 325.

Act. ... The question is, in what manner can the forms of process be made available for the recovery and division of this sum? ... It seems to me that this is a *casus improvisus* under the statute. The 74th section contemplates only the cases of the original trustee dying, resigning, or being removed. ... [T]aking the whole circumstances into consideration, the case falls so entirely within the principle of the section, that I think it is a case for the exercise of the *nobile officium* of the Court. This *casus improvisus* is in all respects parallel to those provided for. I therefore think the prayer of the petition ought to be granted.[55]

Other judges in the case were in agreement. Lord Cowan, for example, said that exercise of the *nobile officium* was, in this case, the only way of resuming the sequestration; if the case had involved the resignation of the trustee, the application should properly have been made to the sheriff, "but this *casus improvisus* falls properly to be dealt with by this Court".[56] Accordingly, the Court granted the prayer of the petition.

In the case of *Young, Petrs*,[57] a petition was made to the *nobile officium* by a representative of one of the commissioners on a sequestrated estate. The petition was brought over 80 years after the sequestration of the bankrupt's estate, the sequestration having originally been conducted under the Payment of Creditors (Scotland) Act 1793.[58] In that period, the bankrupt and trustee had both died, with neither having obtained discharge. A balance remained on the estate. The petition was therefore brought with the agreement of the trustee's testamentary trustees for revival of the sequestration with a view to distributing the balance on the estate. The Court exercised its *nobile officium* to revive the sequestration, ordering that it now be regulated by the Bankruptcy (Scotland) Act 1856 and amending legislation, and remitting to the Lord Ordinary to appoint a meeting of creditors and for the usual process of distribution to follow.

---

[55] At 325–26 per Lord Justice-Clerk Inglis.
[56] At 326 per Lord Cowan.
[57] (1888) 16 R 92.
[58] 33 Geo III, cap 74.

In *Northern Heritable Securities Investment Co Ltd v Whyte*,[59] the bankrupt and trustee in a sequestration had both been discharged. However, certain creditors petitioned the Court to appoint a meeting of creditors to elect a new trustee, alleging that there existed funds belonging to the sequestrated estate which had not been recovered, with outstanding debts remaining. Lord President Inglis described the petition as "properly addressed to the Court in exercise of its *nobile officium*", and noted that the Court had "followed this course which we are here asked to take and have granted the prayer of such petitions in a great many similar cases, beginning with that of *Thomson*".[60] He continued:

> All that is required to sustain such an application, in circumstances similar to the present, is that it shall be averred that there are funds belonging to the sequestrated estate; that the bankrupt has been discharged, not upon a composition, but only by reason of the efflux of time, or by the consent of creditors; and that the petitioners making the application shall be creditors who have not been paid in full.[61]

The Court was unpersuaded by the respondent's argument that there had been abandonment on the part of the trustee, and remitted the matter to the Lord Ordinary. An appeal was made to the House of Lords,[62] but this was dismissed.

In *MacDuff v Baird*,[63] an undischarged bankrupt presented a petition 22 years after discharge of the trustee for a new trustee to be appointed or for a meeting of creditors to be held for the purpose of electing a new trustee. The petitioner explained that he had been successful in business and was now able to pay his creditors in full. Lord President Robertson observed that "the Court has in a whole series of cases exercised the *nobile officium* to the effect of reviving a sequestration, where a trustee was dead

---

[59] (1888) 16 R 100.
[60] At 102 per Lord President Inglis.
[61] At 102 per Lord President Inglis.
[62] *Whyte v Northern Heritable Securities Investment Co Ltd* (1891) 18 R (HL) 37.
[63] (1892) 20 R 101.

or had been discharged".[64] In this case, he noted that there was a question as to what significance lay in the fact that it was not the creditor bringing the petition, but the undischarged bankrupt himself. He concluded that the same considerations applied as in those other cases. Lord Adam stated that the "natural course, in these circumstances, seems to be that the Court should now supply the defect in the machinery of the sequestration and appoint a new trustee".[65] Accordingly, the Court granted the prayer of the petition.

In another set of circumstances, disclosed in *Philip Woolfson Ltd, Petrs*,[66] a trustee had been elected but was found to act for a person opposed to the general interest of the creditors, contrary to section 64 of the Bankruptcy (Scotland) Act 1913 which provided that it shall not be lawful to elect a trustee who holds such an interest. The creditors petitioned the *nobile officium* for a new meeting to be appointed for the election of a trustee, and the Court, without delivering opinions, granted the prayer of the petition.

Occasionally it has not been a trustee whose appointment was sought in the revival or reinvigoration of a sequestration, but that of a judicial factor. In *Moncrieff's Trs v Halley*,[67] the trustee on the sequestrated estates of a deceased debtor died prior to the division of the whole estate. The trustee's representatives obtained an order from the Lord Ordinary to appoint a meeting of creditors for the purpose of electing a new trustee; however, no creditors attended the meeting. The petitioner therefore moved the Lord Ordinary to appoint a judicial factor on the sequestrated estates of the bankrupt. The Lord Ordinary reported the case to the Inner House, which appointed a judicial factor.

The appointment of a judicial factor on a sequestrated estate was likewise sought in *Cheyne's Trs, Petrs*.[68] An individual had

---

[64] At 103 per Lord President Robertson. For additional confirmation of the exercise of the *nobile officium* in a case of discharge, see *Caldwell v Hamilton* 1919 SC (HL) 100 at 109 per Lord Dunedin.

[65] At 103–04 per Lord Adam.

[66] 1962 SLT 252.

[67] (1899) 1 F 696.

[68] 1933 SLT 184.

died in 1849, and his estates were sequestrated in 1850. Progress was made in the sequestration, though delays were encountered in the final realisation of the estate. The trustee continued to lodge annual statutory returns with the sheriff-clerk until around 1860, after which no return was made. The trustee had taken no further step in the sequestration from 1854, and eventually died in 1890. Over 40 years after the death of the trustee – and over 80 years since the award of sequestration – the trustees and executors of a creditor's successor petitioned the Court for the appointment of a judicial factor on the sequestration. The Court granted the prayer of the petition without delivering opinions.

Petition has sometimes been made for the appointment of a meeting of creditors with the purpose of electing a trustee in circumstances other than the trustee's death or discharge. In *Macdonald, Petrs*,[69] a meeting of creditors was appointed to be held at Lochmaddy on North Uist for the purpose of electing a trustee on the sequestrated estate. The bankrupt's agents sent a certified copy of the petition and deliverance by post, but this was not received until one week after the date of the intended meeting in consequence of the correspondence having been detained due to adverse winds. The bankrupt presented a petition to the Court praying for a new meeting of creditors to be appointed for the purpose of electing a trustee. In addition, it was prayed that although the Bankruptcy (Scotland) Act 1856 required that the meeting take place no later than 12 days from the statutory notice of sequestration in the Gazette, the meeting be appointed 25 days in advance, due to the difficulty of communicating with Lochmaddy. The Court granted the prayer of the petition.[70]

---

[69] (1861) 23 D 719.

[70] It is currently required that where a petition for sequestration is presented by a creditor or trustee acting under a trust deed, the sheriff to whom the petition is presented shall grant warrant to cite the debtor to appear before him on a date not less than six nor more than 14 days after the date of citation, to show cause why sequestration should not be awarded: Bankruptcy (Scotland) Act 1985, s 12(2) (as amended by the Bankruptcy and Diligence etc (Scotland) Act 2007).

In *Struthers, Petr*,[71] objections lodged with the sheriff were sustained following the nomination of trustees at a meeting of creditors. Accordingly, no trustees were elected, and there was no provision in the relevant statutes (the Bankruptcy (Scotland) Act 1856 and the Bankruptcy and Real Securities (Scotland) Act 1857) for a second meeting to be held – effectively an instance of statutory omission. In these circumstances, the Court exercised its *nobile officium* to appoint a date for a new meeting of creditors.

In *Steuart v Chalmers*,[72] a meeting of creditors declined to elect a trustee and resolved to abandon the sequestration. One of the creditors who was absent from the meeting petitioned the Court for the appointment of a new meeting of creditors and to remit to the sheriff to proceed with the sequestration. The Court granted the prayer of the petition on the basis that it was incompetent for the meeting of creditors to abandon the sequestration in this way, that a sequestration was capable of recall only by judicial authority, and that appointing a new meeting was essentially the only way forward for the sequestration. Both Lord Justice-Clerk Inglis and Lord Cowan relied on *Thomson, Petr*[73] in the course of their judgments.

A similar state of affairs arose more than a century later in *W & A Gilbey Ltd v Franchitti*.[74] A meeting of creditors had been appointed, though just one creditor attended the meeting and refused to elect a trustee. Subsequently, a different creditor petitioned the *nobile officium* to have another meeting of creditors appointed for the purpose of electing a trustee, it being noted that there was no provision in the Bankruptcy (Scotland) Act 1913 for achieving the same. The bankrupt lodged answers in which it was averred, *inter alia*, that the petitioners were not entitled to invoke the *nobile officium* having failed to attend the first meeting of creditors. The Court was unpersuaded by that averment, and

---

[71] (1861) 23 D 702.
[72] (1864) 2 M 1216.
[73] (1863) 2 M 325.
[74] 1969 SLT (Notes) 18.

granted the prayer of the petition. It is useful to note that the Court found the bankrupt liable in expenses in relation to her opposition to the petition, and at a later date found one of her creditors liable to the petitioning creditor for failing in his duty to elect a trustee.

The actions (or inaction) of creditors may, however, negatively affect the outcome of a petition seeking to breathe new life into a sequestration. An example is furnished in *Abel v Watt*.[75] The estate of a sequestrated individual yielded no dividend. Seven years after the award of sequestration, the trustee was discharged. The bankrupt did not obtain discharge, but carried on trade as a farmer and horse dealer without objection or interference from his creditors. Some 13 years after discharge of the trustee, a petition was presented to the Court by creditors whose debts were subsequent in date to the sequestration. They sought to have a new trustee appointed. However, the original creditors now came forward seeking to revive the sequestration. The Court refused to exercise its *nobile officium*, explaining that the original creditors were barred by acquiescence in the trading activities of the bankrupt.

A few petitions were made in this area which tested the question of competency. It was confirmed that under the Bankruptcy (Scotland) Act 1856, the sheriff was only empowered to appoint a meeting of creditors for the election of a new trustee where the previous trustee had died, resigned or been removed. In other circumstances – such as the discovery of new funds following the discharge of the trustee – it was necessary to petition the Court of Session.[76] It was confirmed in another case that where the bankrupt and trustee had both been discharged and there emerged additional estate for distribution, a petition for the appointment of a new trustee would not fall under the Bankruptcy (Scotland) Act 1913, and would thus be appropriate for presentation to the *nobile officium* of the Inner House.[77]

---

[75] (1883) 11 R 149.
[76] *Hutton, Petr* (1872) 10 M 620.
[77] *Cockburn's Trs, Petrs* 1941 SC 187.

There was also a challenge to the competency of a petition which was disputed by a bankrupt on the basis that it had been made in vacation to the Lord Ordinary on the Bills. The petition then appeared in Single Bills in the Inner House, and the Court ordered intimation and service to be made of new.[78] In another case, an undischarged bankrupt had succeeded to certain heritable property following discharge of the trustee. A creditor petitioned the Court for remit to the Lord Ordinary on the Bills to appoint a meeting of creditors for the election of a new trustee in the sequestration. The Lord Ordinary on the Bills (McLaren) ordered intimation and service, but thereafter the Lord Ordinary on the Bills (Kinnear) refused to pronounce any order on the basis that he had no jurisdiction. The petition thereafter appeared in the First Division of the Inner House, which ordered intimation, advertisement and service to be made of new.[79]

4.4 Loss of process

The Court has exercised its *nobile officium* to facilitate sequestrations in which there has been loss of process. In *Wilson's Tr v Wilson*,[80] for example, most of the original process had been lost, including the creditors' claims. The trustee was unable to locate the papers, but did retain possession of the sederunt book which he regarded as sufficient to enable him to adjudicate on the creditors' claims. The trustee petitioned the Court for authority to proceed in the sequestration notwithstanding the loss of much of the process. The Court, relying on the "identical"[81] authority of *Skirving's Tr, Petr*,[82] granted the prayer of the petition.

In fact, *Skirving's Tr* was not identical, for in that case the entirety of the documents and original process had gone missing, including the sederunt book. The Court nevertheless granted authority to a newly appointed trustee (the previous trustee having

---

[78] *Newton & Son, Petrs* (1900) 8 SLT 221.
[79] *Shaw, Petr* (1884) 11 R 814.
[80] (1899) 1 F 694.
[81] *Wilson's Tr v Wilson* (1899) 1 F 694 at 695 per Lord President Robertson.
[82] (1883) 11 R 17.

left for Canada) to proceed in the sequestration. The Court may in such circumstances order advertisement to be made of new for creditors to come forward and lodge claims, although problems may be encountered if there has been significant passage of time or if original receipts or vouchers previously submitted have been lost.

Another example is *Coull's Tr, Petr*,[83] in which the trustee was discharged and then died. A second trustee was appointed two years later on the bankrupt's succession to further assets, but the second trustee was himself discharged and died. The bankrupt had gone abroad and his location unknown until he reappeared some 30 years after the discharge of the second trustee. There having been further assets to which the bankrupt succeeded, the Court appointed a third trustee. However, the third trustee discovered that most of the sequestration process was lost with the exception of the original petition, the sederunt book and documents relating to the first trustee's discharge. The third trustee petitioned the *nobile officium* for authority to (i) advertise of new for claims and to proceed of new in the sequestration, and (ii) accept entries from the sederunt book as sufficient evidence that creditors were entitled to rank for the amounts appearing in the sederunt book. The Court granted the first part of the prayer, but refused the second.

The *nobile officium* can therefore provide a way forward even when faced with the loss of much or even all of the original process in a sequestration.

4.5 Recall of sequestration

Several petitions have been presented to the *nobile officium* praying for recall of sequestration.[84] This route may be pursued because, for example, of failure to meet a statutory time limit

---

[83] 1934 SC 415.

[84] For the regular procedure on recall, see the Bankruptcy (Scotland) Act 1985, ss 16–17 (as amended) and ss 17A–17G (inserted by the Bankruptcy and Debt Advice (Scotland) Act 2014, s 27, and effective from 1 April 2015).

such as that prescribed in the Bankruptcy (Scotland) Act 1985 that a petition for recall shall be presented within 10 weeks from the date of the award of sequestration.[85] The authority of the Court may therefore be sought to grant recall after the expiry of that time limit.

It appears, however, that petitions to the *nobile officium* for recall have in general not met with success.[86] Instead, where a petition has been viewed positively, the Court has preferred to declare the sequestration at an end.

An example of this can be found in the case of *Anderson, Petr.*[87] Following the appointment of a meeting of creditors at which no creditors appeared, the bankrupt presented a petition for recall of sequestration. Lord Justice-Clerk Inglis noted that the petitioner could not get out of the position of sequestrated bankrupt without the interposition of the Court.[88] Lord Neaves agreed that if the creditors would not accept the diligence in their favour which the sequestration created, then "the Court may take the matter into their own hands".[89] The Court therefore exercised its *nobile officium*, not to grant recall, but instead to declare the sequestration at an end, and the petitioner reinvested in his estates.

Anderson was followed in *Ballantyne, Petr.*[90] An individual's estates were sequestrated and an abbreviate of the deliverance recorded in the General Register of Inhibitions, but no further step was taken in the sequestration. The individual then died intestate and his two creditors agreed to a division of the estate without incurring the expense of bankruptcy administration. A meeting of creditors was appointed for the election of a trustee, but no creditors attended the meeting. One of the creditors therefore petitioned the Court's *nobile officium* for declaration

---

[85] See the Bankruptcy (Scotland) Act 1985, s 16(4).

[86] As noted, it is no longer competent to petition the Court of Session for recall as a matter of ordinary course.

[87] (1866) 4 M 577.

[88] At 578 per Lord Justice-Clerk Inglis.

[89] At 578 per Lord Neaves.

[90] (1900) 2 F 1077.

that the sequestration was at an end, the Court granting the prayer of the petition.

The petitioners in *Macleish's Trs, Petrs*[91] sought alternative prayers, namely for recall of sequestration or declaration that the sequestration was at an end. The estates of a deceased had been sequestrated, and part of those estates included heritable property burdened with a bond and disposition in security. The property was vested in the bankrupt's testamentary trustees, who obtained discharge after having paid to the trustee the value of the reversion. The sequestrated estates were then divided and the trustee discharged. The testamentary trustees then petitioned the Court, which held that it was inappropriate to recall a sequestration which had run its full course, and instead granted declarator that the sequestration was at an end.

Alternative prayers for recall of sequestration or declaration that the sequestration was at an end were also sought by creditors in *Craig & Co Ltd, Petrs*.[92] The petition was presented on the basis that an arrangement had been reached between the trustee on the estate and the creditors on the distribution of the assets of the sequestrated firm. They agreed that continuation of the sequestration was no longer necessary or desirable. Section 31 of the Bankruptcy (Scotland) Act 1913 provided, however, that no petition for recall of sequestration shall be competent after the expiry of 40 days from the deliverance awarding sequestration, though with the exception that nine-tenths in number and value of the creditors ranked on the estate may at any time apply for recall by petition to the Court. The petition was therefore presented to the *nobile officium* on the view that, as the creditors had not yet ranked on the estate, the provisions of the Act did not allow for the presentation of a statutory petition. Lord Justice-Clerk Cooper stated that recall of sequestration was a specific statutory remedy available only under certain conditions prescribed by the Act, and as such it was appropriate

---

[91] (1896) 24 R 151.
[92] 1946 SC 19.

to declare the sequestration at an end.[93] The Court accordingly did so. According to Lord Mackay, this was the "fifth time in a century" that the Court had used its *nobile officium* to declare a sequestration at an end.[94]

If it was beginning to appear that the Court would categorically decline to exercise its *nobile officium* to grant recall of sequestration; however, that doubt was dispelled in the more recent case of *Wright v Tennent Caledonian Breweries Ltd.*[95] A debtor petitioned the *nobile officium* for authority to lodge a petition for recall outside a statutory time limit. Section 16(4)(a) of the Bankruptcy (Scotland) Act 1985 required that a petition for recall be presented within 10 weeks from the date of sequestration, but the debtor had not been able to petition for recall within that period due to various proceedings leading to the award of sequestration being made more than 10 weeks after the relevant date. The petition was refused, but not on point of competency. Lord President Hope explained that the failure to comply with the time limit was not the fault of the petitioner. Her being deprived of the statutory remedy was due to an "unforeseen circumstance, for which the Act makes no provision", and accordingly "this is the kind of case where the inherent equitable jurisdiction of the Court of Session may be exercised to make good the situation which has occurred". It would be:

> appropriate to extend the time for the presentation of the petition for recall by a suitable period on the ground that compliance with the statutory timetable was impossible, provided always that we were persuaded that the petitioner has reasonable grounds for seeking a recall.[96]

Lord President Hope then went on to deal with the respondent's contention that the remedy of reduction of the award of sequestration was open to the petitioner, and that therefore the petition to the *nobile officium* was incompetent. He took the view

---

[93] At 22 per Lord Justice-Clerk Cooper.

[94] At 23 per Lord Mackay.

[95] 1991 SLT 823.

[96] At 826 per Lord President Hope.

that this was a matter of relevancy rather than competency, and that in the present circumstances the remedy of recall would have been more appropriate. He concluded:

> The appropriate remedy here would have been to apply for a recall and, but for the view which I have taken on the argument on the construction of the documents, I would have been in favour of permitting the petitioner to do this in the exercise of the *nobile officium*.[97]

As noted, the petition was dismissed for other reasons.

A final twist in the tale is that the Court may regard a petition to the *nobile officium* for recall to be incompetent. This was the conclusion in *Brown v Middlemas of Kelso Ltd*.[98] The sheriff principal had pronounced decree in absence against a partnership and the partners thereof both as partners and individuals. The petitioner denied that he was a partner and alleged that he was unaware of the proceedings in the sheriff court and of the service of a charge. He alleged, *inter alia*, that the first he learned of the proceedings was in a letter from the interim trustee awarding sequestration over the petitioner's estate. The Bankruptcy (Scotland) Act 1985 provided in section 16(4)(a) that a petition for recall of sequestration must be presented within 10 weeks after the date of sequestration; however that period had since expired. The petitioner therefore petitioned the Court for recall of the award of sequestration in exercise of its *nobile officium*. Lord Justice-Clerk Ross, delivering the opinion of the Court, distinguished the case of *Wright v Tennent Caledonian Breweries Ltd* as one in which there had been an unforeseen circumstance, whereas no such unforeseen circumstance arose in the present case. The Court was of the view that there was no *casus improvisus* in the statute and that, if it granted the prayer of the petition, it would effectively be extending a statutory time limit.[99] The petition was ultimately dismissed.

---

[97] At 827–28 per Lord President Hope.

[98] 1994 SC 401.

[99] For further discussion on judicial treatment of the extension of statutory time limits by exercise of the *nobile officium*, see pp 232–35.

4.6 Discharge from sequestration

Petitions have been successfully presented to the *nobile officium* for discharge from sequestration. Such petitions would most obviously be brought by sequestrated persons,[100] though they might equally be brought by other parties.[101]

The *nobile officium* is of course not the ordinary route to securing discharge,[102] and there should be some compelling or unusual reason why recourse to the *nobile officium* is sought (and even more so after recent statutory reforms[103]). The cases reveal some examples of such situations.

In *White, Petr*,[104] the trustee in a sequestration went incommunicado, apparently no longer at his original address and incapable of being contacted. It was suspected that he had gone abroad some time ago. The trustee had not, however, produced a statutory report before doing so, and as a result it was not possible for the bankrupt to secure discharge. The bankrupt therefore petitioned the Court for a substitute report to be produced by the Accountant in Bankruptcy. The petition was successful, with the Court appointing its intimation and remitting to the Lord Ordinary on the Bills.

It may be that no statutory report has been furnished – thus practically preventing discharge from being obtained in the ordinary way – because the trustee has died. This occurred in both *Meldrum, Petr*[105] and *Mackay, Petr*.[106] In both cases petitions were successfully presented by the bankrupt for the Court to

---

[100] *White, Petr* (1893) 20 R 600; *Meldrum, Petr* (1895) 2 SLT 405; *Mackay, Petr* (1896) 24 R 210; *Cruickshank v Gowans* (1899) 1 F 692; *Aitken v Robson* 1914 SC 224; *Laing, Petrs* 1962 SC 168; *Black, Petr* 1964 SC 276; *Fraser v Glasgow Corporation* 1967 SC 120.

[101] As, eg, in *Gray's Executrices, Petrs* 1928 SLT 558, in which the petition was brought by executrices-nominate.

[102] See the Bankruptcy (Scotland) Act 1985, ss 54–56, as amended by, *inter alia*, the Bankruptcy and Debt Advice (Scotland) Act 2014 (including the inserted ss 54A–54G and 55A–55B).

[103] See p 82, fn 4.

[104] (1893) 20 R 600.

[105] (1895) 2 SLT 405.

[106] (1896) 24 R 210.

exercise its *nobile officium* to remit to the Accountant of Court to prepare a statutory report in lieu of the trustee, paving the way for discharge to be obtained.

It may be that discharge is sought at some earlier point in proceedings, in particular when the sequestration has stalled. In *Aitken v Robson*,[107] the creditors elected a trustee at their statutory meeting, but did not decide on the sufficiency of caution, meaning that no bond of caution was lodged and that, consequently, the sheriff refused to confirm the election of the trustee. No further steps were taken in the sequestration for seven years, after which the bankrupt petitioned the Court for discharge. Lord Salvesen noted that there was no statutory provision for obtaining discharge in these circumstances, and the Court exercised its *nobile officium* to grant discharge.

Similar facts arose in *Laing, Petrs*,[108] with no further steps being taken for eight years after the sheriff's refusal to confirm the election of the trustee. In addition, creditors representing over 95 per cent in value of the debts due by the petitioners agreed to waive and renounce their claims. Unable to secure discharge due to the failure of the sequestration to run its course, the bankrupts petitioned the Court for discharge in exercise of its *nobile officium*. Lord President Clyde noted that there was "no statutory machinery" to secure discharge in these circumstances, and the Court, relying on *Aitken v Robson* as authority, granted discharge.

Both *Aitken v Robson* and *Laing* were relied on in *Black, Petr*,[109] in which the trustee failed to lodge a bond of caution within seven days as required by the Bankruptcy (Scotland) Act 1913. As in previous cases, no further progress was made in the sequestration. The bankrupt averred that there was a *casus improvisus* in the statute and that he had been deprived of his statutory right to discharge. Accordingly, he petitioned the *nobile officium*. Lord President Clyde agreed that a *casus improvisus*

---

[107] 1914 SC 224.
[108] 1962 SC 168.
[109] 1964 SC 276.

had arisen, and that the "door is open" for exercise of the *nobile officium*.[110] The Court granted discharge to the bankrupt.

Black was itself followed in *Fraser v Glasgow Corporation*.[111] Sequestration in that case proved abortive at an even earlier stage, with no creditors attending the statutory meeting, no trustee being elected, and no further steps being taken. There being no provision for this situation in the Bankruptcy (Scotland) Act 1913, the bankrupt petitioned the Court for discharge in exercise of its *nobile officium*, arguing that a *casus omissus* had arisen. Lord President Clyde noted that sequestration is a statutory procedure, that the bankrupt had done everything statutorily required of him, and that the bankrupt could not be blamed for the failure of the creditors to attend the statutory meeting. He continued:

> [W]here someone is sequestrated and a trustee has not been appointed, and the statutory machinery has consequently broken down, there is no provision in the Bankruptcy Act to enable that bankrupt to be discharged. It would obviously be unjust that anyone, even in the position of a bankrupt, should be left indefinitely in this situation, and this is the very set of circumstances in which it has always been the practice to invoke the *nobile officium* of this Court.[112]

Lord President Clyde said that the respondents – Glasgow Corporation, a creditor for unpaid rates – "received the intimation to which they were entitled under the statute, and if they chose to do nothing in the face of that intimation, then the consequences of their lying back will rebound upon their own heads".[113] The Court granted discharge to the bankrupt in exercise of the *nobile officium*.

A lack of adequate statutory machinery had also been a motivating factor in the Court's intervention in *Gray's Executrices, Petrs*.[114] Executrices-nominate of a deceased had presented a petition under the Bankruptcy (Scotland) Act 1913 for the discharge of both the estates of the deceased and the

---

[110] At 277 per Lord President Clyde.
[111] 1967 SC 120.
[112] At 123 per Lord President Clyde.
[113] At 124 per Lord President Clyde.
[114] 1928 SLT 558.

executrices-nominate. The petition was heard in the Bill Chamber. As Lord Mackay explained in his judgment, the deceased was never properly insolvent. The issue raised by the case was that the Act did not appear to provide for a situation such as that presented: what was sought was not discharge on composition, because either the creditors did not desire payment, or they had been paid in full. As such, Lord Mackay said:

> The provisions of the fasciculus dealing with Discharge without Composition appear, perhaps by the occurrence of a *casus improvisus*, not to apply in express terms to the discharge of the estate, or of the representatives of a deceased bankrupt, but only to the bankrupt himself. I am of opinion, however, that in these circumstances there is an inherent jurisdiction residing in the Court in dealing with matters of bankruptcy which enables it under its *nobile officium* to refuse to be tied by such technical fetters, and to grant an effective order terminating the sequestration and declaring the estate and the representatives free of debt.[115]

Lord Mackay then cited several authorities which he regarded as supporting that position. One of those was the case of *Keiller, Petr*,[116] of which he said that "the Court ... regarded some substituted declaration by the representative as a pre-requisite to discharge, but did not hold themselves precluded by the strict terms of the statute from equitably granting a complete relief of the estate and the representative". However, he regarded the case of *Roberts, Petrs*,[117] in which the requirement for the statutory declaration was dispensed with, as overruling the requirement for a substituted declaration laid down in *Keiller*. He also referred to the unreported case of *Cuthbert*,[118] in which the Lord Ordinary received a declaration from the bankrupt and granted discharge with the concurrence of a majority in number of four-fifths in value of the estate. However, in the present case the concurrence of a majority of creditors would not be necessary, as creditors who

---

[115] At 560 per Lord Mackay.
[116] (1842) 4 D 742.
[117] (1901) 3 F 779.
[118] 31 Dec 1909 and 12 Feb 1910, Bill Chamber, unreported.

had received full satisfaction would no longer have title to oppose it. In the end, the Court pronounced an interlocutor granting discharge.

A final case worthy of mention – and one in which the petition was unsuccessful – is *Cruickshank v Gowans*.[119] The trustee had been discharged after preparing a statutory report which was lodged with the Accountant of Court. The bankrupt then alleged that certain facts had been omitted from the trustee's report, and given that the (now discharged) trustee refused to report on the facts, the bankrupt was prevented from obtaining discharge. He therefore petitioned the Court to exercise its *nobile officium* to ordain the former trustee to deliver a report which included those alleged facts, or to remit to the Accountant of Court to furnish such a report, and thereafter give notice to his creditors and discharge him from bankruptcy.

The petitioner sought to rely on *White*,[120] but the Court refused the petition as incompetent. Lord President Robertson distinguished *White* as a case in which no report had been lodged and the trustee had disappeared. That gave rise to the Court stepping in to have a report furnished by the Accountant of Court. In the present case a report had been produced, and whether it was a good report or a bad report was for the judge in the sequestration to decide. Accordingly, the Court took the view that the bankrupt should have made his arguments before the court of sequestration.

4.7 Invalidation of company dissolution

Though company dissolution is not squarely within the context of insolvency, petitions have been presented to the *nobile officium* for declaration that the dissolution of a company is void.[121] These petitions have, however, tended to be unsuccessful. The essential

---

[119] (1899) 1 F 692.

[120] *White, Petr* (1893) 20 R 600.

[121] For the normal statutory course of action, see the Companies Act 2006, ss 1029–1033. See also *Stair Memorial Encyclopaedia*, Corporate Insolvency Reissue at paras 402–403.

rationale of such petitions has been to effectively "turn back the clock" so that the dissolved company may do something that only an undissolved company could do.

One such thing would be to convey property. This was the basic issue in *Campbell, Petr*.[122] A building society had been dissolved by an instrument of dissolution. At that date, the building society was infeft in certain heritable subjects and the trustee of the building society had sold those subjects on to a third party, as authorised by the instrument of dissolution. The purchaser objected, however, that the trustee was unable to give valid title inasmuch as a dissolved entity could not grant a conveyance of the subjects in question.

The trustee petitioned the Court to authorise and empower him to execute and deliver the necessary dispositions and conveyances, without completing a feudal title in his person. The Court refused the petition. Lord President Inglis explained that the office of trustee was in this case entirely statutory. The statute must either have given the trustee the power to sell and dispose of the subjects without making up a feudal title in his own person, or it had withheld that power. In the former case, the intervention of the Court would be unnecessary; in the latter case the Court had no jurisdiction to "dispense with the ordinary forms of conveyancing in the case of dissolved companies of this kind".[123] In other words, the petitioner:

> either has a good title to convey, and in that case he does not need our authority, or he has not a good title to convey, and in that case we are not in a position to give him a good title.[124]

This was "not a case in which there can be any appeal to the *nobile officium*, because it is a matter depending entirely on the construction of the words of the statute".[125] There were other, well-known, means of testing the issue of good title.[126] To give

---

[122] (1890) 18 R 149.
[123] At 151 per Lord President Inglis.
[124] At 152 per Lord Kinnear.
[125] At 151 per Lord President Inglis.
[126] At 151 per Lord McLaren.

the petitioner a good title would in essence be a circumvention of statute.[127]

A different perspective arose in *Collins Brothers & Co Ltd, Petrs*,[128] in which a company in liquidation had sold its assets to a new company and was then dissolved. Ten years later the new company discovered that it had not obtained a formal conveyance of certain property which had been included in the transfer, and thereafter petitioned the Court for declaration that the dissolution was void and to authorise the liquidator to grant a conveyance. The petitioners argued that section 223 of the Companies (Consolidation) Act 1908 could not be set in motion as it only applied where an application to void a dissolution was brought within two years of the date of dissolution, and that the circumstances therefore required a petition to the *nobile officium*. The Court, noting the "special circumstances of the case", granted the prayer of the petition.

Collins was distinguished, and *Campbell* followed, in *Lord Macdonald's Curator Bonis, Petrs*.[129] A marble quarrying company had been dissolved having gone into voluntary liquidation. Section 223 of the Companies (Consolidation) Act 1908 provided that the Court may declare the dissolution of a company as void within a period of two years from the date of dissolution. Almost eight years had elapsed since the dissolution of the company, when a petition was presented to the Court by its former liquidator. The company had been the proprietor of a feu consisting of three pieces of ground, two of which had never been sold. The petitioner sought to have the dissolution declared void for the purpose of granting a disposition of the two pieces of ground under the feu charter. As the Act did not provide for the Court to declare void a dissolution after the lapse of a period of two years from the date of dissolution, an alleged *casus improvisus*, the petitioner prayed for the Court to exercise its *nobile officium*. However, the Court refused the petition, Lord President Clyde explaining that the feus

---

[127] At 152 per Lord McLaren.
[128] 1916 SC 620.
[129] 1924 SC 163.

had become *bona vacantia*, and that "there seems to be no reason whatever for interfering, by an exercise of the *nobile officium*, with the law of Scotland which applies to caduciary estate".[130] In other words, there were already rules of law which governed this state of affairs; as Lord Sands noted in the same case, "the petition must be dismissed, on the ground that the *nobile officium* can be called into play only if matters are inextricable".[131]

Lord Macdonald's Curator Bonis was followed in *Forth Shipbreaking Co Ltd, Petrs*.[132] A company had gone into voluntary liquidation and, after the liquidator had entered into an agreement for transfer of the whole assets of the old company to a new company, the old company was dissolved in terms of the Companies (Consolidation) Act 1908. The new company obtained possession of the heritable property transferred, but did not obtain a formal conveyance. The new company itself went into liquidation. The Act provided that the Court may make an order declaring a company dissolution to have been void within a period of two years from the date of dissolution of the company. However, more than two years after the old company had been dissolved, the liquidators and the new company petitioned the Court to declare, in exercise of its *nobile officium*, the dissolution of the old company to have been void and for the liquidator of the old company to be authorised to grant a formal conveyance of the heritable property. The Court did not agree with the petitioner's averment that the case presented a *casus improvisus*, however. Lord President Clyde was of the opinion that the ordinary law provided a remedy, and that in any event the case was not materially different from *Lord Macdonald's Curator Bonis*. Accordingly, the Court refused the prayer of the petition.

However, *Champdany Jute Co Ltd, Petrs*[133] concerned a petition for declaration of the dissolution of a company as void presented *within* two years of dissolution, under section 223

---

[130] At 166 per Lord President Clyde.
[131] At 166 per Lord Sands.
[132] 1924 SC 489.
[133] 1924 SC 209.

of the Companies (Consolidation) Act 1908. This was for the purpose of receiving a repayment of excess profits duty from the Inland Revenue. The Court granted the prayer of the petition in amended form, but Lord President Clyde pointed out in his judgment that this was a petition presented under section 223 of the Act, and that the reporter was "mistaken" in regarding the petition as involving any appeal to the *nobile officium*.[134] The petition was not, after all, presented outside the two-year statutory period.

A final case to note in this section is *Scottish Fluid Beef Co Ltd v Auld*.[135] A company had gone into voluntary liquidation. The liquidator made a return to the registrar of a meeting of creditors held for the purpose of laying his account before it, as required by the Companies Act 1862. The statute provided that on the expiry of three months from the date of registration of the return the company would be deemed dissolved.[136] However, several weeks later the company and liquidator presented a petition to the Court to suspend the operation of that statutory provision, because it had been discovered that the company had not been fully wound up in that a sum of money was due to the company by one of its directors, and that proceedings were being taken against the director for recovery of that sum. The Court was of the view that the petition was incompetent inasmuch as it sought to suspend the operation of a statutory provision whilst requiring the Court to anticipate the outcome of the separate proceeding relating to the recovery of the sum of money from the director. Accordingly, the Court dismissed the petition.

4.8 Other

It remains to address several miscellaneous cases which have arisen in the field of bankruptcy, insolvency and sequestration, but which do not fall neatly under the above headings.

---

[134] At 211 per Lord President Clyde.
[135] (1898) 25 R 1056.
[136] Companies Act 1862, s 143.

A case which did not explicitly mention the *nobile officium*, but which raised a relevant question of competency as to a sheriff-substitute's actions, was *Mann v Dickson*.[137] A trustee was elected at a meeting of creditors. The sheriff declared that election to be null and void on the basis that the party elected trustee had induced creditors to vote for him by offering remuneration for support. The sheriff appointed a new meeting of creditors to be held, but an order of this nature has tended to be made by the Court of Session in exercise of its *nobile officium*. There was recognition of some potential controversy here – the case report notes that:

> The only difficulty the Sheriff-substitute had was as to the course of the future procedure in the sequestration. There does not appear in the Act to be any express power given to order a meeting for a new election of a trustee in circumstances like the present; and as the case was a novel one, and of some importance in the construction of the New Bankrupt Statute, the Sheriff-substitute took the opinion of the Sheriff-principal. In conformity with the views indicated by the Sheriff, and with the practice of the Court of Session under the old statute of 54 Geo. III c. 37 ... and also being anxious to construe the statute beneficially for the interest of the estate, the Sheriff-substitute has decided that he may order a meeting to be held for the election of a new trustee. He has accordingly appointed the creditor-objector, who has appeared, to intimate it in the Gazette, which is the course directed by the statute to be taken in certain analogous cases.[138]

An appeal was brought to the Court of Session against the decision of the sheriff-substitute, but not on point of alleged incompetency. The Court dismissed the appeal, but none of the opinions elicit any discussion of the competency of the sheriff appointing a new meeting of trustees. It may be noted that Lord Justice-Clerk Hope was absent.

In *Central Motor Engineering Co v Gibbs*,[139] we see an example of the Court declining to exercise its *nobile officium*

---

[137] (1857) 19 D 942.
[138] At 943 (Note).
[139] 1917 SC 490. See also *Central Motor Engineering Co v Galbraith* 1918 SC 755.

where a regular procedural option was available. The sequestrated persons petitioned the *nobile officium* for declaration that the proceedings in the sequestration were void *ab initio*. This was prayed on two bases: first, in non-compliance with the Bankruptcy (Scotland) Act 1913, the person who took the oath as to the debt of the petitioning company was not one of the persons authorised to do so by the Act; and second, also in non-compliance with the Act, the correct procedure for citation had not been observed. The Court regarded the petition as premature or incompetent. In particular, the petitioners could have brought an action of reduction under the ordinary forms of process. As such, the Court refused the prayer of the petition.

In *Muir, Petr*,[140] no commissioners were elected and all creditors and their mandatories refused to accept the office of commissioner. The trustee petitioned the Court for the appointment of the Accountant of Court to act in lieu of the commissioners, and particularly to fulfil their duties under the Bankruptcy (Scotland) Act 1856. The Court granted the prayer of the petition.

In *Stark's Trs, Petrs*,[141] a petition was presented by certain creditors to the *nobile officium* for the repayment to them of certain unclaimed dividends from the King's and Lord Treasurer's Remembrancer. The Bankruptcy (Scotland) Act 1913 provided for the transfer of unclaimed dividends to the Remembrancer in certain circumstances. The *nobile officium* was petitioned on the basis that, due to the provisions in a schedule of the Bankruptcy (Scotland) Act 1913 which repealed a particular section of the Court of Session Consignations (Scotland) Act 1895, there was a defective link in the statutory machinery such that the *nobile officium* represented the only way of recovering the dividends. However, Lord President Clyde was of the view that the petition should not have been presented to the *nobile officium*, as a petition could have been presented under certain provisions of the 1895 Act. He therefore invited the petitioners to amend their petition

---

[140] (1894) 2 SLT 316.
[141] 1932 SC 653.

so that it was not addressed to the *nobile officium*, and having done so, the Court made an order in accordance with the prayer of the petition as sought.

An instance of the Court dispensing with a procedural requirement was provided in *Roberts, Petrs*.[142] A bankrupt presented a petition for discharge under the Bankruptcy (Scotland) Act 1856. The petition was initially opposed, then unopposed, and the Lord Ordinary found the petitioner entitled to discharge and appointed him to appear and make a statutory declaration. The bankrupt thereafter became insane and had a curator *bonis* appointed. The curator *bonis*, who was sisted in place of the bankrupt, moved the Lord Ordinary to allow a statutory declaration to be made to the best of his knowledge and belief, or to dispense with the statutory requirement of declaration. The Lord Ordinary reported the case to the Inner House. Lord President Balfour was of the view that it was unsatisfactory to substitute a declaration by the curator *bonis*, who would not have enough knowledge of matters to which his declaration would relate. However, the Lord President opined that the bankrupt should not be deprived of discharge when all of the other statutory requirements had been complied with, and therefore recommended that the proper course would be to exercise the *nobile officium* to dispense with the statutory requirement for declaration. The Court accordingly dispensed with that requirement.

The case of *Bell's Trs v Bell's Tr* did not make mention of the *nobile officium*, though may have involved an exercise of it.[143] The estate of a solvent deceased person had been sequestrated. Before the settlement of all claims, the heir-at-law raised an action against the trustee for conveyance to him of the surplus heritable estate to which he was heir, amounting to some £30,000. Lord Justice-Clerk Moncrieff described this as an "unusual application", but one "founded on the highest equity". He noted that it would be a "great hardship" to the heir-at-law if he were

---

[142] (1901) 3 F 779.

[143] It should be noted however that the case involved the defender reclaiming after a decision of the Lord Ordinary.

kept out of his property.[144] Lord Craighill added that the statute did not provide for a situation in which not all of the debts had been paid out of the estate, and yet where there was "more than enough" in the estate for as yet undischarged payments.[145] The Court found in favour of the heir-at-law.

An unusual case which fell on the insufficiency of argument was *Munro v Graham*.[146] An heir of entail petitioned the Court for sequestration of an estate on the ground that a pupil, whom the heir of entail would succeed, was a "supposititious child". This was argued with the aim of establishing that the succession had opened to the petitioner. He alleged that the child was not really the son of the "parents" in question. The Court was insufficiently persuaded by the strength of the petitioner's submissions, however, and it noted that the child in question had always been acknowledged by his "parents". Accordingly, the Court refused the prayer of the petition.

In the field of company insolvency, *Ker v Hughes*[147] concerned the Companies Act 1862, which empowered the Court to summon before it certain persons connected with a company with regard to which a winding-up order had been made, and also to order the production of related deeds, documents, papers etc. The liquidator of a company was unable to obtain possession of the company books and papers from the company secretary, and sought warrant from the Lord Ordinary for court officers to search for and seize the company books and papers. The Lord Ordinary found the application meritorious, but doubted whether he had power to grant it. As such, he reported the liquidator's note to the Inner House "in order that their Lordships may, if they think fit, in the exercise of their *nobile officium*, grant warrant in such terms as they think right".[148] The Inner House granted warrant as sought, with Lord Justice-Clerk Macdonald "very clearly of

---

[144] (1882) 10 R 370 at 371 per Lord Justice-Clerk Moncrieff.
[145] At 372 per Lord Craighill.
[146] (1849) 11 D 1202.
[147] 1907 SC 380.
[148] At 382–83 (note).

opinion" that the Court had "power to make the order which is asked",[149] and Lord Stormonth-Darling speaking of "powers we undoubtedly possess".[150] Neither judge elaborated on what power they were exercising, and no explicit reference was made by the Inner House to the *nobile officium*.[151]

In *Liquidator of the Clyde Marine Insurance Co Ltd, Petr*,[152] a creditor was appointed to apply to the Court for appointment of a committee of inspection at the first meeting of creditors in the voluntary winding-up of a company. The Companies (Consolidation) Act 1908 required that such application be made within 14 days; however, the creditor inadvertently failed to apply within the statutory time limit. He petitioned the *nobile officium* for the appointment of the committee of inspection. The Court granted the prayer of the petition, Lord President Clyde noting that this was "a clear case for the exercise of the power, which the *nobile officium* gives us, to rectify what is a pure mistake, and to supply machinery which, owing to that mistake, is deficient".[153]

An interesting case relevant to the *nobile officium*, but which did not involve a petition to that jurisdiction, is found in *Jamieson, Petrs*.[154] A number of licensed insolvency practitioners petitioned the Outer House concerning the fallout from a House of Lords case, *Powdrill v Watson*,[155] which, although its effect was reversed by the Insolvency Act 1994, gave rise to a number of problems in dealing with insolvencies. The petitioners averred that over two hundred receiverships may be affected notwithstanding the 1994 Act, involving over 1,300 employees and giving rise to a maximum of £12.5 million in aggregated potential claims. The petition prayed for all claimants to complete a questionnaire giving details of their claim prior to bringing or continuing court proceedings, in order to ease the administrative difficulties

---

[149] At 383 per Lord Justice-Clerk Macdonald.
[150] At 383 per Lord Stormonth-Darling.
[151] This would now be governed by the Insolvency Act 1986, ss 234–237.
[152] 1921 SC 472.
[153] At 473–74 per Lord President Clyde.
[154] 1997 SC 195.
[155] [1995] 2 AC 394.

in dealing with those claims. The Lord Ordinary doubted the competency of what was prayed as a matter of jurisdiction, and reported the case to the Inner House. The Inner House was of the view that to grant the prayer of the petition would be to impose an additional requirement on claimants which did not feature in the Insolvency Act 1986 nor in the Rules of Court applicable to either the Court of Session or the sheriff court, and that it had no power under the statute to give the directions sought by the petitioners.

The petitioners queried whether the Court might do so in exercise of its *nobile officium*. The Court stated that it could not give a concluded opinion on this issue, but it appeared that the *nobile officium* could not be used to extend statutory provisions or the Rules of Court in this way,[156] and in any event there appeared to be no *casus improvisus* or exceptional circumstances which would justify exercise of the *nobile officium*. The preliminary view of the Court was therefore that the *nobile officium* could not be used in this way, and the present petition was refused as incompetent.

Finally, it has been suggested that "the court's equitable jurisdiction" might be useful in recognising a shareholder's entitlement to bring proceedings for the benefit of a company, in circumstances where the company had been wrongfully disabled from bringing proceedings itself.[157]

---

[156] For discussion of the effective extension of statutory provisions by the *nobile officium*, see pp 232–35.

[157] See *Anderson v Hogg* 2000 SLT 634 at 643 per Lord Reed. This was a reference to the *nobile officium*.

CHAPTER 5

CUSTODY OF CHILDREN

The *nobile officium* has been exercised to safeguard the welfare of children. This is done in the spirit of assisting vulnerable and dependent parties, one of the ethical cornerstones of the *nobile officium*. With regard to children, it has principally manifested in questions of custody. It was said by Lord Robertson that:

> There is an inherent power in the Court of Session to exercise in its *nobile officium*, as *parens patriae*, jurisdiction over all children within the realm, and an application by anyone able to demonstrate an interest may bring a petition to the *nobile officium* if the interests of a child is involved or threatened.[1]

Lord Templeman described this as an "inherent broad equitable jurisdiction" by which the Court would make orders of custody and access which "may be made upon the application or in favour of any person (whether or not a parent of the child) who can demonstrate a sufficient interest in obtaining the relief sought".[2]

There is some degree of relation between the Court's *nobile officium* and its *parens patriae* jurisdiction. The term *parens patriae* literally translates from Latin as "parent of the nation", and is also seen in its male version *pater patriae*, "father of the nation". This is a reference to the protective jurisdiction of the monarch over persons unable to act for themselves, including, but not limited to, children:

> The guardianship of all unprotected persons, by reason of weakness of understanding, by extreme youth, natural infirmity of talent, by

---

[1] *Beagley v Beagley* 1984 SC (HL) 69 at 83 per Lord Robertson.
[2] At 94 per Lord Templeman. See also *Syme v Cunningham* 1973 SLT (Notes) 40 at 40 per Lord Keith; and Frederick Parker Walton, *A Handbook of Husband and Wife According to the Law of Scotland* (W Green, 1893) at 72.

nature or disease, was formerly vested in the Crown. The King, as *pater patriae*, was clothed with authority to do this; and, as a matter of course, where persons, within the years of pupillarity, have neither testamentary tutors appointed to them, nor a tutor at law served to the office, his Majesty, through his Exchequer, still bestows a gift of tutory on some one to protect the pupil. It was his Majesty's privilege and right to name protectors, at his pleasure.[3]

The Court's claim to the *parens patriae* jurisdiction is through its inheritance of jurisdiction from the Court of Exchequer: the "whole power, authority and jurisdiction" of the latter was transferred by section 1 of the Exchequer Court (Scotland) Act 1856 to the Court of Session, which was simultaneously designated the Court of Exchequer in Scotland. The Court's protective jurisdiction to appoint judicial factors was suggested to have "developed alongside, and largely in substitution for, the *parens patriae* jurisdiction of the Court of Session as the Court of Exchequer in Scotland",[4] although it was stated that if the possibility of appointments being made under the *parens patriae* jurisdiction was obstructed due to the repeal of the statutory provision entitling the Court of Session to exercise powers formerly enjoyed by the Court of Exchequer, it could still be argued that the *nobile officium* could be used to make the appointments.[5]

Some have merged the jurisdictions, perhaps taking a conceptual rather than a technical view of the matter. Lord Chancellor Campbell said of a particular case that the "Court of Session had undoubted jurisdiction", for by its "*nobile officium*, conferred upon them by their sovereign as *parens patrie* [sic], it is their duty to take care of all infants who require their protection, whether domiciled in Scotland or not".[6] More recently, Sheriff Wilkinson and Kenneth Norrie argued that the "[s]uperintendence

---

[3] *Bryce v Grahame* (1828) 6 S 425 at 433 per Lord Cringletie.
[4] *Law Hospital NHS Trust v Lord Advocate* 1996 SC 301 at 314 per Lord President Hope.
[5] *Law Hospital NHS Trust v Lord Advocate* at 328 per Lord Cullen.
[6] *Stuart v Moore* (1861) 23 D 902 at 908 per Lord Chancellor Campbell.

of guardians belonged at common law to the Court of Session as *parens patriae* in the exercise of its *nobile officium*".[7]

Others have maintained a degree of separation or distinction between the jurisdictions. Lord President Hope described the origin of the Court's "tutory jurisdiction" as lying in the sovereign as *parens patriae* rather than in the Court's residual *nobile officium*, adding that the *parens patriae* jurisdiction existed not only with regard to minors, but also to adults of unsound mind, such as a patient in a persistent vegetative state.[8] Lord Clyde likewise maintained the distinction between the *parens patriae* jurisdiction and the *nobile officium*: if the power to authorise discontinuation of treatment for a patient in a persistent vegetative state was not to be located in the Court's *parens patriae* jurisdiction traceable to the sovereign, then there would be:

> no difficulty in holding that the Court of Session would have such a power under its general residual jurisdiction to which the label of *nobile officium* may be attached if only to distinguish it from what might technically be seen as a *pater patriae* jurisdiction.[9]

Lord Clyde added that this could have practical implications in terms of invoking the correct procedure in a given case. In any event, the *parens patriae* jurisdiction is clearly of more specific application than the broader *nobile officium*, and may be regarded as capable of invocation via the *nobile officium* or, as appropriate, by another process.[10] Whether or not the *nobile officium* is appropriately viewed as a vehicle for the *parens patriae* jurisdiction, it is in principle capable of fulfilling the same function.

---

[7] A B Wilkinson and Kenneth McK Norrie, *Law Relating to Parent and Child in Scotland* (3rd edn, 2013, W Green) at 187. See also Wilkinson and Norrie, *Law Relating to Parent and Child in Scotland* (1st edn, 1993) at 188 which states that "control of parental power is based on the *nobile officium* of the Court of Session which acts as *parens patriae*".

[8] *Law Hospital NHS Trust v Lord Advocate* at 314 per Lord President Hope.

[9] *Law Hospital NHS Trust v Lord Advocate* at 324 per Lord Clyde.

[10] It is worth noting that the *parens patriae* jurisdiction is, like the *nobile officium*, an equitable jurisdiction, and this may feed into the conceptual and jurisprudential location of the *nobile officium* itself – see Section 1.3.

The *nobile officium* was originally the jurisdiction by which custody was contended and awarded. The principal object and guiding principle was and remains the interests of the child:[11] "the benefit of the infant is the foundation of the jurisdiction, and the test of its proper exercise".[12] At one time the only ground for exercising the *nobile officium* to remove a child from the custody of his father was endangerment of the physical or moral interests of the child.[13] The jurisdiction could also be used to direct interim custody and education.[14]

Lord Justice-Clerk Thomson said that custody was "originally a matter entirely for the *nobile officium* and competent only in the Inner House".[15] Whilst applications for the custody of children were presented to the Inner House, the Rules of Court later permitted such applications to be made to the Outer House notwithstanding that they were applications to the *nobile officium*.[16] In 1962 it was provided that statutory petitions could be made to the Outer House, and in 1970 this was extended to include petitions at common law.[17]

Issues of custody and access increasingly came under statutory regulation, beginning with the Conjugal Rights

---

[11] *Stuart v Moore* (1861) 23 D 902 at 910 per Lord Cranworth; *Cheetham v Glasgow Corporation* 1972 SC 243. Where the Court was essentially called upon to exercise its auxiliary jurisdiction by sanctioning an award of custody pronounced by a foreign court, it took into account the welfare of the child before giving effect to the foreign decree (*Radoyevitch v Radoyevitch* 1930 SC 619). On the auxiliary jurisdiction, see p 35, fn 18.

[12] *Stuart v Moore* (1861) 23 D 902 at 908 per Lord Chancellor Campbell.

[13] *Lang v Lang* (1869) 7 M 445 at 447; *Stevenson v Stevenson* (1894) 21 R 430.

[14] *Stuart v Moore* (1860) 23 D 51.

[15] *McArthur v McArthur* 1955 SC 414 at 416 per Lord Justice-Clerk Thomson. See also *Heriot-Hill v Heriot-Hill* (1906) 14 SLT 182 at 183 per Lord Mackenzie; and *Brown v Brown* 1948 SC 5 at 11 per Lord Mackay. For other examples of custody by exercise of the *nobile officium*, see *Muir v Milligan* (1868) 6 M 1125; *Brand v Shaws* (1888) 16 R 315; *Edgar v McKillop* (1893) 21 R 59; and *Stevenson v Stevenson* (1894) 21 R 430. Unsuccessful examples are found in *Kennedy v Steele* (1841) 4 D 12; and *Gillan v Parish Council of Barony Parish, Glasgow* (1898) 1 F 183.

[16] *Syme v Cunningham* 1973 SLT (Notes) 40 at 41 per Lord Keith.

[17] *Hogg v Dick* 1987 SLT 716 at 718 per Lord Cullen.

(Scotland) Amendment Act 1861.[18] The view has been taken, however, that the enactment of statutory provisions did not necessarily abrogate the general basis for awarding custody in proper cases,[19] even although in most modern cases recourse to the *nobile officium* would be unnecessary, and statutory enactments subsequent to the 1861 Act have made that recourse even less necessary.[20] Whilst the *nobile officium* is no longer the default mode for obtaining custody, it was stated in 1956, after a number of statutory enactments, that it was even then "clear that in virtue of the *nobile officium* the Court of Session has power to deal with all questions of custody of children".[21] More recently still, it was confirmed that the *nobile officium* can be resorted to where there is a gap in provision under a particular statutory framework, with the jurisdiction being utilised to achieve some object for the welfare of the child.[22] It was also confirmed in the House of Lords that if exceptional circumstances arose after the making of an adoption order which affected the welfare of the child, and which were unforeseen by Parliament, the divested parent may apply to the *nobile officium* for an appropriate order to the extent that this would not conflict with statute.[23]

---

[18] Key statutory milestones include the Guardianship of Infants Act 1886, the Guardianship of Infants Act 1925, the Illegitimate Children (Scotland) Act 1930, the Children (Scotland) Act 1995, the Children's Hearings (Scotland) Act 2011 and the Children and Young People (Scotland) Act 2014.

[19] *McCallum v McCallum* (1893) 20 R 293; *S v S* 1967 SC (HL) 46 at 50–52 per Lord Reid; *Beagley v Beagley* (1984) SC (HL) 69 at 83 per Lord Robertson; Walton, *Handbook of Husband and Wife* at 323. See also *Lang v Lang* (1869) 7 M 445 at 447 per Lord Benholme; and *AB v CB* (1906) 8 F 973 at 974 per Lord McLaren. See, however, *Beagley v Beagley* at 94 per Lord Templeman.

[20] See Lord Reid's comments in *S v S* 1967 SC (HL) 46 at 52, in particular; *Murray v Forsyth* 1917 SC 721 at 725, 726–27 and 728 per Lords Skerrington, Johnston and Mackenzie, respectively; *Campbell v Campbell* 1956 SC 285 at 289–90 per Lord President Clyde; and *Richardson v Burns* 1963 SLT (Sh Ct) 26 at 27 per Sheriff-Substitute Middleton.

[21] *Campbell v Campbell* at 289 per Lord President Clyde.

[22] *Beagley v Beagley* (1984) SC (HL) 69 at 93 per Lord Keith of Kinkel.

[23] *D v Grampian Regional Council* 1995 SC (HL) 1 at 7 per Lord Jauncey of Tullichettle.

Among some of the earlier cases, the Lord Ordinary on the Bills had competently exercised an effective delegation of the *nobile officium* during vacation to interdict a mother's removal of her children from the jurisdiction, and to remove them from her custody.[24]

In *Nicolson v Nicolson*,[25] the *nobile officium* was used to grant custody of a child to his father. The Court went on to find that it was not entitled to interfere in the father's custody of the child unless it would be expedient to do so, thus apparently imposing a standard of expediency. Lord Ardmillan set out the particular state of the law of Scotland at that time as follows:

> The general rule in regard to the custody of children is beyond all doubt. The legal right to the custody of a lawful child is in the father; and a court of law will enforce that right by the appropriate compulsitors. But that right is not absolute. It is not beyond the control of the law. It is within the power and the duty of a court of justice, and more particularly of this Court, which is a Court both of law and of equity, to mitigate, in the exercise of a cautious discretion, the severity of the general rule by interposing in exceptional cases. The exceptions must be few, and must rest on clear grounds; and these grounds must be found in considerations of danger to the life, health, or morals of the child. Both in this country and in England, a court of justice, when the interests of the child in regard to life, health, or morals have required it, has refused to permit the father to retain the custody. This has been done in Scotland, in the exercise of the *nobile officium* of this Court.[26]

In another case, a young boy had boarded with a friend of his father at Crieff, whilst his father resided in India.[27] When his father (predeceased by his mother) died, his trust settlement made no provision for the boy's custody or for the appointment of a tutor. A petition was presented by the boy's grandmother, uncles and aunts for custody of the boy to be transferred to his grandmother. The Court refused the petition on the basis that the petitioners had

---

[24] *Earl of Buchan v Lady Cardross* (1842) 4 D 1268. See also *Bergius v Bergius* 1924 SC 537. See, however, *Stuart v Moore* (1860) 22 D 1504.

[25] (1869) 7 M 1118.

[26] At 1124 per Lord Ardmillan.

[27] *Smith v Smith's Trs* (1890) 18 R 241.

no legal basis for making their demand, as the boy was strictly without a legal guardian, and that it would be inexpedient that the existing arrangement be altered. Lord President Inglis noted that there was evidence that the boy's parents had been highly satisfied with his custodial arrangements, and that it would be "rash and inadvisable" to interfere with the existing arrangement.[28]

Among more recent cases is that of *Humphries v X and Y*,[29] in which a man who was the father of one child, and the stepfather of another, had been charged with the murder of another of his children. His trial was due to take place at a later date. Meanwhile, the two surviving children were detained at a place of safety under section 37 of the Social Work (Scotland) Act 1968, and warrant for this was extended on three occasions. The reporter to the children's panel noted that the hearing of evidence for the circumstances regarding the child's death under the Act was due to take place prior to the father's trial, and that this may prejudice the father's defence at the trial. Accordingly, the reporter petitioned the *nobile officium* to authorise the local authority to detain the surviving children for a period beyond the trial diet, in excess of the statutory period. The Court granted the prayer of the petition. Lord President Emslie explained that although the *nobile officium* could not be used to defeat an express or implied statutory intention, or to extend the scope of a statute, the present case would constitute neither of those. Instead, the Court would merely be supplying deficient machinery for the highly special circumstances of the case, namely securing a balance in the "major conflict" between the children's interests under the Act, and the father's interests (and the public interest) under the criminal law.[30]

In *Sloan, Petr*,[31] certain children from Orkney were to be detained at a place of safety on the Scottish mainland under section 37 of the Social Work (Scotland) Act 1968. A hearing

---

[28] *Smith v Smith's Trs* (1890) 18 R 241 at 243 per Lord President Inglis.
[29] 1982 SC 79. See also *Ferguson v TP* 1989 SC 231.
[30] *Humphries v X and Y* at 83–84 per Lord President Emslie.
[31] 1991 SC 281.

was arranged to take place in Kirkwall; however, the reporter to the children's panel petitioned the *nobile officium* for the hearing to be conducted elsewhere in the sheriffdom on the ground that it was not in the best interests of the children to return to Kirkwall. There was no appropriate statutory provision under which this change of place could be directed. The Court, noting that the statutory machinery for achieving the same was lacking, exercised its *nobile officium* to ordain the sheriff to hear the children's evidence at Inverness.

Finally, in *R v Kennedy*,[32] the Court dismissed a petition to the *nobile officium*. The petitioner was a father of three children who had been subject to supervision requirements at a children's hearing, with one of those children having been the victim of an offence under the Criminal Procedure (Scotland) Act 1975. The petitioner appealed to the Court of Session, but abandoned the appeal. The child victim later retracted her allegation against the petitioner. However, the children's hearing decided that supervision should remain in place, and the petitioner sought unsuccessfully to have the Secretary of State order the termination of the supervision requirement under section 52 of the Social Work (Scotland) Act 1968.

The petitioner then sought to invoke the *nobile officium* to have the grounds for referral reheard by the sheriff on the basis that additional evidence was now available which cast doubt on the credibility of his daughter's original allegation that she was a victim of the aforesaid offence. The Court held that there was no statutory provision allowing for additional evidence to be heard, that the sheriff's decision was rendered final by the statute except on a point of law or in cases of irregularity in proceedings, and that there had been no oversight in the statute's failure to provide for a procedure for reconsidering the grounds for referral. There had been no exceptional or unforeseen occurrence in the present case, and the petition fell to be dismissed as incompetent. However, in another case the *nobile officium* might be used to remove a case

---

[32] 1993 SC 417; followed in *H, Petrs* 1997 SLT 3.

from a children's hearing which ought not to be before it, on the basis that there were exceptional circumstances such as mistaken or incomplete information on a material point.[33]

It can be seen that the *nobile officium* has moved from being the default mode for obtaining custody of children to a residual, exceptional mechanism for marginal cases. It retains its utility particularly in cases which fail to be adequately governed by relevant statutory provisions, continuing to be directed by the welfare of the child in the spirit of equitable intervention. Where procedural modification or alleviation would be in the best interests of the child, but which is not capable of achievement under the relevant statutory framework, the *nobile officium* may provide a valuable course for securing that alleviation. This might apply with regard to a children's panel, but its scope for application is, in principle, open-ended.

---

[33] *R v Kennedy* at 426.

CHAPTER 6

PUBLIC OFFICERS

The *nobile officium* has been used with regard to public office and its administration. It was not uncommon for public officers to be appointed on an interim basis by exercise of the *nobile officium*, either because of a lack of statutory provision for an emergent set of circumstances, or because to follow the course of statutory procedure would take a length of time detrimental to public administration, thus commending a speedier, interim appointment.

The *nobile officium* was also used to assist with the administration of public affairs in a way which related to the holding of public office, such as with disruption to the normal course of administration caused by vacancy of office. The jurisdiction has also been used to deprive persons of office.

6.1 Interim appointment of public officer

The *nobile officium* was used with relative frequency to appoint public officers on an interim basis. Vacancy of office, such as upon the death or illness of the officeholder, would sometimes give rise to a situation either unprovided for by the relevant statutory framework, or provided for but which process would take a length of time detrimental to public administration. In these scenarios, petition was typically made by an interested party to the Court, praying for the interim appointment of a relevant public officer until the position be regularly filled.[1]

Sometimes there would be an additional aspect to the case in hand, such as a pressing matter of administration which would be jeopardised by the vacancy of the public office. The emphasis in

---

[1] More, *Lectures on the Law of Scotland* at 250.

such cases was on the expedient conduct of public administration, and by appointing an officer on an interim – rather than a tenured – basis, the Court would be able to strike a balance between facilitating the regular course of public administration, whilst ensuring respect for the basic legal framework for the ordinary appointment of public officeholders.

The range of public offices subject to such petitions was wide. They encompass the interim appointment of judicial and administrative officeholders at both the local and national level. Petitions have secured the interim appointment of such offices as sheriff, sheriff-clerk, commissary, Keeper of the Register of Hornings, Keeper of the Great Seal for Scotland and Lyon King-at-Arms.

The petitioner in such cases would usually be an interested party, and could himself be the party seeking interim appointment.[2] Where a petitioner did not personally seek appointment,[3] he could propose the name of a candidate for the Court's consideration, or leave that matter to the Court. We find the Lord Advocate bringing such petitions on several occasions.[4] It should of course be noted that nowadays there will usually be a statutory framework dealing with the appointment of a given public officer upon vacancy.[5] This chapter nevertheless presents a backdrop to the current legal position and a repository of case law demonstrating the potential for the *nobile officium* to be utilised in this area if, for some reason, even the modern statutory framework for appointments proves inadequate.

Interim appointment in the case of the death of an incumbent public officer was perhaps the least controversial of the reasons

---

[2] As in *Dundas, Petr* (1837) 15 S 398.

[3] As in *Gracie, Petr* (1840) 2 D 839.

[4] Such as in *Lord Advocate, Petr* (1860) 22 D 555; *Lord Advocate, Petr* (1885) 12 R 925; and *Lord Advocate, Petr* (1890) 17 R 293.

[5] For example, in the event of a vacancy in the office of the Keeper of the Registers of Scotland, the functions of that office shall be performed by such member of the staff of that office or such other person as may be authorised by the Scottish Ministers: Public Registers and Records (Scotland) Act 1948, s 1(6) (as amended).

for the Court ordering interim appointment by exercise of its *nobile officium*. Petitions have been successfully presented upon the death of the incumbent for interim appointment of the offices of sheriff,[6] sheriff clerk,[7] commissary,[8] Director of Chancery,[9] Keeper of the Register of Hornings,[10] Keeper of Her Majesty's Signet for Scotland,[11] Writer to the Privy Seal,[12] Keeper of the Great Seal for Scotland,[13] and Lyon King-at-Arms.[14]

Whilst the Court was generally willing to appoint interim public officers in these circumstances, it would not do so if it did not consider itself to have jurisdiction or if, for some other reason, appointment did not seem apposite. For example, the Court declined to appoint an interim judge in the High Court of Admiralty following the death of a judge in that court, and a petition made by the clerk of that court for said appointment. Even though the petitioner highlighted the expediency of such an appointment for the business of the High Court of Admiralty, the view of the Court of Session was that no vacancy had arisen as, by reference to the Admiralty Court Act 1681, the High Admiral was the Judge of the High Court of Admiralty.[15]

It is worth noting an argument advanced in a case from 1744 that the Scots Privy Council was "in use" to make interim appointments.[16] As example, a case was cited from 1703 concerning the interim appointment of sheriff-deputes following

---

[6] *Lynd and Sandilands, Petrs* 1744 Mor 7433; *Earl of Dumfries, Petr* 1745 Mor 7434.

[7] *Speirs, Petr* (1842) 5 D 388.

[8] *Lorrain, Petr* 1755 Mor 7445; *Gracie, Petr* (1840) 2 D 839. See also *Winram, Petr* 1739 Mor 7432. The Court also confirmed its jurisdiction to appoint an interim commissary clerk: *Christie, Petr* 1742 Mor 7433.

[9] *Dundas, Petr* (1837) 15 S 398.

[10] *Case anent the Register of Hornings*, 12 Dec 1696, 4 Brown's Sup 340.

[11] *Logan, Petr* (1890) 17 R 757.

[12] *Goldie, Petr* 1741 Mor 7432.

[13] *Lord Advocate, Petr* (1885) 12 R 925.

[14] Unreported case of February 1866 in Mackay, *The Practice of the Court of Session*, vol 1 at 210, note (e).

[15] Act of 1681 concerning the jurisdiction of the admiral court, *APS* viii 351, c 82.

[16] *Lynd and Sandilands, Petrs* 1744 Mor 7433.

the death of the Sheriff Principal of Edinburgh. The petitioners identified this power as "formerly vested in the Privy Council", suggesting that the power has a long pedigree.

There is an instance of an interim appointment being made in the case of illness. The keeper of a county register of sasines having become insane, the Lord Advocate petitioned the Court for appointment of an interim keeper. The Court exercised its *nobile officium* to make the appointment, Lord President McNeill noting that the matter was "pressing".[17]

It appears, however, that the illness of the incumbent officeholder would have to be sufficiently serious before the Court would make an interim appointment. The unreported case of *Glassford Bell, Petr*[18] may be taken as an example. The Sheriff of Lanarkshire petitioned the Court for an interim appointment to be made for the period of his temporary illness. The Court instead suggested that the sheriff apply to the Crown for leave of absence, an application that was subsequently refused. The then law officers were of the opinion that no such interim appointment could be made.

In one case the Clerk of the Peace for Ayrshire had resigned.[19] The Lord Advocate petitioned the Court to have an interim clerk appointed, though Lord President Inglis enquired as to whether there was any precedent for an appointment by the Court in the case of resignation. The Lord Advocate referred the Court to a case of interim appointment of the Clerk of the Peace for Forfarshire in 1888, and the Court went on to make the appointment.

The case of *Walker, Supplicant*[20] concerned the aftermath of the election of magistrates for the Burgh of Inverkeithing, which had been set aside by the Court for bribery and corruption. With no magistrates being thereby elected, a petition was brought by the Town Clerk of Inverkeithing for the Court to authorise the

---

[17] *Lord Advocate, Petr* (1860) 22 D 555.
[18] See Mackay, *The Practice of the Court of Session*, vol 1 at 211.
[19] *Lord Advocate, Petr* (1890) 17 R 293.
[20] 1761 Mor 7447.

bailies from the preceding year to act as interim bailies until new officeholders were established, particularly so as to allow for the proper administration of infeftments in the burgh. Authority was cited by the petitioner with regard to a similar case from Edinburgh in 1746, and from Linlithgow in 1755. The Court granted the prayer of the petition.

Another case in which an election of magistrates had been set aside was *Reekie v Gardiner*.[21] The resulting lack of magistrates led to a petition being presented to the Court for the interim appointment of managers of the Burgh of Kilrenny until the regular appointment of magistrates. The Court appointed the petitioners as interim managers, being those persons last elected to the magistracy of the burgh.

Circumstances relating to the Jacobite Rebellion in Edinburgh gave rise to several cases, in one of which a petition prayed for the appointment of a person to receive a resignation and grant infeftment in Edinburgh. The Court, granting the prayer of the petition, appointed a former bailie.[22] In a case heard just two days later, the Court appointed certain persons to act as interim bailies in exercising bailiary powers (receiving resignations, giving sasines etc) in Edinburgh.[23] Another saw the Court appointing interim bailies to process applications from "indigent prisoners for debt", on petition from an Edinburgh candlemaker who had been imprisoned for debt.[24] In a further case from that month, a petition was presented submitting that, by want of a Dean of Guild in Edinburgh, "many inconveniences had arisen in the town" including "buildings... carried on contrary to law" and trading by unfree persons. The petition prayed that a Dean of Guild and Council be appointed. Having "considered the disturbance of the public police of the city", the Court granted the prayer of the petition.[25]

---

[21] (1829) 7 S 379.
[22] *Denham and Wallace, Supplicants* 1746 Mor 7435.
[23] *City Clerks of Edinburgh, Petrs* 1746 Mor 7436.
[24] *Braidwood, Petr* 1746 Mor 7436.
[25] *Town Clerks of Edinburgh, Petrs* 1746 Mor 7437.

In *Duff v Magistrates of Elgin*,[26] the Town Clerk of Elgin had succeeded to certain heritable property, and petitioned the Court to authorise and ordain the Magistrates of Elgin to appoint the sheriff clerk in Elgin to execute the office of town clerk for the purpose of taking all necessary infeftments in favour of the petitioner. The magistrates objected to the petition, including on the basis that this would take the Court beyond the extent of its *nobile officium*, however the Court dismissed the objections and granted the prayer.

In *Magistrates of Rothesay v Carse*,[27] there was a dispute between burgh magistrates and a town clerk whom they had purported to dismiss from office by resolution. The petitioners had brought a case in the Court of Session for declarator of the validity of their resolution to dismiss the town clerk, meaning that the legality of the dismissal was still at issue. In the meantime, the administration of the burgh was detrimentally affected. The petitioners therefore sought to have an interim town clerk appointed until the case seeking declarator had come to a conclusion – in other words, for an interim town clerk to be appointed pending a ruling on the legality of the purported dismissal. The Court considered that it was in the public interest that an interim appointment be made, and exercised its *nobile officium* to make that appointment.

A final class of cases which demonstrates other circumstances warranting interim appointment is that concerning municipal elections – in particular, scenarios in which the normal operation of the process for appointment of a returning officer could not take effect, and petitioners sought to have the Court appoint a returning officer on an interim basis.

There were at least five such cases toward the end of the nineteenth century. In the first of these, *Magistrates of Dunfermline, Petrs*,[28] the Provost and three retiring bailies of Dunfermline fell to leave office by rotation. By operation of the Burghs (Scotland) Act

---

[26] (1823) 2 S 117.
[27] (1902) 4 F 641.
[28] (1877) 5 R 47.

1852,[29] it fell to one of the bailies to act as returning officer on the day of the election; however that bailie was incapacitated due to severe illness. The Act did not prescribe a course of action in these circumstances, and the case rubric indeed described it as a *casus improvisus*. A petition was therefore presented to the Court by the Provost and four bailies to authorise and appoint the Provost, whom failing one of the three retiring bailies, in respective order of seniority, to act as returning officer in the forthcoming election. The Court granted the prayer of the petition.

The remaining cases present similar facts. In *Police Commissioners of Kirriemuir, Petrs*,[30] the operation of the Parliamentary and Municipal Elections Act 1873 required the Provost of the Burgh of Kirriemuir to act as returning officer. However, he was seeking re-election and therefore could not competently act as returning officer. The Act failed to specify what should happen in this event. The Commissioners of Police of the burgh therefore petitioned the Court praying that it exercise its *nobile officium* to appoint a returning officer. The petitioners prayed that the sheriff-substitute at Forfar be appointed, whom failing, the junior magistrate who did not retire; but the Court appointed the junior magistrate as returning officer.

Similar facts were presented in *Royal Burgh of Renfrew, Petrs*,[31] whilst in *Muirhead, Petr*[32] the magistrate upon whom the duty of returning officer devolved had died. The Court appointed a returning officer in both instances. In *Town-Council of Stromness, Petrs*,[33] the petitioners sought not only the appointment of a returning officer, but also the authority to make up and certify a roll of electors. The Court granted the prayer of the petition as to the appointment of the returning officer, but declined to grant the remainder of the prayer. These cases may be considered instances of statutory omission or deficiency.

---

[29] Also known as the Municipal Elections Act 1852.
[30] (1884) 12 R 103.
[31] (1897) 25 R 18.
[32] (1886) 14 R 18
[33] (1891) 19 R 207.

6.2 Assistance with administration of public office

There have been cases in which there has not been interim appointment of a public officer, but in which the Court has exercised its
nobile officium to assist with the administration of public office.

In the early case of *Goldie, Petr*,[34] the son of the late Writer
to the Privy Seal presented a petition to the Court. His father had
died whilst in office. The Court authorised the petitioner to write
out and record whatever writs may be necessary to allow the work
of that office to continue in the interim, until a new commission
be granted.

In *Cowper, Petr*,[35] the Court authorised a town clerk and
keeper of a burgh register of sasines to collate the records of writs
recorded by his predecessor, and to subscribe the record, which
his predecessor had omitted to do. In *Provost, Magistrates and
Town Council of Elgin, Petrs*,[36] the town clerk of Elgin had died
having been unable through illness to carry out his duties for over
a month prior to his death. A petition was successfully presented
to the *nobile officium* for the new town clerk to grant and sign
certificates of registration, and to complete their registration, with
regard to deeds and instruments presented during his predecessor's
period of incapacity. The Court granted the prayer of the petition.

Finally, in *Hepburn, Petr*,[37] the Court exercised its *nobile
officium* to grant authority to the town clerk of a royal burgh to
authenticate and subscribe minutes of 434 deeds presented for
registration in the burgh register of sasines, which had not been
authenticated by his predecessors, and to record the petition and
warrant in the burgh register of sasines.

6.3 Deprivation of public office

The Court has also exercised its *nobile officium* to deprive persons
of office. In *Incorporated Society of Law-Agents in Scotland v*

---

[34] 1741 Mor 7432.

[35] (1885) 12 R 415. The case cites an unnamed authority from 1861.

[36] (1885) 12 R 1136. See also *Duff v Magistrates of Elgin* (1823) 2 S 117.

[37] (1905) 7 F 484.

Laing,[38] a petition was presented to the Court to have two notaries public deprived of office. One of the notaries had been convicted of embezzlement in the High Court of Justiciary, whilst the other had been convicted of breach of trust and embezzlement. The Society furnished authority to show that notaries should be of good standing, and that the Court had on at least two occasions removed notaries from office on the ground of malpractice. The Court was persuaded of its authority to deprive notaries of office, and granted the prayer of the petition.

---

[38] (1893) 21 R 267.

CHAPTER 7

STATUTORY OMISSIONS

One of the characteristic applications of the *nobile officium* has been the supply of legal norms deemed absent or omitted from the law. The *Stair Memorial Encyclopaedia* states that it "has generally been accepted, particularly in recent years, that the power *ex nobile officio* is normally exercised in modern times only to provide for a *casus omissus* of a procedural nature".[1] Typically there will be a prescribed process or framework in the statute but, through oversight, there is no provision for a given set of circumstances. Lord President Hope said of the *nobile officium*:

> The power may be exercised in highly special or unforeseen circumstances to prevent injustice and oppression. If the intention of a statute is clear but the necessary machinery for carrying out that intention in special or unforeseen circumstances is lacking, the power may be invoked to provide that machinery.[2]

Situations of this kind can arise in the context of legislation or some other document or instrument, such as a trust deed. The focus of this chapter is on omissions in primary and secondary legislation. Statutory omissions generated a greater volume of jurisprudence in certain areas, such as bankruptcy.[3] That area is principally addressed elsewhere in the book,[4] with only selected cases discussed in the present chapter. Any degree of overlap is kept to a minimum, and it is useful to consider such cases in the particular context of statutory omissions in their own right. This

---

[1] Civil Jurisdiction, vol 4, para 4.
[2] *R v Kennedy* 1993 SC 417 at 421 per Lord President Hope. See also *Pringle, Petr* 1991 SLT 330 at 332 per Lord President Hope.
[3] *Dunedin Encyclopaedia*, vol X at 325 described bankruptcy as the "chief head" in the area of statutory omissions.
[4] See Chapter 4.

chapter is primarily concerned with statutory omissions under the jurisdiction of the Court of Session. For statutory omissions under the jurisdiction of the High Court of Justiciary, see Section 9.1.

7.1 Terminology and context

Instances of omission have principally been designated a *"casus improvisus"* (a case unforeseen) or *"casus omissus"* (a case omitted). These terms appear to have been used somewhat interchangeably by the courts, though the former term has appeared with more frequency. Neither has been used exclusively in the context of the *nobile officium*. A third term, *"casus incogitatus"* (a case unconsidered), has appeared still less frequently.

James Maclaren defined the *nobile officium* in general as:

> the equitable power vested in the Court of Session to make provision for cases arising out of statutes, but for which no provision has been made in said statutes; or for unexpected, or exceptional, happenings, whether arising from statute or otherwise.[5]

Maclaren then itemised the heading of "statutory *casus improvisus*", which he defined as follows:

> Where a statute provides for a certain thing to be done, and omits to state the manner in which it is to be done, the Court may provide the means, or may not, depending upon whether the omission has been slight or serious.[6]

Despite their apparently interchangeable usage, the *casus improvisus* and *casus omissus* received separate treatment in John Trayner's *Latin Maxims and Phrases*. He defined the *casus improvisus* as:

> An unforeseen case; and therefore a case not provided for. This phrase is of frequent occurrence, and admits of varied illustration. Thus, if an Act of Parliament has been passed for the removal of some inconvenience, or the suppression of some evil, and specified the circumstances or

---

[5] James Maclaren, *Court of Session Practice* (1916, W Green) at 100.
[6] Maclaren, *Court of Session Practice* at 100.

cases in which it is to have application, and a case occurs which is not specified by the Act, in which, nevertheless, the application of the Statute would be beneficial, this is a *casus improvisus*, and neither the procedure nor the provisions of the Act can be applied to it. The Statute cannot be strained so as to be made applicable to a case for which it does not provide.... When a *casus improvisus* occurs, it must be disposed of according to the rules of the common law.[7]

Of the *casus omissus*, Trayner recorded two entries:

Casus omissus et oblivioni datus dispositioni communis juris relinquitur – A case omitted and forgotten is left to be disposed of according to the rules of the common law. On the subject of this maxim, reference is made to what has been said above (see *Casus improvisus*), and to what immediately follows.

Casus omissus pro omisso habendus est – A case (or class of cases) omitted is to be held as (intentionally) omitted. This is a rule to be observed in the construction of statutes, and in considering whether they are applicable to certain cases analogous to the cases therein provided for. An illustration of this phrase will be found in Stair, B. 3, T. 2, § 49.[8]

Stair gave an early illustration of the maxim *casus omissus pro omisso habendus est*. In the seventeenth-century case of *Grierson v Closeburn*, a reference to composition in an Act of 1469 did not appear in a subsequent Act, even although reference was made to the former Act. Stair observed that "[the Lords] thought it not competent to them to extend the said composition *ad pares casus*, where it did so much appear that the Parliament of purpose had omitted it".[9]

Trayner also included a separate entry for the *casus incogitatus*:

Casus incogitati – Circumstances unthought of, unprovided for. Where questions arise regarding which there is no rule of law, they are decided according to rules drawn by analogy, or on equitable grounds (Stair, B. 1, T. 1, § 6).[10]

---

[7] John Trayner, *Latin Maxims and Phrases* (4th edn, 1894, W Green; rep 1986, Caledonian Books) at 70–71.

[8] Trayner, *Latin Maxims* at 71.

[9] Stair, III, 2, 49. Intentional omissions are further considered below.

[10] Trayner, *Latin Maxims* at 71.

This term was also used by Stair, who wrote that "in statutes, the lawgiver must at once balance the conveniences and inconveniences, wherein he may, and often doth, fall short; and there do arise *casus incogitati*, wherein the statute is out, and then recourse must be had to equity".[11] In addition, although not writing with specific regard to statutory omissions, Stair argued that:

> though men's laws be profitable and necessary for the most part, yet being the inventions of frail men, there occur many *casus incogitati*, wherein they serve not, but equity takes place: and the limitations and fallencies, extensions and ampliations of human laws are brought from equity.[12]

A pleading of *casus incogitatus* was made in the early case of *Russell v Trustees for repairing the roads leading to Glasgow*.[13] The case concerned a Turnpike Act which rendered final the decisions of justices of the peace, but a road which lay in two counties – and was thus subject to the jurisdiction of the justices of the peace of both counties – had contradictory judgments rendered upon it. The Court of Session found itself competent to review these judgments, repelling a comment to the competency of the action, the suspenders having argued that:

> As this road lies within two counties, the Quarter Sessions of which have pronounced contradictory judgments, this is a *casus incogitatus* that does not fall under the act, and the matter would be inextricable without the interposition of this Court.[14]

Although there may remain technical distinctions between the *casus improvisus*, *casus omissus* and *casus incogitatus*, these distinctions are not maintained in the present discussion largely because the terms appear to have been used interchangeably in the cases. This chapter, like the book as a whole, opts for

---

[11] Stair, I, 2, 15.

[12] Stair, I, 2, 6.

[13] 1764 Mor 7353.

[14] *Russell* at 7354. This case may now be more appropriately considered an exercise of the supervisory jurisdiction.

the more neutral term "statutory omission", which is intended to embrace the *casus improvisus, casus omissus* and *casus incogitatus*. They are treated as a single category whereby there has been an omission by oversight of the legislature. The use of any one of these Latin terms rather than "statutory omission" corresponds to its appearance in particular cases, but the cases are discussed on the presumption that the terms can be used interchangeably.

7.2 Omissions not always dealt with under the *nobile officium*

The *nobile officium* has not been ubiquitously cited in instances of statutory omission. In some cases – perhaps most – resort would be had to rules and principles of statutory interpretation. This may be unsurprising as a matter of judicial policy, with courts addressing ambiguities, open texture and potential "gaps" by way of interpretation. It also seems less controversial in constitutional terms. By contrast, equitable interposition at least has the appearance of a more contestable and exceptional way in which to address gaps in a statute, for even when the court insists that it is guided by legislative intent, it ostensibly acts as "gap filler". To cite an exercise of the *nobile officium* in the course of filling statutory gaps would surely amplify that appraisal. Whether this is the rationale for the courts' differential treatment of cases is a matter of conjecture, though it perhaps illuminates why there may have been a disinclination to resort to the *nobile officium* in all such cases.[15] A perceptive observation made in the Land Court was that where the legislative framework is generally expressed, it may be more accurate to describe the court as "filling in the details" rather than "filling in the gaps".[16] This may be a useful distinction in the boundary between statutory interpretation and judicial gap-filling. Nevertheless, the point remains that the

---

[15] It was written at the beginning of the 20th century that this application of the *nobile officium* was exercised rarely and cautiously: Brodie-Innes, *Comparative Principles* at 278.

[16] *Cameron v Duke of Argyll's Trs* 1981 SLT (Land Ct) 2 at 8.

courts have appeared to enter the realm of gap-filling without recourse to the *nobile officium.*

An example of a case in which the Court dealt with a statutory omission without reference to the *nobile officium* is that of *Perth Quarter Sessions, Petrs.*[17] The case addressed an omission as a matter of statutory interpretation, though was discussed by Maclaren in a section entitled "statutory *casus improvisus*", which appeared under the general heading of "*nobile officium*".[18]

In another case cited by Maclaren in the same section,[19] there was also no reference to the *nobile officium*. Unlike in *Perth Quarter Sessions*, the Court refused to intervene. Lord President Inglis stated that the case involved:

> a question which has arisen by accident – an accident which is due, I think, to an oversight on the part of the Legislature, in altering the law in so far as the division of the parishes is concerned without making any provision as to the effect of that alteration on the law of residential settlement. ... But that is exactly what the Legislature ought themselves to have settled, and what, in my opinion, nobody but the Legislature can settle. It cannot be a question of common law, for common law on the subject there is none. It is not a question of statute law, for the statutes on the subject are silent. The difficulty is a difficulty created by the Legislature, and the Legislature alone can remove it. I am therefore for dismissing the case.[20]

The Court dismissed the case on the basis that it presented no question of law. This is an example of a case where there was a form of statutory "omission", but not one which the Court was prepared to fill by exercise of its *nobile officium.*

Likewise, in *West Highland Railway Co v County Council of the County of Inverness*[21] – also cited by Maclaren and containing

---

[17] (1861) 24 D 221.

[18] Maclaren, *Court of Session Practice* at 100.

[19] *Parochial Board of the Parish of Borthwick v Parochial Board of the Parish of Temple* (1891) 18 R 1190.

[20] *Parochial Board of the Parish of Borthwick* at 1192. Evidently, not every "lacuna" is regarded as one for the courts to fill: see *Hatcher v Harrower* 2011 JC 90 at 93 per Lord Bonomy; and also *HM Advocate v Harris (No 2)* 2011 JC 125 at 134 per Lord Justice-General Hamilton.

[21] (1904) 6 F 1052.

no reference to the *nobile officium* – Lord Young stated that whereas the legislature had "thought it desirable" to include a particular clause in the Light Railways Act 1896, the fact that it did not include such a clause in the West Highland Railway Guarantee Act 1896 led to the presumption that "the Legislature thought that such a clause was not necessary".[22] This would be an application of the maxim *casus omissus pro omisso habendus est*, dealing with what are regarded as intentional omissions on the part of the legislature.[23]

A more recent example of a statutory omission being addressed other than by way of the *nobile officium* is in *Aberdeen City Council v Wokoma*.[24] The Education (Scotland) Act 1980 provided that a parent may make a placing request for their child to attend a particular school. Under section 28A(3), the authority was entitled to refuse the placing request on certain grounds. A further ground for refusal was inserted by the Education (Scotland) Act 1996, designated section 28A(3A) of the 1980 Act. It was provided in the 1980 Act that a parent whose placing request was refused may appeal to a committee and thereafter to the sheriff, each of which was entitled to confirm the education authority's refusal if satisfied that one or more of the grounds in section 28A(3) existed. There was no reference therein to the additional ground provided in section 28A(3A).

The case concerned a placing request refused by Aberdeen City Council, one of the grounds for which was that provided in section 28A(3A). The child's mother appealed unsuccessfully to the committee, and thereafter appealed to the sheriff. The sheriff found no reference to section 28A(3A) in the grounds on which he was entitled to confirm the education authority's refusal. He refused to confirm the

---

[22] At 1065. Maclaren also referred to *Duke of Argyll v Muir* 1910 SC 96, another case concerning a *casus improvisus* which was deemed to exist in a statute, but which made no reference to the *nobile officium* (*Court of Session Practice* at 101). For further cases on municipal elections and putative statutory omissions, see Section 6.1.

[23] See further *Harper, Petr* 1982 SLT 232 at 233.

[24] 2002 SC 352.

decision, and referred in his note to the existence of a *casus omissus*.

Aberdeen City Council therefore petitioned the Court for judicial review of the sheriff's decision on the basis that he erred in law. Lord Drummond Young, sitting in the Outer House, stated that the courts are "ever mindful that their constitutional role in this field is interpretative", and that they "must abstain from any course which might have the appearance of judicial legislation".[25] In his opinion, however, the 1980 Act as amended contained an "obvious drafting error",[26] and it was held that the statute should be read as containing a reference to section 28A(3A).

This judgment is interesting for present purposes for two reasons. First, the case could potentially have been dealt with by way of the *nobile officium*. There was deemed to be a statutory omission, and the *nobile officium* could have been invoked to supply the omission. Instead, the Court essentially adopted an interpretative approach whereby the relevant sections were reconstructed to achieve their apparent intention. There was no express reference to equitable intervention on the part of the Court.

Second, the case was heard in the Outer House. Had attempt been made to address this by way of petition to the *nobile officium*, it would have had to be made to the Inner House under rule 14.3(d) of the Rules of Court. Of course, the petitioners approached the question as one of the sheriff erring in law and that was putatively an appropriate petition to the supervisory jurisdiction, competently heard in the Outer House. The petitioners could, however, have constructed their case differently by seeking to petition the *nobile officium* on the basis of a statutory omission in the 1980 Act. There may have been strategic reasons for preferring the route adopted, and it may even have been necessary to overcome the potential obstacle of judicial review being considered an available remedy which would count against an invocation of the *nobile officium*.

---

[25] At 359 per Lord Drummond Young.
[26] At 359–60 per Lord Drummond Young.

However, the important point is that the end result, so far as the "corrected" form of the statute is concerned, could have been achieved by way of a petition for judicial review or a petition to the *nobile officium*. In the former case it could competently be transacted in the Outer House, whereas in the latter case it would have required presentation to the Inner House. The question may be posed as to whether, if the latter case would have required resort to the extraordinary equitable jurisdiction of the Court, and to exceptional, equitable intervention on its part, it is sound policy or practice to enable the same result to be achieved by way of a "lesser" equitable jurisdiction in the form of the supervisory jurisdiction, invoked in the context of judicial review.[27] In any event, the case is a neat illustration of the fine and perhaps indeterminate line between statutory interpretation and intervention *ex nobile officio* for the supply of a statutory omission.

Finally, at issue in *Esso Petroleum Co Ltd v Hall Russell & Co Ltd*[28] was what could potentially have been construed as an omission in the Rules of Court. The case arose in the context of alleged inordinate and inexcusable delay in bringing an action, and it was argued that the courts had an inherent power to regulate their own procedure, giving them the necessary authority to dismiss the action. Lord Johnston stated that:

> The Court of Session obviously has an inherent power enshrined in the *nobile officium* and, putting aside whether a Lord Ordinary could exercise that power, a problem which could be avoided by reporting the case to the Inner House, the essential question is whether or not the necessary *casus improvisus* exists in the present context to enable such a power to be taken or created.... Fundamentally the procedure of the court is regulated by statutory instrument, namely Rules of Court, and I consider that one could only reach the point of even considering whether such a power existed if the Rules of Court were not only silent on a particular point, but plainly silent by reason of error or oversight.

[27] Perhaps that is always a conundrum so far as the *nobile officium* is concerned, for one is typically required to utilise other remedies (including in bodies inferior to the Inner House) before a petition to the *nobile officium* would be competent.

[28] 1995 SLT 127.

This I am quite unable to infer from a study of the rules. ... It is plain to my mind that the draftsmen of the rules intended certain consequences to arise in the event of such circumstances occurring, but the very fact the rules are silent as to whether a power to dismiss an action for delay alone can be exercised would suggest the draftsmen might have had such in contemplation and deliberately eschewed it ... [O] ne must assume that the draftsmen have dealt with the problem of delays to the extent that is intended and that the ensuing silence is eloquent of an express intention not to confer the power demanded by the defenders.[29]

This would again be an application of the maxim *casus omissus pro omisso habendus est*. The view that the absence of a specific rule in the Rules of Court should not necessarily be approached as one of omission was also taken in *Tonner v Reiach and Hall*.[30]

7.3 Court of Session

(a) Failure to carry out statutory duty or obtemper statutory process

In the first class of cases, a statutory omission is encountered where there is a failure to carry out a statutory duty or to obtemper a statutory process, and the statute does not provide adequate machinery for dealing with that failure.

A relatively early example of such an omission was in the Royal Burghs (Scotland) Act 1833. In *Herron v Town Council of Renfrew*,[31] the council of a royal burgh failed to elect magistrates as required by the Act, with an equal number of councillors divided as to one of two sets of proposed magistrates. The Court ordained the councillors to fulfil their statutory duty and appointed a meeting for that purpose.

A number of cases concerned an omission arising in the Salmon Fisheries (Scotland) Act 1862. Sections 18 and 19 of the Act provided for the constitution of a district fishery board within three months following the publication of any by-law

---

[29] At 129–30.
[30] [2007] CSIH 48 at para [93].
[31] (1880) 7 R 497.

constituting the district. Section 24 provided that the fishery board would continue in office for a period of three years, and that the proprietors of the relevant salmon fisheries should meet every three years for the purpose of electing a new board. However, the Act omitted to specify what should happen in the event that such a meeting did not take place, and how a district fishery board should be reconstituted in those circumstances. This occurred in several cases where the relevant parties failed to call a meeting of the board as required by statute.

In *Campbell, Petrs*,[32] a district fishery board for the River Awe had lapsed following a failure to call a meeting for the purpose of electing a new board, so that the district was without a board following the end of the statutory period. A petition was presented for reconstitution of the board, citing urgency due to an increase in illegal fishing. The Court remitted to the sheriff with instructions on how to arrange for the reconstitution of the board in accordance with the Act.

The issue of intimation arose in other cases concerning reconstitution of district fishery boards. In *Duke of Argyll, Petrs*,[33] though the petitioners argued that it was not the practice of the Court to order intimation, the Court directed for the petition to be intimated to the then Secretary for Scotland and to be advertised in certain newspapers. The issue of intimation again arose in the case of *Sandeman's Trs, Petrs*,[34] in which the petition had been served on the Secretary of State for Scotland and advertised in certain newspapers. The Court directed that there should be service on the Lord Advocate, who subsequently did not lodge answers, and so the Court granted the prayer of the petition for reconstitution of the board.

Finally, in *West Highland Woodlands Ltd, Petrs*,[35] where another district fishery board had lapsed following a failure to call meetings for the purpose of electing a new board, Lord President

---

[32] (1883) 10 R 819. See also *Brodie, Petr* (1884) 21 SLR 309.
[33] (1896) 23 R 991.
[34] 1947 SC 304.
[35] 1963 SC 494.

Clyde acknowledged that there was no provision in the Act for the reconstitution of a board which had lapsed, and stated that the "appropriate method of securing that object is accordingly a petition to the *nobile officium* of this Court".[36] Noting that this was the course adopted in other relevant cases, the Court granted the prayer of the petition.

Two better known cases arose due to an omission in the Licensing (Scotland) Act 1959. In *Maitland, Petr*,[37] a publican's provisional licence would not become effective until declared final at a general half-yearly meeting of a licensing court, in terms of the Act. Application was made to that meeting on behalf of the publican. The licensing court dealt with a large number of similar applicants, and *per incuriam* omitted to make any pronouncement on the publican's application, though it had intended to declare the licence final. The statutory process was therefore not followed. The publican petitioned the *nobile officium* to authorise the licensing court to meet for the purpose of declaring the licence final, there being no statutory machinery for doing so. The Court granted the prayer of the petition, Lord President Clyde explaining that the *nobile officium* "enable[s] justice to be done where, *per incuriam*, some formal step has been omitted and quite unnecessary delay and expense would be involved if the procedure had to be gone through all over again".[38]

In *McLaughlin, Petr*,[39] the petitioner sought to rely on *Maitland*. She had failed to complete a form received from the licensing court prior to its next general half-yearly meeting. When she returned the form, it was received by the clerk to the court after the conclusion of its half-yearly meeting. The petitioner averred that she had no experience of the licensed trade and was unaware that she had to apply prior to the meeting. In these circumstances, the Licensing (Scotland) Act 1959 made no provision for special meetings of the licensing court. However,

---

[36] At 496.
[37] 1961 SC 291.
[38] At 293 per Lord President Clyde.
[39] 1965 SC 243.

the Court refused the prayer of the petition. Lord President Clyde explained that to grant the prayer of the petition would be to contradict the express provisions of the statute, which sought to secure that all applications were submitted prior to the relevant meeting. It would be "quite wrong" for the Court to exercise its *nobile officium* "or any other common law powers to alter the statutory provisions of an Act of Parliament or enable anything to be done which is expressly rendered ineffective by the Act".[40] This would broadly conform with the Court's position that the *nobile officium* is not appropriately used to correct a blunder.[41]

The case of *Black, Petr*[42] concerned an omission in the Bankruptcy (Scotland) Act 1913. A meeting of creditors was convened and a trustee elected. However, the trustee failed to lodge a bond of caution within seven days, as required by the Act. Lord President Clyde explained that the bankrupt's estate had therefore never been effectively vested in the trustee and, as such, the statutory route for discharge was not available as it required a report to be submitted to the court by the trustee, and a trustee had not been confirmed in office. Accordingly, "[a] *casus improvisus* has therefore arisen, so far as the statute is concerned, and the door is open for the exercise by this court of the *nobile officium*".[43] The Court granted discharge to the bankrupt.

In a case concerning a private Act of Parliament,[44] the Banffshire Roads Act 1866, road trustees had failed *per incuriam*

---

[40] At 245 per Lord President Clyde. Another case involving an apparent omission in licensing legislation was *Bell's Executor, Petr* 1960 SLT (Notes) 3. However, it was opined by Lord President Clyde in two subsequent cases that *Bell's Executor* should not be regarded as authoritative in future cases: see *Maitland, Petr* at 293–94; and *McLaughlin, Petr* at 246. He stated that it was not possible to ascertain the Court's reasoning in *Bell's Executor* given the lack of opinions in that case; however it seems that the difficulty encountered appears to have been at least partly attributable to an oversight on the part of the petitioner's solicitors. In *Maitland*, Lord President Clyde stated that the *nobile officium* would "be invoked in vain if it were to be used as a mere cloak for incompetence on the part of the applicant's representatives" (*Maitland, Petr* at 293). See further Section 10.3.

[41] See pp 223–24.

[42] 1964 SC 276.

[43] At 277 per Lord President Clyde.

[44] *Banff County Road Trs, Petrs* (1881) 9 R 20.

to make up a list of bridges within a period of time stipulated by the Act. The trustees petitioned the Court for authority to make up the list with the statutory period having expired. Lord President Inglis stated that this was "quite a case for the exercise of our equitable jurisdiction",[45] and the Court granted authority as prayed. It is not expressly stated in the brief case report that there was an omission in the Act, and not every failure of a statute to provide for an extension of time would or should be regarded as an omission. Nevertheless, the Court was prepared to exercise an equitable jurisdiction to effectively extend the statutory period.

Finally, in *Ferguson, Petrs*,[46] two persons entitled to vote in a general election examined the electoral register for the registration area in which they resided. They found that their names were not on the register, and subsequently ascertained that the electoral registration officer had removed their names on the basis of information received from a third party that they were deceased. Under regulation 11(3) of the Representation of the People (Scotland) Regulations 1950, the electoral registration officer was required to give notice of an objection to the inclusion of a name on the register to the person to whom the objection related, but had failed to do so. The two persons concerned petitioned the *nobile officium* for reinstatement of their names on the register.

The Court found that the electoral registration officer had acted *ultra vires*, Lord President Clyde noting that there was "no machinery in the statutes or in the regulations for dealing with this situation", and that the *nobile officium* was:

> devised just to meet a situation of the kind with which we are presented in these two applications. . . . The two applications disclose the omission of a procedural step in the compiling of the electoral register, i.e., the failure by the registrar to intimate to the petitioners the proposed alteration in the voting list. No remedy for the registrar's deletion of the two names without intimation to the petitioners is available in the regulations, and it is not now disputed that the petitioners are qualified to have their names in the register.[47]

---

[45] At 20 per Lord President Inglis.
[46] 1965 SC 16.
[47] At 19.

The Court granted the prayer of the petitions, and authorised and ordained the electoral registration officer to insert the names of the two petitioners in the current register of electors.[48]

(b) Statutory process fails to achieve anticipated result

A second class of cases in which statutory omissions have been encountered is where the statutory process has been observed, but has for some reason failed to achieve its anticipated result, and there is no adequate provision for that breakdown in the statutory machinery.

A number of bankruptcy cases have arisen in this way, primarily due to a breakdown in the machinery of the Bankruptcy (Scotland) Acts 1856 and 1913.[49] A principal cause of breakdown has been where a meeting of creditors held for the purpose of electing a trustee over the bankrupt's estate has failed to elect a trustee, with the statutory framework failing to provide for what should happen in such circumstances. In *Struthers, Petr,*[50] for example, objection was made at the meeting of creditors to the parties proposed as trustee, with no valid election being made. There was no statutory provision available for the purpose of convening a second meeting of creditors, and so the Court, in exercise of its *nobile officium*, appointed a new meeting to be held.

In *Steuart v Chalmers,*[51] no trustee was elected at the meeting of creditors, and the creditors resolved to abandon the sequestration. Lord Justice-Clerk Inglis regarded this as "utterly incompetent",[52] and Lord Cowan deemed it *ultra vires,*[53] the proper course having

---

[48] An alternative approach might have been to declare the *ultra vires* act void *ab initio*, so that in law the names had never been removed from the register.

[49] Lord Pearson stated that "[w]here a *casus improvisus* arises in the course of a sequestration, necessitating the intervention of the Court in aid of the statutory procedure, no doubt resort must be had to the *nobile officium*": *Duke v Somervell* (1903) 11 SLT 289 at 289.

[50] (1861) 23 D 702.

[51] (1864) 2 M 1216.

[52] At 1219.

[53] At 1220.

been to apply for recall of the sequestration. Nevertheless, one of the creditors, who was not present at the meeting, petitioned the *nobile officium* to appoint a meeting of creditors for the purpose of electing a trustee so that the sequestration may continue. The Court granted the prayer of the petition. Lord Justice-Clerk Inglis said that the "leading consideration" was that:

> There is here a depending process of sequestration which has come to a dead lock, and which, so far as I can see, is inextricable under the statute, so that unless we can interfere, that process can, apparently, neither proceed nor be extinguished. Without a trustee being elected it is plain that there can be no proceedings in a sequestration; and it is equally clear that a sequestration without a trustee cannot be brought to a termination; and, therefore, the effect of refusing to interpone would be to leave the bankrupt for ever in the position of a sequestrated bankrupt, and to lock up his estate from himself as well as from others, and render it inaccessible in any legal manner. That state of matters presents a strong case for the intervention of the Court.[54]

In *Aitken v Robson*,[55] the meeting of creditors elected a trustee, but failed to decide on the sufficiency of caution offered as required by section 72 of the Bankruptcy (Scotland) Act 1856.[56] The sheriff therefore refused to confirm the election, and no bond of caution was lodged with the sheriff-clerk. No further steps were taken in the process of sequestration, which had dragged on for around seven years. The bankrupt petitioned the *nobile officium* for discharge; however, the petition was challenged by one of the creditors who argued that, in such circumstances, it was for the bankrupt to have a trustee appointed and confirmed, and then to proceed with the process of sequestration. Lord Dundas considered that he did "not think that in the circumstances that would be an appropriate, or a right and equitable, course to adopt", and that it would be "the proper and the just course" to grant discharge.[57] Lord Salvesen likewise thought this "a case

---

[54] At 1218.
[55] 1914 SC 224.
[56] This aspect is also capable of being classed as failure to carry out a statutory duty.
[57] At 227.

for the exercise of the *nobile officium* of the Court, because the Bankruptcy Statutes provide no means by which this petitioner can obtain a discharge in his sequestration".[58] Lord Guthrie agreed, adding that requiring the bankrupt to obtain discharge by having a trustee appointed to take up the matter anew would be unnecessary.[59] Accordingly, the Court exercised its *nobile officium* to grant discharge.

A similar situation encountered in *Laing, Petrs*[60] was deemed subject to the same principles under the 1913 Act. A trustee was elected at the meeting of creditors, but the statutory requirement for lodging a bond of caution was not satisfied.[61] The sheriff-substitute refused to confirm the election of the trustee, and no further steps were taken in the sequestration for eight years. In addition, creditors representing over 95 per cent of the value of the debt due had waived their claims. The bankrupts petitioned the *nobile officium* for discharge, which the Court granted. Lord President Clyde noted that:

> [f]aced with a situation in which there is no statutory machinery to secure their discharge, the petitioners have presented this application to the *nobile officium* of the Court. In our view, it is proper that that power should be exercised by us with a view to granting this discharge.[62]

In *Fraser v Glasgow Corporation*,[63] a meeting of creditors had been appointed by the sheriff-substitute under the 1913 Act. The meeting was advertised in the Edinburgh and London Gazettes and otherwise in accordance with the Act; however no creditors attended the meeting. Consequently, no trustee was elected, and no further progress took place in the sequestration. The Act omitted to provide for this occurrence, and the bankrupt was

---

[58] At 227.

[59] At 228.

[60] 1962 SC 168.

[61] As in *Aitken v Robson*, this aspect is capable of being classed as a failure to carry out a statutory duty.

[62] *Laing, Petrs* at 170.

[63] 1967 SC 120.

in a situation whereby the statute failed to provide a means of obtaining discharge. He therefore petitioned the *nobile officium* to obtain discharge. Lord President Clyde observed that, the statutory machinery having "broken down", and in which there was "no provision ... to enable [the] bankrupt to be discharged", it would:

> obviously be unjust that anyone, even in the position of a bankrupt, should be left indefinitely in this situation, and this is the very set of circumstances in which it has always been the practice to invoke the *nobile officium* of this Court.[64]

The Court granted discharge to the bankrupt.[65]

Another situation in which a statutory omission was encountered in the context of bankruptcy legislation was where funds emerged after the discharge of the trustee. This occurred in *Thomson, Petr*,[66] where under the 1856 Act certain estates were sequestrated and divided. New funds emerged after the trustee's exoneration and discharge. However, the bankrupt had not obtained discharge, and there was no longer a trustee over the estate to effect distribution. The trustee petitioned the *nobile officium* of the Court to appoint a meeting for the purpose of electing a new trustee.

Lord Justice-Clerk Inglis regarded the circumstances as "extraordinary" and the petition "unprecedented". It revealed "great practical embarrassment in the working of the Bankrupt Act", for it had contemplated cases in which the trustee died, resigned or was removed, but not the present circumstances. Accordingly:

> taking the whole circumstances into consideration, the case falls so entirely within the principle of the section [of the Act], that I think it is a case for the exercise of the *nobile officium* of the Court. This *casus improvisus* is in all respects parallel to those provided for.[67]

---

[64] At 123.

[65] An alternative way of dealing with this situation may have been to appoint a judicial factor: see *Moncrieff's Trs v Halley* (1899) 1 F 696.

[66] (1863) 2 M 325.

[67] At 325–26.

Lord Benholme expressed the view that "[t]he section of the Act was apparently intended to exhaust the cases in which the appointment of a new trustee is necessary", but that "[i]t has not exhausted them, for here is a case not provided for".[68] Lord Neaves added that the case "comes under the words, certainly under the spirit, of the enactment",[69] and the Court directed for a new meeting to be appointed.

In the case of *Shaw, Petr*,[70] the undischarged bankrupt had succeeded to heritable property following the discharge of the trustee, and the Court exercised its *nobile officium* to direct for a meeting of creditors for the purpose of electing a new trustee in the sequestration.

A similar state of affairs arose in *Abel v Watt*,[71] with the emergence of new funds following the discharge of the trustee, but the bankrupt having not obtained discharge. Lord President Inglis confirmed that this was a situation of *casus improvisus*.[72] However, a key difference was that the new funds were acquired by the undischarged bankrupt through trading activities over the course of 13 years since the trustee's discharge, with no interference from the creditors. Despite the statutory omission, the creditors were held barred from insisting on their right to the exclusion of new creditors on the basis of acquiescence. It appears to have been acquiescence that was the fatal issue, and not the mere passage of time, for in another case the Court exercised its *nobile officium* to revive a sequestration some 80 years after it first commenced.[73]

In *MacDuff v Baird*,[74] a petition was presented to the *nobile officium* for the revival of a sequestration 22 years after the

---

[68] At 326.

[69] At 326.

[70] (1884) 11 R 814.

[71] (1883) 11 R 149.

[72] At 151.

[73] *Young, Petrs* (1888) 16 R 92. See also *Northern Heritable Securities Investment Co Ltd v Whyte* (1888) 16 R 100, and *Whyte v Northern Heritable Securities Investment Co Ltd* (1891) 18 R (HL) 37.

[74] (1892) 20 R 101.

trustee had been discharged, the undischarged bankrupt having since been successful in business and allegedly now able to pay all of his creditors in full. In this case, however, it was not the creditor or discharged trustee who petitioned the Court, but the bankrupt himself. Lord Kinnear noted that in *Thomson, Petr*,[75] the case of the discharge of a trustee prior to the full conclusion of the sequestration "had not been foreseen by the Legislature", and that it was "therefore held that in the exercise of the *nobile officium* the Court has a discretion to supply the omission in this respect", treating the matter as a statutory omission. In the present case it was therefore "a mere question of discretion whether the Court is to exercise its *nobile officium* on the application of the creditors or of the bankrupt himself".[76] Lord President Robertson was of the view that the same considerations applied in both sets of circumstances, and the Court, being in agreement, granted the prayer of the petition to direct for a meeting of creditors to be appointed for the purpose of electing a new trustee.

It was confirmed in another case that where the bankrupt and trustee had both been discharged, and a petition sought to have a new trustee appointed, there was "no provision under the Bankruptcy Act for that set of circumstances", and "the application is properly made under the *nobile officium* in the Inner House".[77]

This section concludes with three non-bankruptcy cases. In the first, section 5 of the Burghs (Scotland) Act 1852 provided that, in a case in which the provost and all of the magistrates were among the one third of a council going out of office by rotation, they shall retain and continue to exercise their powers and functions until the election and coming into office of their successors. However, in *Magistrates of Dunfermline, Petrs*,[78] one magistrate remained in office, but by reason of illness was unable to discharge his duties as returning officer in the election. This

---

[75] (1863) 2 M 325.
[76] *MacDuff v Baird* at 104 per Lord Kinnear.
[77] *Cockburn's Trs, Petrs* 1941 SC 187 at 188 per Lord President Normand.
[78] (1877) 5 R 47.

situation was not captured by the Act. The Court exercised its *nobile officium* to authorise the provost, whom failing one of the three retiring bailies, to act as returning officer.[79]

In a case concerning licensing,[80] a half-yearly meeting of a licensing court was not quorate in terms of the Licensing (Scotland) Act 1903. Accordingly, the meeting could not be validly constituted or adjourned. The next meeting fell under the Act to be held some months after all the licences in the county would expire. The Act made no provision for the licensing court to meet on another date; therefore a petition was presented to the Court to appoint a meeting prior to the expiry of the licences. The Court granted the prayer of the petition.

Finally, in *Humphries v X and Y*,[81] the Court exercised its *nobile officium* to detain certain children at a place of safety beyond the period of a trial diet, as this was "merely to provide machinery which is lacking to secure, in the highly special circumstances of this case, the overriding intention of Parliament as we understand it".[82]

(c) Power lacking

Some cases have encountered a statutory omission in circumstances where a power is essentially lacking in the statutory framework. In such cases, there is neither a failure to follow a statutory process, nor a process or provision that has failed to achieve its anticipated result, but an essential power is omitted from the statute. The *nobile officium* must be used cautiously in such cases to ensure that the Court does not assume a legislative function.

In *Thom, Petr*,[83] the Police Commissioners of the Royal Burgh of Linlithgow resolved to sell or feu a parcel of land. However, it was averred that the relevant statute, namely the

---

[79] This case is discussed at pp 132–33.
[80] *Buchanan, Petrs* 1910 SC 685.
[81] 1982 SC 79. See p 124.
[82] At 84 per Lord President Emslie.
[83] (1887) 14 R 444.

General Police and Improvement (Scotland) Act 1862, did not contain any provisions authorising the sale of property which had ceased to be of use to them. The Court, in an apparent exercise of its *nobile officium*, authorised the Commissioners to sell the land by public auction. This could potentially have been classed as an intentional omission.

In *Registrar-General for Scotland, Petr*,[84] duplicate registers of death had been rendered useless as records due to damage caused by dampness whilst at the General Register Office in Edinburgh. The Registrar-General for Scotland petitioned the *nobile officium* for an order that new duplicate registers be prepared from duplicates in the custody of local registrars, to be duly authenticated by the Registrar-General. Lord President Cooper explained that the Registration of Births, Deaths and Marriages (Scotland) Act 1854 contemplated the possibility of a register being lost, destroyed or damaged when in the custody of a local registrar, but made no provision for its loss, destruction or damage following its arrival at the General Register Office. It was therefore "appropriate and necessary" that the Court exercise its *nobile officium* to supply the statutory omission, granting the prayer of the petition.[85]

Where the Companies Act 1948 required companies to keep minutes of meetings of its directors, but made no provision as to the inspection of minute books, the Court exercised its *nobile officium* to ordain a company to make available those minute books for inspection.[86]

Finally, in *Skinner, Petr*,[87] certain funds had been made over in an antenuptial contract of marriage. The two named trustees died without having assumed a trustee to act with them, and so the heir of the last surviving trustee petitioned the *nobile officium* for declarator that he was entitled to assume office as a trustee. The Court held that there was a statutory omission in the Succession

---

[84] 1949 SLT 385.
[85] At 385–86 per Lord President Cooper.
[86] *McCusker v McRae* 1966 SC 253.
[87] 1976 SLT 60.

(Scotland) Act 1964. Previously, such a right would have been established under the Titles to Land Consolidation (Scotland) Act 1868, but the relevant sections thereof were repealed by the Succession (Scotland) Act 1964. The repealing section was itself repealed by the Statute Law (Repeals) Act 1974, but there had been no revival of the original statutory right. The heir of provision was entitled to assume the office of trustee, but the statutory machinery was now lacking for its realisation. As such, it was "right and proper" that the Court should exercise its *nobile officium* to supply the statutory omission. This is an example of a statutory omission arising by an apparent oversight in statutory repeal mechanisms.[88]

7.4   Judicial approach to statutory omissions

It is apparent from the cases discussed in this chapter that a lack of statutory machinery appropriate to a particular case is, in general, insufficient to be regarded as a statutory omission. In addition, the statute which would otherwise have regulated the case should bear some evidence or indication that the legislature (or secondary legislator where appropriate) has not contemplated, or has overlooked, a particular set of circumstances. If it appears that the "omission" or failure to provide was intended, the Court will decline to recognise the case as one of statutory omission appropriate for exercise of the *nobile officium*, in accordance with the maxim *casus omissus pro omisso habendus est.*

In considering whether there is a statutory omission, the court will typically have regard to the general framework of the statute and the presumed intention of Parliament. The Court is cautious to ensure that in exercising its *nobile officium* it is not extending the scope of a statute – and it is on that basis that what appear to be deliberate failures to provide for a set of circumstances are not interpreted as cases of omission.

---

[88] See also *Dobbie v Coltness Iron Co Ltd* 1920 SC (HL) 121 at 137 per Lord Dunedin.

For example, in *Smart v Registrar General for Scotland*,[89] a woman whose marriage had been celebrated and registered in Scotland obtained a decree of divorce in the Netherlands Antilles and sought, by virtue of section 5 of the Registration of Births, Deaths and Marriages (Scotland) Act 1855, for this to be recorded against the relevant entry in the Register of Marriages. The section made no specific provision for the rectification of an entry of marriage with regard to a decree of divorce obtained in a foreign court. The Court took the view that the Act applied only to Scotland, and to Scots processes and officials, and accordingly that to exercise its *nobile officium* in the manner sought would have the effect of extending the scope of the Act. On that basis, the petition was refused. The judicial policy against using the *nobile officium* to extend the scope of Acts of Parliament is explored further in Section 10.3.

The *nobile officium* received mixed treatment with regard to an omission in the case of *London and Clydeside Estates Ltd v Aberdeen District Council*.[90] Lord Hailsham of St Marylebone appeared somewhat dismissive of the *nobile officium*, referring to "the jurisdiction peculiar to Scottish law, which goes by the imposing name of *nobile officium*", and to "the more arcane aspects of *nobile officium*".[91] Lord Fraser of Tullybelton added that:

> [The] fact that Parliament has not provided for the legal consequences to follow from a failure to carry out the statutory procedure does not give rise to a *casus improvisus*. The consequences of such failure have to be ascertained according to the general rules of law. They may include a right to recover damages, or to have a document reduced, or to obtain a decree of declarator or some other redress but there is no impasse of the kind that has hitherto been regarded as suitable for solution by an exercise of the *nobile officium*. That is an exceptional power and the court "does not view with favour its indefinite extension".[92]

---

[89] 1954 SC 81.
[90] 1980 SC (HL) 1.
[91] At 28–29.
[92] At 36.

Although Lord Fraser may have regarded the case as failing to present a situation of statutory omission, the generality of his statement does not appear to sit comfortably with, for example, the salmon fisheries cases already discussed, in which the "failure to carry out the statutory procedure" was precisely deemed to give rise to a statutory omission in several cases.[93] This may signal the adoption of a stricter approach to the question of omission, and it is notable that it is made in one of the few discussions of the *nobile officium* in the House of Lords.

A final but important point is that the Court will be slow to regard a lack of provision for appeal in a statute as an omission. In *Fife & Kinross Motor Auctions Ltd v Perth and Kinross District Licensing Board*,[94] the petitioner averred that the licensing board had erred in a material fact. It was argued that as the Licensing (Scotland) Act 1976 failed to provide for a mechanism of appeal, it was justified to invoke the *nobile officium* to challenge the erroneous decision. However, the Court held that the intention of Parliament was that there be no appeal in the circumstances, and the petition was dismissed. Reliance was placed on Lord President Clyde's dictum in *Maitland, Petr* that the jurisdiction could not be invoked "to give a remedy to someone other than the parties to whom Parliament has chosen to give a remedy".[95] In any event, the petitioner was not without a remedy as sufficient time had elapsed such that it was entitled to make a fresh application to the licensing board within the statutory framework.

---

[93] See Section 7.3(a).
[94] 1981 SLT 106.
[95] *Maitland, Petr* 1961 SLT 291 at 293.

CHAPTER 8

MISCELLANEOUS PROCEDURE

The *nobile officium* is broad in substantive scope despite being a relatively narrow procedural device. The book has thus far given an overview of the jurisdiction's utilisation in those areas of law in which it has featured more than others, or in which there were recurring themes. Inevitably, however, there have been numerous other applications of the jurisdiction. These are collected in the present chapter as miscellaneous exercises of the *nobile officium*. They are typically concerned with procedural issues, and have as far as possible been further organised by sub-category.

8.1 Authority to change name

The *nobile officium* was used to grant authority to persons who had been admitted to their profession by the Court to change their names. The general position was stated by Lord McLaren:

> [i]t is in accordance with practice that authority may be given to use a new name when the application is by some one who has been admitted to his profession by the Court. If so, where the name is entered on a roll to which the authority of the Court is given, or which is under the control of the Court, it may be necessary to present an application for authority to change the name in order that the roll may be kept in order.[1]

In an example of the exercise of this power, the Court granted authority to a writer to the signet to assume an additional surname, and ordained that a deliverance to that effect be recorded in the

---

[1] *Robertson, Petr* (1899) 2 F 127 at 127–28 per Lord McLaren. See also More, *Lectures on the Law of Scotland* at 250; and Mackay, *The Practice of the Court of Session*, vol 1 at 210.

Books of Sederunt.[2] In another case, a solicitor petitioned the *nobile officium* for authority to assume a name by which he was generally known, to direct the Registrar of Solicitors to alter his name in the Roll of Solicitors, and to ordain the petition and the deliverance thereon to be recorded in the Books of Sederunt. The Court, without delivering opinions, directed the Registrar of Solicitors to alter the petitioner's name, but refused the remainder of the petition.[3]

The categories of person required to obtain the authority of the Court in this way was relatively narrow. A chartered accountant, for example, did not require the Court's authority to change his name.[4] Lord Adam explained that:

> A notary is an imperial officer, and a person holding a public office may require authority. So in the case of a Writer to the Signet and other persons whose names are entered on a register. But there is nothing to prevent a private individual from changing his name.[5]

Lord Adam stated in another case that:

> Any person in Scotland may, without the authority of the Court, call himself what he pleases, and, accordingly, when a petition for such a purpose is presented, we are in use to dismiss it as unnecessary, unless sufficient reason is shewn for the application.[6]

The Court thus refused to exercise its *nobile officium* to grant authority to change a surname where the petitioner had merely been requested in his mother's settlement to assume a surname in her remembrance.[7] Although the petitioner relied on two authorities,[8] the Court found nothing of relevance in either. Lord President Inglis noted that the petitioner was neither a Crown nor public officeholder.

---

[2] *Inglis, Petr* (1837) 16 S 111.

[3] *Silverstone, Petr* 1935 SC 223.

[4] *Robertson, Petr* (1899) 2 F 127.

[5] At 127 per Lord Adam.

[6] *Johnston, Petr* (1899) 2 F 75 at 76 per Lord Adam. See also *Young, Petr* (1835) 13 S 262.

[7] *Forlong, Petr* (1880) 7 R 910.

[8] *Sempill* (A S, 30 June 1757); *Grant* (10 July 1841, unreported).

The Court has exceptionally granted authority to change a name where the person was neither a Crown nor public officeholder in the strict sense. This occurred in *Johnston, Petr*,[9] in which the Court granted authority for a clergyman to formally assume his adopted name, due to a bishop refusing to insert any name in the petitioner's letters of orders but that on his certificate of baptism.

8.2 Evidence and witnesses

The *nobile officium* has been invoked to permit or facilitate alterations to the normal manner in which evidence is obtained or witnesses cited. The jurisdiction could, for example, be competently invoked to obtain the leave of the court to take the evidence of a witness on commission and to lie *in retentis* pending the hearing of an appeal.[10] In another case, the shorthand writer's notes of the testimony of certain witnesses in a proof in the sheriff court had been accidentally destroyed. The Court exercised its *nobile officium* to remit to the sheriff to take the evidence of those witnesses of new, though Lord President Inglis opined that the sheriff may have proceeded without obtaining such authority.[11]

In *Galloway Water Power Co v Carmichael*,[12] a company petitioned the *nobile officium* for the appointment of a commissioner to take the evidence of their engineer before proceeding to arbitration. The engineer was going to take up an appointment in Australia for several years, and it was proposed that in view of this fact, and the complicated and technical character of the evidence, it should be obtained prior to his departure to lie *in retentis*. The Court granted the prayer of the petition. Lord Justice-Clerk Aitchison emphasised that the general rule was that

---

[9] (1899) 2 F 75.

[10] *McLachlan v Lewis* 1925 SC 577. However, the motion in this case was refused. See also Aeneas J G Mackay, *The Practice of the Court of Session* (1879, T & T Clark) vol 2 at 77.

[11] *Yates v Robertson* (1891) 18 R 1206 at 1207 per Lord President Inglis.

[12] 1937 SC 135.

there must be a pending process in which an application of this kind could be made, and that this rule could only be relaxed in exceptional circumstances.[13]

An example of an unsuccessful case is found in *Dobie v Aberdeen Railway Co*,[14] in which a motion directed to the *nobile officium* for the examination of a witness by commission, on the ground of his wife's serious illness, was refused.

As to the general power of the Court under this head, Lord Curriehill said: "[t]here is, no doubt, in our law a rule, which at one time was enforced a good deal, that the Court, in the exercise of its *nobile officium*, might subject a party to a judicial examination before itself".[15]

8.3 Contempt of court in civil proceedings

It is competent to petition the *nobile officium* of the Court of Session to challenge a sentence imposed for contempt of court in civil proceedings in the sheriff court.[16] Indeed, it is competent to challenge such a decision only in the Court of Session, and it is not competent to petition the *nobile officium* of the High Court in such cases.[17]

The *nobile officium* of the Court of Session was successfully invoked in *ADM, Petr*[18] to challenge a finding of contempt of court in civil proceedings. A husband was ordered by the sheriff court in divorce and related proceedings to make an interim payment of aliment; however the sheriff later found him in contempt of court for breach of the order of interim aliment. The Court of Session granted the husband's petition to the *nobile officium* on the basis that a failure to make payment of an

---

[13] At 140 per Lord Justice-Clerk Aitchison.

[14] (1856) 19 D 195.

[15] *AB v Binny* (1858) 20 D 1058 at 1065 per Lord Curriehill.

[16] *Stair Memorial Encyclopaedia*, Civil Procedure Reissue at para 290. For contempt of court in criminal proceedings, see Section 9.7.

[17] *Cordiner, Petr* 1973 JC 16; *M v S* 2011 SLT 918 at 919 per Lord Justice-Clerk Gill.

[18] 2014 SC 165. Another successful petition is found in *AB and CD, Petrs* [2015] CSIH 25.

alimentary debt cannot amount to contempt, and that the sheriff had not been entitled to short-circuit certain statutory provisions by a finding of contempt. In another successful petition, presented in *Paxton v HM Advocate*,[19] the Court exercised its *nobile officium* to recall a finding of contempt made by the sheriff in civil proceedings in circumstances where the sheriff had left the bench and there were no proceedings in which contempt could arise.

Instead of averring incompetency in the decision or sentence of contempt of court, a petition might aver that the sentence imposed by the sheriff was harsh, oppressive or disproportionate.[20] However, where these grounds were averred in the case of *M v S*,[21] the Court was unpersuaded in view of the petitioner's conduct which included obstructing the progress of a sheriff court action, disregarding legal advice, making grave and unsubstantiated allegations against another person, and submitting a false undertaking to the Court. That undermined the merits of the petition, but not its competency.

Likewise, in *G v B*,[22] a mother had been sentenced to imprisonment for contempt of court. She petitioned the *nobile officium* for suspension of the finding of contempt and the sentence. The Court was unpersuaded that the sentence was excessive, taking the view that this was an attempt by a custodial parent to sever the bond between her child and the father by way of delay, manipulation, making false assurances and defying the interlocutor of the sheriff. Finally, a petition has been competently (though unsuccessfully) presented to challenge a finding of contempt and an associated fine imposed by the vacation judge in the Court of Session.[23]

---

[19] 1984 SLT 367.
[20] Whilst not technically a case of contempt, *Johnson v Grant* 1923 SC 789 gives an interesting insight into the Court exercising "clemency", as Lord President Clyde described it, in ordering the liberation of persons imprisoned for breach of interdict.
[21] 2011 SLT 918.
[22] 2011 SLT 1253.
[23] *Simpson, Boath & Co, Petrs* 1981 SC 153.

8.4 Authorisation of sheriff officers

A cluster of cases demonstrate a very practical application of the *nobile officium* for the facilitation of the recovery of debts. These have in general occurred with regard to debts or assets in or relating to remote areas – typically the Northern Isles and the Outer Hebrides – where the necessary personnel were either absent or inconveniently placed for the recovery of debts.

The Court exercised its *nobile officium* to grant warrant to have a summons served by a sheriff officer in Orkney, as there was no messenger-at-arms in the county, and it would incur great expense to serve the summons in the ordinary way.[24] In another case, a person sought to arrest funds in Orkney having obtained decree against the Earl of Orkney. Statute provided for a sheriff officer to execute a summons, but not diligence. There being no messenger-at-arms in Orkney, the Court granted warrant to a sheriff officer to execute the arrestment.[25]

In *North of Scotland Bank Ltd, Petrs*,[26] a petition was presented to the *nobile officium* for warrant to sheriff officers to charge, arrest and poind in terms of an extract decree. The petitioners had obtained decree against a merchant in Lerwick, but there was no messenger-at-arms in Shetland, the nearest being at Wick on the Scottish mainland. There was no statutory provision for sheriff officers in such areas to execute diligence in these circumstances, and the Court granted warrant as prayed. In *Robertson, Petrs*,[27] a charge was given on a bill with the acceptor holding property in Shetland. A petition was successfully presented to the *nobile officium* to grant warrant to a sheriff officer in Orkney or Shetland to carry into execution the extract by arrestment, poinding and sale, there being no messengers-at-arms resident in either Orkney

---

[24] *Cooper, Petrs* (1854) 16 D 1104.

[25] *Schweitzer, Petr* (1868) 7 M 24. The case report makes no mention of the *nobile officium*; however the case was cited as authority in similar petitions to the *nobile officium*, such as in *North of Scotland Bank Ltd, Petrs* (1891) 18 R 460, and *Robertson, Petrs* (1893) 20 R 712. See, however, *Miller's Trs, Petrs* (1856) 19 D 139.

[26] (1891) 18 R 460.

[27] (1893) 20 R 712.

or Shetland, and the expense of sending a messenger-at-arms to Shetland being out of proportion to the sum involved.

In a case relating to the Outer Hebrides,[28] certain funds belonging to a debtor against whom an action was being raised were in the hands of a party on Lewis. There was, however, no messenger-at-arms on Lewis and it was averred that it would involve great expense, inconvenience and delay if a messenger-at-arms was sent from the Scottish mainland or Skye. On report from the Lord Ordinary on the Bills, the Court granted warrant for letters of arrestment *jurisdictionis fundandae causa*, and granted warrant to sheriff officers on Lewis to execute the arrestment.

8.5 Correction of errors, clerical mistakes and procedural omissions

The *nobile officium* has been used to correct errors, clerical mistakes and procedural omissions. In *Drew, Petrs*,[29] there had been a clerical error in writing out the Lord Ordinary's interlocutor so that an appointment was erroneously stated to be with regard to a minor. The relevant trustee petitioned the *nobile officium* for rectification of the clerical error in the Records of Session, averring that no party's interests would be prejudiced by correcting the error. The Court granted the prayer of the petition.

In *Liquidators of Benhar Coal Co Ltd, Petrs*,[30] the liquidator of a company obtained a decree for authority to sell the superiority of feued subjects. It was subsequently discovered that the dates entered for the feu contract were erroneous, and the error carried through to the extract decree. The Court authorised the correction of this error. Where an extract decree gave an erroneous designation to a successful party in litigation, it was not necessary to have that error corrected by invoking the *nobile*

---

[28] *Kennedy, Petr* (1862) 24 D 1131.

[29] (1839) 1 D 467.

[30] (1891) 19 R 108.

officium in the Inner House, for it could be competently corrected by the Lord Ordinary.[31]

Other procedural omissions, such as those relating to bankruptcy[32] or statutory omissions,[33] are discussed elsewhere in the book.

8.6 Substituted authority to subscribe

The Court has used its *nobile officium* to authorise the subscription of documents and instruments in substitution for the rightful signatory. This has been appropriate in circumstances where it has not been possible or feasible to obtain the subscription of that person, such as an inability or unwillingness of the rightful signatory to subscribe the document or instrument.

Where a recalcitrant bondholder refused to sign a discharge of bonds, even in defiance of an order of the Court for him to sign it, the *nobile officium* was exercised to grant authority to the Clerk of Court to sign the discharge in his place.[34] Lord President Clyde explained that the Court was justified in taking this course of action as it would carry into effect a joint minute which had the backing of judicial authority, to prevent its being "annulled or defied by the obstinacy of one of the parties to it".[35]

The Court likewise authorised the Clerk of Court to sign an assignation in place of a recalcitrant bankrupt, though added that it would not adopt this course in the case of a refusal by a trustee to sign a document, dealing with trust property, which it was said to be his duty as trustee to sign.[36]

In *Lennox, Petrs*,[37] a *pro indiviso* proprietor refused, following a decree of division and sale of heritable subjects and

---

[31] *Miller v Lindsay* (1850) 12 D 964. See also *Clark & Macdonald v Bain* (1895) 23 R 102 on the correction of a court extract, where "£14" was recorded instead of "£41".

[32] See Chapter 4.

[33] See Chapter 7.

[34] *Wallace's Curator Bonis v Wallace* 1924 SC 212.

[35] At 216 per Lord President Clyde.

[36] *Pennell's Tr, Petr* 1928 SC 605.

[37] 1950 SC 546.

their sale by public auction, to sign a disposition of that property, and stated in a letter that she would never sign such a disposition. The Court, on petition of the purchasers and the remaining *pro indiviso* proprietors, exercised its *nobile officium* to authorise the Deputy Principal Clerk of Session to sign the disposition in place of the recalcitrant proprietor. Similarly, in another case, the Court exercised its *nobile officium* to authorise the Clerk of Court to sign a disposition of heritable subjects in place of a seller who refused to do so.[38]

In a final example,[39] the seller of a house left Edinburgh for Nigeria without signing a disposition for the conveyance of the house. Two successive dispositions were sent to Nigeria for signature, neither of which was returned. The purchaser, experiencing consequent financial and liability difficulties, petitioned the *nobile officium* for the Court to authorise the Deputy Principal Clerk of Session to sign the disposition in place of the seller in order for the transaction to be completed. The Court granted the prayer of the petition. Lord President Clyde regarded the case as analogous to those in which a party had persistently refused to sign a document which he was under an obligation to sign.[40]

It can be seen that the principle of the Court's intervention in these cases is an intention not to permit legal processes to be obstructed by what are typically recalcitrant persons who have not only a right, but an obligation, to sign a particular document or instrument. As seen in the final case, the power may also be exercised where it is not certain that the rightful subscriber is refusing to sign the document or instrument, but where it is nevertheless proving impossible to obtain subscription. In each case, the Court has authorised a clerk or deputy clerk of court to sign in place of the rightful subscriber. As such, the Court ensures that a practical solution is found where it would be inequitable to allow an obstruction or defeat of the realisation of legal rights.

---

[38] *Mackay v Campbell* 1966 SC 237.

[39] *Boag, Petr* 1967 SC 322.

[40] At 324 per Lord President Clyde.

8.7 Application of substantive equity and equitable discretion

There is a case worth singling out for its illustration of a more substantive equity applied by the Court, and which does not fall neatly into the other categories. That is the case of *Grahame v Magistrates of Kirkcaldy*.[41] A burgh resident successfully obtained interdict against the magistrates of the burgh from erecting stables or other buildings on a bleaching green in Kirkcaldy. Prior to interdict being sought, the building of stables was already underway on the bleaching green and most of the building contracts had been entered into. The stables were completed at a cost of £2,000 before interdict was obtained. The original interdictor sought for the Court to order the removal of the buildings and to restore the ground to its former state. The magistrates, having expressed regret at the situation, offered to make available a new bleaching green which was twice as large as the original green, around a quarter of a mile away.

The Court thus had to decide whether or not to order removal of the buildings. Lord Young stated that the test to be applied was whether the interest was sufficiently great against ordering the removal of the buildings that the Court, in exercise of its reasonable discretion, would refuse to direct their removal.[42] He noted that the building exercise had not been undertaken contumaciously, but in the interests of the community, and that it would not be in the interests of the community to both sanction a loss of £2,000 in community expense and to remove the municipal stables. Lord Gifford found the magistrates' offer of an alternative, enlarged bleaching green to be a "fair and reasonable proposal", and that although they had done wrong in building on the bleaching green, they had "made offer of a fair equivalent to the community".[43] He added that he had "no doubt as to the equity of the case at all".[44]

---

[41] (1881) 8 R 395. See also the appeal at (1882) 9 R (HL) 91.
[42] At 400 per Lord Young.
[43] At 398–99 per Lord Gifford.
[44] At 399 per Lord Gifford.

Lord Justice-Clerk Moncrieff expressed the view that it was "within the equitable power of the Court" that, where satisfied that no interest will be endangered, and no great loss incurred, a party may be authorised to accept an equivalent in place of a strict vindication of legal right (namely an insistence on the letter of the interdict).[45] In other words, the Court had the power to order equitable compensation in lieu of ordering the removal of the buildings in compliance with the original interdict. The Court therefore held that the alternative offer by the magistrates should be accepted in substitution for the pursued order of removal.

It is worth pointing out that there is no mention of the *nobile officium* in the case report. The term does, however, appear in the rubric, and the case may be fairly characterised as an instance of it. The Court exercised an equitable jurisdiction to pronounce what was regarded as an ad hoc equitable resolution in a way which fell outside the ambit of regular remedies. This may be distinguished from those cases in which the courts have been said to have an equitable power to prevent abuse of process – a power which this author submits is not an exercise of the *nobile officium* – because that is a power common to all courts (including the sheriff court) to ensure procedural regularity, orderliness and fairness as intrinsic aspects of judicial process. By contrast, it is submitted that *Grahame v Magistrates of Kirkcaldy* involves the exercise of a particular kind of equitable power which only the Court of Session would have in a civil context, namely a specific capacity to apply "equity" over "law".[46] Even if both instances would lead to equitable results, one is a generic capacity of courts to maintain the integrity of the judicial process, whilst the other is a specific equitable award which dispenses with strict legal requirements, and which in this case sanctioned non-compliance with the Court's own decree.

---

[45] At 402 per Lord Justice-Clerk Moncrieff.
[46] See also *Burnett v St Andrew's Episcopal Church, Brechin* (1888) 15 R 723.

8.8 Dispensing with other procedural requirements

The Court has dispensed with other procedural requirements by exercise of the *nobile officium*. This has included dispensing with the citation of a next of kin,[47] the *induciae* of a summons,[48] and the *induciae* in an action to preserve a petitioner's *pari passu* ranking.[49] As discussed,[50] the Court has also exercised its *nobile officium* to dispense with the statutory requirement for a bankrupt to take a declaration where the bankrupt had become insane.[51]

The case of *Dunnachie, Petr*[52] is marked in its rubric as an instance of the *nobile officium*, however it is unclear if that is an accurate designation of the case. Section 5 of the Married Women's Property (Scotland) Act 1881 provided that:

> Where a wife is deserted by her husband, or is living apart from him with his consent, a Judge of the Court of Session or Sheriff Court, on petition addressed to the Court, may dispense with the husband's consent to any deed relating to her estate.

A woman whose husband was confined in a lunatic asylum petitioned the Court under section 5 of the Act to dispense with the requirement for her husband's consent to a bond and disposition, or to related dispositions and deeds. The Court granted the prayer of the petition, but it did so without delivering opinions, and it is unclear whether the case was an instance of statutory interpretation, whereby section 5 would include a husband who was confined in a lunatic asylum (who has presumably not deserted his wife, and who is not necessarily living apart from his wife by consent), or whether the Court exercised its *nobile officium* to dispense with the requirement. Indeed, it is not clear if the exact circumstances of the case could have been competently transacted by the sheriff court.

---

[47] See *Buchan, Petrs* (1873) 11 M 662.
[48] *McKidd, Petr* (1890) 17 R 547.
[49] *Barnett and Mandatory, Petr* (1894) 2 SLT 371.
[50] See pp 114 and 233–34.
[51] *Roberts, Petrs* (1901) 3 F 779.
[52] 1910 SC 115.

In another case concerning a marital relationship, the *nobile officium* was exercised on the petition of a wife to dispense with her husband's consent in her election between *legitim* and testamentary provisions where there would have been serious partiality.[53]

8.9 Public records

A cluster of cases concerned the utilisation of the *nobile officium* for the protection and preservation of public records. This has taken the form of a general supervisory jurisdiction over public records and registers, with the Court being described in one case as "stand[ing] in the position of guardian and custodier of all deeds recorded in the Books of Council and Session for the benefit of all interested in the deeds".[54]

Several cases involved petition to the Court for permission to remove documents from the jurisdiction. The reports for those cases have rarely cited the *nobile officium*, but it would seem that they either did involve an exercise of the *nobile officium*, or at least a closely related power. The view was expressed that in deciding such matters, the Court was acting not on a question of law, but of administration.[55] Where the Court has granted permission for documents to be removed from the jurisdiction, in particular for the facilitation of processes in foreign courts, this would invoke similar principles to those underlying the auxiliary jurisdiction.[56]

Where petition has been granted, the Court has often ensured that precautionary measures are taken for the protection and preservation of the documents, imposing conditions such as finding caution and the deposit of an authenticated extract in place of the original. These and similar conditions were imposed where permission was granted for deeds and documents to be

---

[53] *Sillars v Sillars* 1911 SC 1207.

[54] *Macdonald, Petr* (1877) 5 R 44 at 46 per Lord President Inglis.

[55] *King's Remembrancer, Petr* (1902) F 559 at 561 per Lord McLaren.

[56] See p 35, fn 18; and *Young, Petr* (1866) 4 M 344 at 347 per Lord President McNeill.

removed for production in courts in England,[57] Ireland,[58] and the East Indies.[59] The Court sometimes required that a nominated public officer, such as a deputy keeper of registers, proceed with the documents in their custody to the foreign court for their production.[60] Sometimes, however, a simple undertaking to return the documents was sufficient,[61] or an undertaking combined with a penalty for failure to return them.[62] On occasion the Court did not appear to impose any conditions and simply granted permission for the documents to be removed from the jurisdiction.[63] There would have to be "highly exceptional" circumstances warranting the removal of documents from court to process outside the jurisdiction.[64]

In general, the Court would have to be satisfied that it was necessary to remove the documents from the jurisdiction. In *Western Bank of Scotland and Liquidators, Petrs*,[65] the Court refused a petition for warrant to obtain delivery from the sheriff clerk of a deed for production in the Supreme Court of New York, being not satisfied that it was necessary to produce the original. In another case, the Court refused warrant to remove an extracted process to an English court of divorce.[66] The Court also refused a petition for entire registers to be removed from the jurisdiction

---

[57] *Dunlop v Deputy-Clerk Register* (1861) 24 D 107; *Macdonald, Petr* (1877) 5 R 44; *Inglis, Petr* (1882) 9 R 761.

[58] *Jolly, Petr* (1864) 2 M 1288.

[59] *Duncan v Lord Clerk Register* (1842) 4 D 1517. See also *Garrett, Petrs* (1883) 20 SLR 756.

[60] *Bayley, Petrs* (1862) 24 D 1024; *Shedden, Petr* (1862) 24 D 1446; *King's Remembrancer, Petr* (1902) F 559; *Pheysey, Petr* (1906) 8 F 801; *Campbell, Petrs* 1934 SC 8 – each for production in a court in England. However, sending a court officer a great distance from Scotland may be "out of the question" – see *Duncan v Lord Clerk Register* (1842) 4 D 1517. See also the "great doubts" expressed in *Adamson, Petr* (1852) 14 D 1045 and *Chalmers v Thomson* 1922 SLT 364, in which deeds were to be conveyed by the sheriff clerk for production within Scotland.

[61] *The United Telephone Co Ltd v Maclean* (1882) 9 R 710.

[62] *Adamson, Petr* (1852) 14 D 1045.

[63] *Earl of Euston, Petr* (1883) 11 R 235; *Pheysey, Petr* (1906) 8 F 801.

[64] *Whitehall v Whitehall* 1957 SC 30 at 43 per Lord Sorn.

[65] (1868) 6 M 656.

[66] *Power v Lord Clerk Register* (1859) 21 D 782.

for production in the High Court of Justice in England,[67] though it seems that entire volumes were removed from Scotland in other cases.[68] Warrant has also been refused for the removal of certain deeds from the Books of Council and Session for production in an English court when their return could not be ensured.[69]

Not every case has involved the removal of documents from the jurisdiction, for some have seen petitions for authority to remove documents from public registers and records for use elsewhere in Scotland. In one example of this, the *nobile officium* was exercised to grant warrant to a sheriff clerk to transmit a will and codicils from the Sheriff Court Books at Elgin to the Clerk of the First Division for inspection before the Court of Session.[70] There have also been other instances of this application of the Court's power, with documents being removed for use in both judicial[71] and administrative[72] processes.

A potentially different application of the *nobile officium* with regard to public records was seen in *Macdonald v Keeper of the General Register of Sasines*.[73] A petition was presented to the *nobile officium* to ordain the Keeper of the General Register of Sasines to record a deed of settlement in the Register of Sasines. The Court refused the petition on the basis that the Keeper had acted within his discretionary limits, though this did not mean that the Court might not, in other circumstances, accede to such a request.

An unsuccessful application was made in *Smart v Registrar General for Scotland*,[74] which concerned a wife who had been married in Scotland and was later divorced by decree of a court in the Netherlands Antilles. On the view that the relevant section

---

[67] *Kennedy, Petr* (1880) 7 R 1129.
[68] *Earl of Euston, Petr* (1883) 11 R 235; *Pheysey, Petr* (1906) 8 F 801.
[69] *Young, Petr* (1866) 4 M 344.
[70] *Jamieson's Trs v Jamieson* (1899) 2 F 96.
[71] *Mansfield v Stuart* (1840) 2 D 1235; *Shedden, Petr* (1862) 24 D 1446; *Chevenix-Trench, Petr* 1917 SC 168; *Chalmers v Thomson* 1922 SLT 364.
[72] *Gordon, Petr* (1871) 8 SLR 445. *Gordon* was described as an instance of the *nobile officium* – *Chalmers v Thomson* at 366 per Lord Ashmore.
[73] 1914 SC 854.
[74] 1954 SC 81. This case is also discussed at p 159.

of the Registration of Births, Deaths and Marriages (Scotland) Act 1855 did not provide for rectification of her marriage entry in the Register of Marriages, she petitioned the *nobile officium* to authorise the Registrar General to record the decree of divorce in the Register. The Court took the view that the intention of Parliament had been that the statute in question only applied to Scots processes and officials, and that there was no *casus improvisus* requiring exercise of the *nobile officium*. This exercise of the jurisdiction would extend its scope and, as such, the prayer of the petition was refused.

The protective jurisdiction of the *nobile officium* over public records also extends to their physical integrity and preservation.[75] It may, in addition to the cases discussed, be seen where the Court has facilitated public officers in the conduct of public administration,[76] and in the context of statutory omissions.[77]

8.10   Other

The case of *The Royal Bank of Scotland plc v Gillies*[78] is an excellent illustration of the *nobile officium* being deployed to resolve a procedural impasse. The Royal Bank of Scotland had obtained decree for payment against a debtor in the sheriff court. A charge was served and expired without payment. The bank sequestrated the debtor; however, an arrangement for settlement was entered into with the debtor. The Court of Session was critical of taking a decree of default in the circumstances of the sequestration, and counsel for the bank advised that the Court would be likely to recall the sequestration. The Court apparently indicated that it would be advisable not to insist in the sequestration and, accordingly, the bank consented to recall of the award of sequestration.

However, the debtor failed to make any of the repayments under the arrangement for settlement. The bank therefore sought

---

[75] See *Registrar-General for Scotland, Petr* 1949 SLT 385, discussed at p 157.

[76] See Chapter 6.

[77] See Chapter 7.

[78] 1987 SLT 54.

to resume its pursuit of the debt. However, it encountered something of a procedural impasse. The bank was advised that the effect of the recall of the award of sequestration was to impugn that decree as obtained in breach of an undertaking which had not been advised to the debtor's solicitors. This jeopardised any diligence on the decree. The bank was also advised that any further action in pursuit of the debt would be subject to a plea of *res judicata*, and that whereas the debtor had not taken any steps to reduce the decree for payment, the petitioners were themselves advised that it would not be competent for them to seek to reduce the decree, for reasons articulated in the case. There was no competent avenue of appeal, and in short there was no other procedural mechanism by which the bank could pursue the recovery of the debt than by petition to the *nobile officium*.

The Court was persuaded of the necessity of the petition. Lord Justice-Clerk Ross stated that in the Court's opinion "it would not be in accordance with justice that the petitioners should be unable to seek repayment of the alleged debt merely because the decree can be impugned".[79] It was explained that the effect of granting the prayer would be to place the parties in the position in which they were prior to the decree for payment. As such, the bank would be able to pursue the debtor of new, and the debtor would be able to state any relevant and competent defence if he so desired. This appeared to the Court to be "a reasonable result in the special circumstances of this case".[80] In other words, the Court was prepared to cure a procedural impasse by essentially turning back the clock, returning the parties to a prior condition where matters could be taken afresh.

The *nobile officium* can be used to order or ordain a person to perform an act or observe a process. The jurisdiction has thus been used to ordain a sheriff to state a case following the refusal of the sheriff to allow a person to be represented at a hearing.[81]

---

[79] At 55 per Lord Justice-Clerk Ross.
[80] At 56 per Lord Justice-Clerk Ross.
[81] See *C v Kennedy* 1991 SC 68.

Where a statute provided that an award of costs by a tribunal "may be enforced in like manner as a decree of the Court of Session",[82] but where the extractor refused to issue an extract of such an award on the basis that it was not competent for him to do so, the Court exercised its *nobile officium* to authorise the extractor to issue an extract in line with statutory intention.[83] The jurisdiction can be competently invoked to compel an arbiter to proceed in a submission.[84] It has also been used to ordain a respondent wife to disclose her true private address in her answers, which had been withheld on the basis of an averment that her husband would subject her to further ill treatment if her true address was disclosed.[85] Where industrial action was taken by clerks of court, making a litigant unable to obtain a commission and diligence in the sheriff court, the Court of Session granted a commission and diligence by exercise of the *nobile officium*.[86]

The case of *B's Executor v Keeper of the Registers and Records of Scotland*[87] disclosed another potential application of the *nobile officium*. An executor presented a petition to the *nobile officium* for the Court to ordain the Keeper of the Registers and Records of Scotland to record only such parts of a will in the Books of Council and Session as were relevant and of testamentary effect, or alternatively to exclude certain passages from any extract of the will. The relevant passages were said by relatives of the testatrix to be defamatory. As the Writs Execution (Scotland) Act 1877 effectively did not provide for the recording of portions of deeds, the Court refused the prayer of the petition as seeking to have the Court direct the Keeper to do something contrary to his statutory obligations. However, Lord Justice-Clerk Aitchison observed that there might arise an

---

[82] Road and Rail Traffic Act 1933, s 15(12)(b).

[83] *London, Midland and Scottish Railway Co, Petrs* 1937 SC 643.

[84] *Watson v Robertson* (1895) 22 R 362 at 366 per Lord President Robertson. The petition in that case was dismissed. See also, however, *Edmund Nuttall Ltd v Amec Projects Ltd* 1992 SC 133.

[85] *Stein v Stein* 1936 SC 268.

[86] *Manson v British Gas Corporation* 1982 SLT 77.

[87] 1935 SC 745.

exceptional case in which the Court may, "in the exercise of its inherent equitable jurisdiction as the Supreme Court of Scotland", declare that certain passages in a deed were extraneous and to be treated *pro non scripto*, thus meaning that the Keeper would indeed record the deed whilst omitting passages as directed by the Court.[88]

In another instance, the *nobile officium* was exercised to authorise the disinterment and cremation of the bodies of three Norwegian seamen, and to have their cremated remains conveyed to Norway for reinterment. The seamen had been interred in Scotland due to circumstances at the time of their death, when Norway was occupied by German forces. The Court, without delivering opinions, granted the prayer of the petition.[89]

It even lies within the power of the Court to authorise an act in contravention of its own decree. This occurred in *Bowie, Petrs*,[90] in which the *nobile officium* was exercised to authorise an act in contravention of its own decree of perpetual interdict. The interdict had been obtained in 1863 against a committee of parish heritors, prohibiting them from certain building uses of a family burial ground. In 1965, the church congregational board approved a plan for a new session house and offices to be built on the burial ground. A petition was presented to the *nobile officium* on behalf of the board for authority to build on the burial ground, though without seeking to reduce the perpetual interdict. The Court granted the prayer of the petition, authorising an act which was technically in contravention of the perpetual interdict. Although the decree of interdict was in this case substantially left intact, the *nobile officium* may even be used to invalidate the Court's own decrees.[91]

The *nobile officium* can be competently invoked to set aside a judicial decision on the basis of apparent bias or an appearance of

---

[88] At 750 per Lord Justice-Clerk Aitchison.

[89] *Solheim, Petrs* 1947 SC 243. See also *Mitchell, Petr* (1893) 20 R 902.

[90] 1967 SC 36. See also *Grahame v Magistrates of Kirkcaldy* (1881) 8 R 395, discussed at pp 170–71.

[91] See *University of Edinburgh v The Torrie Trs* 1997 SLT 1009.

compromised impartiality and objectivity.[92] It was also said that the *nobile officium* could potentially be invoked where a statutory order made by a district court (now a justice of the peace court) is so defective as to be meaningless or impossible of compliance to such an extent that it causes oppression or injustice.[93]

---

[92] *Davidson v Scottish Ministers (No 2)* 2003 SC 103; *Helow v Advocate General* 2007 SC 303 (the petition in *Helow* was refused on its merits).
[93] See *MacPherson, Petrs* 1990 JC 5 at 14 per Lord Justice-General Hope.

CHAPTER 9

THE HIGH COURT OF JUSTICIARY

The *nobile officium* of the High Court of Justiciary appears historically less remarked than its counterpart jurisdiction in the Court of Session. It was described as rarely invoked between the time of the institutional writers and the late 1960s, in contrast to the "liberal smattering" of petitions in the Court of Session.[1] In more recent times, the High Court has been in receipt of twelve times the number of petitions presented to the Court of Session,[2] though exhibiting a markedly lower rate of success, with under 28 per cent of petitions successful in the High Court, contrasted with 67 per cent of petitions successful in the Court of Session. As these figures indicate, however, the *nobile officium* retains considerable utility and potential for application in the criminal sphere.

The Carloway Review was critical of the ends to which the *nobile officium* is sometimes employed. It was regarded as a way of attempting to undermine existing decisions of the High Court,[3] such as in effectively seeking to reverse a refusal by the High Court of leave to appeal.[4] In particular, as there is no equivalent in summary procedure of the finality provision expressed in section 124 of the Criminal Procedure (Scotland) Act 1995 for solemn proceedings, the Review regarded the *nobile officium* as an additional potential avenue of appeal in

---

[1] C N Stoddart, "The *nobile officium* of the High Court of Justiciary" 1974 SLT (News) 37 at 37.

[2] Based on figures from 2004 to 2013 inclusive: see Appendix 2.

[3] *Carloway Review* at para 8.1.37.

[4] *Carloway Review* at paras 8.1.19, 8.1.37 and 8.1.39. The Review noted, at para 8.1.22, an unsuccessful attempt by a party who had been refused leave to appeal by stated case, to circumvent that decision by lodging a bill of suspension and a petition to the *nobile officium*: see *Shepherd v Procurator Fiscal, Dornoch* [2010] HCJAC 114.

summary cases.[5] The possibility for one mode of appeal to interfere with another would inevitably cause delay, uncertainty and expense, and with regard to the need for certainty and finality, "cannot be justified in a modern system of appellate justice".[6] The High Court should be "alert to the potential abuses which this equitable procedure can create",[7] and the situation is now changed with the existence of the Scottish Criminal Cases Review Commission ("SCCRC").[8] The Review even considered whether petitions to the *nobile officium* of the High Court should be abolished altogether, but was "ultimately persuaded that the power ought to be retained on the basis that it should continue to be available to deal with circumstances which are truly extraordinary or unforeseen and where there is no other remedy available".[9]

David Hume described the *nobile officium* of the High Court as its "exclusive... power of providing a remedy for all extraordinary occurrences in the course of criminal business".[10] He cited several examples of the *nobile officium* being utilised by the High Court from as early as 1711, though there is the outstanding problem of defining the boundary between the *nobile officium* proper and a more general equitable discretion that has for centuries been endemic to the judicial exercise in Scotland. In any event, the *nobile officium* likely grew out of a general sense of the supreme courts' wide powers of equitable superintendence. Among the early exercises of the High Court's *nobile officium* enumerated by Hume were the interim appointment of public officers, the assignment of aliment to prisoners, the assignment of

---

[5] *Carloway Review* at para 8.1.22. It was recommended that there should be a statutory provision which attaches finality to summary appeal decisions in the same manner as to solemn decisions. At the time of writing, this recommendation was reflected in clause 81 of the draft Criminal Justice (Scotland) Bill, proposed as section 194ZA of the Criminal Procedure (Scotland) Act 1995. See *Express Newspapers plc, Petrs* 1999 JC 176.

[6] *Carloway Review* at para 8.1.38.

[7] *Carloway Review* at para 8.1.40.

[8] *Carloway Review* at paras 8.1.36, 8.1.38 and 8.1.39. See p 194.

[9] *Carloway Review* at para 8.1.40.

[10] See Hume, *Commentaries*, vol II at 59.

particular places for imprisonment, the liberation of prisoners at danger in their confinement, and provision for witnesses. Hume was keen to point out, however, that this list was not exhaustive.[11]

In similar terms, Archibald Alison described the *nobile officium* as the "exclusive power of providing a remedy for all extraordinary or unforeseen occurrences in the course of criminal business".[12] He summarised the essence of the jurisdiction as follows:

> that wherever the interposition of some authority is necessary to the administration of justice, and there exists no other judicature by whom it can competently be exercised, or which has been in use to exercise it, the Court of Justiciary is empowered and bound to exert its powers, on the application of a proper party, for the furtherance of justice.[13]

Alison also described the "general controlling power which the Justiciary Court possess, and the interference in mitigation of otherwise irremediable evils, which, in virtue of their *nobile officium*, they frequently exercise".[14] Henry Moncreiff referred to the *nobile officium* as enabling the Court to "interfere in extraordinary circumstances to prevent injustice or oppression where there is no judgment or warrant to review".[15] Moncreiff wrote that there were numerous instances of this power being used in older cases,[16] and himself detailed examples including a petition for recalling a sentence and relief from the penalty in a bond of caution, and a petition for interim liberation pending appeal.[17]

The following excerpt from a judgment of Lord Justice-General Emslie is often cited as an authoritative statement of principle on the *nobile officium* of the High Court:

---

[11] Hume, *Commentaries*, vol II at 59–60.

[12] Alison, *Practice of the Criminal Law of Scotland* at 23.

[13] Alison, *Practice of the Criminal Law of Scotland* at 25.

[14] Alison, *Practice of the Criminal Law of Scotland* at 662.

[15] Moncreiff, *Law of Review in Criminal Cases* at 218.

[16] Moncreiff did not explore these earlier decisions, though given that the cases he did discuss date from no earlier than 1858, it can be assumed that the older cases to which he referred fall prior to that date.

[17] Moncreiff, *Law of Review in Criminal Cases* at 264–71.

> [*following citation of several authorities*] These classical descriptions of the power have been accepted by this court as authoritative in all cases in which the scope of its power under the *nobile officium* has been called in question, and as the cases show, have been interpreted to mean that the power will only be exercised where the circumstances are extraordinary or unforeseen, and where no other remedy or procedure is provided by the law ... To complete this review of the nature, scope and limits of the power we have only to add that the *nobile officium* of this court, and for that matter of the Court of Session, may never be invoked when to do so would conflict with statutory intention, express or clearly implied.[18]

In broad accordance with this statement of principle, it has generally been held that a competent exercise of the *nobile officium* would require extraordinary or unforeseen circumstances, some element of fairness or justice warranting equitable intervention, the unavailability of another remedy or procedure for invocation, and that equitable intervention would not be contrary to statutory intention, express or implied. These are not entirely freestanding requirements, and are in any case without prejudice to more general limitations on the scope of the jurisdiction.[19]

The requirement for the existence of extraordinary or unforeseen circumstances is a recurring theme in cases dealing with petitions to the *nobile officium* of the High Court,[20] and a failure to satisfy this criterion has proved problematic or detrimental in a number of petitions.[21] On what counts as "extraordinary or unforeseen circumstances" it has been elaborated that:

> That expression does not, in our view, refer simply to the question whether the circumstances are unusual. ... It also refers to the question

---

[18] *Anderson v HM Advocate* 1974 SLT 239 at 240 per Lord Justice-General Emslie.

[19] See Chapter 10.

[20] *Perrie, Petr* 1992 SLT 655 at 658 per Lord Justice-General Hope; *Windsor, Petr* 1994 JC 41 at 54 per Lord Sutherland; *Newland, Petr* 1994 JC 122 at 126 per Lord Justice-General Hope; *McIntosh, Petr* 1995 SLT 796 at 798; *Cooney v HM Advocate* 1999 GWD 28-1322; *Birrell v HM Advocate* 2011 JC 27 at 31 per Lord Malcolm.

[21] See, eg, *Anderson v HM Advocate* 1974 SLT 239; *HM Advocate v Greene* 1976 SLT 120; *Ferguson v HM Advocate* 1980 JC 27; *Harper, Petr* 1982 SLT 232; and *Manson, Petr* 1991 SLT 96.

whether the situation is one for which no provision is made, or is one which cannot be made good by the taking of any alternative steps, that is to say steps other than by use of the court of its *nobile officium*.[22]

As noted below, an anomaly in the scheme of a requirement for "exceptional or unforeseen circumstances" is that the *nobile officium* is a standard means of challenging a finding of contempt of court.[23]

It has been said in the criminal context that "the *nobile officium* cannot be exercised to override the express provisions of a statute or where to do so would conflict with statutory intention express or implied"[24] and that "the *nobile officium* of this court ... may never be invoked when to do so would conflict with statutory intention"[25] – a core principle of the *nobile officium*. For example, a petition for restoration of a legal aid certificate was dismissed as incompetent on the basis that it conflicted with rule 164(2) of the Act of Adjournal (Consolidation) 1988.[26] In *Perrie, Petr*, Lord Justice-General Hope stated that "it is clear that we cannot exercise the *nobile officium* on grounds which would have been the proper subject of an appeal had a further right of appeal been available under the statute".[27] He continued:

> The purpose of the *nobile officium* is to prevent injustice or oppression where the circumstances are extraordinary or unforeseen and where no other remedy or procedure is provided by the law. But the power cannot be exercised in order to review on the merits a decision taken by the court under the statutory provisions for appeal. That is not to say that the court could never, in the exercise of the *nobile officium*,

---

[22] *Bryceland, Petr* 2003 SLT 54 at 57 per Lord Justice-General Cullen.

[23] See Section 9.7.

[24] *Evans v HM Advocate* 1992 SLT 401 at 404 per Lord Justice-General Hope, drawing on very similar comments in *Anderson v HM Advocate* 1974 SLT 239 at 240 per Lord Justice-General Emslie. These comments were endorsed in *Pickett v HM Advocate* 2008 SLT 319 at 330. See also *Lang, Petr* 1991 SLT 931 and Chapter 10.

[25] *Perrie, Petr* 1992 SLT 655 at 657 per Lord Justice-General Hope.

[26] *McGettigan, Petr* 1996 SLT 76.

[27] At 658 per Lord Justice-General Hope.

alter or correct an order which has been pronounced by the court in the exercise of its appellate jurisdiction under the Act. Indeed counsel for the petitioner was able to provide us with a recent example of a case where that has been done.[28]

However, Lord Justice-General Hope appeared to suggest in another case that sufficiently extraordinary or unforeseen circumstances *may* justify exercise of the *nobile officium* in conflict with statutory intention.[29]

As noted, there should generally be no other remedy open to the intending petitioner for a petition to the *nobile officium* to be competent (including a right of appeal),[30] the essence of the jurisdiction being "to redress all wrongs for which a particular remedy is not otherwise provided".[31] Lord Justice-General Emslie's reference to no other remedy or procedure being provided by law has been said "not to be read as covering the situation when an available remedy has not been employed and can no longer be employed".[32] In other words, the *nobile officium* is not ordinarily available where a person has failed to utilise some remedy or procedure, and they now seek rescue from that failure. The cases also show that the Court will not look sympathetically upon the lack of an available remedy simply where existing remedies have been unsuccessfully pursued, largely because the jurisdiction is not a general mode of appeal, and is by no means intended to be a natural extension of the appeal process.

---

[28] At 658 per Lord Justice-General Hope.

[29] See *Beattie, Petr* 1993 SLT 676 at 678 per Lord Justice-General Hope, discussed at pp 195–96.

[30] *Cordiner, Petr* 1973 JC 16 at 18 per Lord Justice-General Emslie; *Anderson v HM Advocate* 1974 SLT 239 at 240 per Lord Justice-General Emslie; *Evans v HM Advocate* 1992 SLT 401; *Clayton, Petr* 1992 SLT 404; *Perrie, Petr* at 658 per Lord Justice-General Hope; *Windsor, Petr* 1994 JC 41 at 53–54 per Lord Sutherland; *Drummond, Petr* 1998 SLT 757; *La Torre v Lord Advocate and Scottish Ministers* 2008 JC 72 at 74 per Lord Nimmo Smith, *Paterson v HM Advocate* 2008 JC 230; *Birrell v HM Advocate* 2011 JC 27 at 31 per Lord Malcolm. See further Section 10.4.

[31] *Fenton, Petr* 1982 SLT 164 at 164.

[32] *Cobanoglu, Petr* 2012 SCL 604 at 610 per Lord Clarke.

What counts as a "remedy" in these circumstances may be open to debate,[33] though so far as the *nobile officium* of the High Court is concerned it does not necessarily mean a remedy within the criminal justice system. For example, where an act is amenable to judicial review in the Court of Session, that is a "remedy" which would exclude the *nobile officium* of the High Court being used to challenge the matter in question.[34] It is, on that note, worth pointing out that practitioners should ensure that a petition to the *nobile officium* is being directed to the correct court, in order to avoid a petition being regarded as incompetent on point of jurisdiction:

> There is no doubt that the High Court of Justiciary has a power in the exercise of the *nobile officium*, similar to that of the Court of Session, to provide a remedy in extraordinary or unforeseen circumstances. But it is equally clear that these two courts do not exercise a concurrent jurisdiction in the exercise of this power. The High Court of Justiciary has exclusive jurisdiction in the exercise of the *nobile officium* in relation to matters which can properly be described as criminal business, while exclusive jurisdiction in the exercise of the *nobile officium* in all civil matters lies with the Court of Session.[35]

One should bear in mind the equitable essence of the *nobile officium* and its general appeal to notions of fairness and justice. After quoting Lord Justice-General Emslie's statement of principle, Lord Justice-General Cullen stated:

> We would add that it is plain that, even if a case can be brought within the general requirements to which we have referred, it still requires to be shown that there is a compelling case for the exercise of the power, consistent with considerations of what is fair and just in the circumstances.[36]

---

[33] See the discussion on whether the possibility of referral by the SCCRC is a "remedy" at p 194, fn 65.

[34] *British Broadcasting Corporation, Applicants* 2012 SCL 347.

[35] *Newland, Petr* 1994 JC 122 at 126 per Lord Justice-General Hope. See, eg, *Cordiner, Petr* 1973 JC 16. As pointed out in *Renton and Brown's Criminal Procedure* at para 34-01, the *nobile officium* of the High Court may be utilised by persons affected by criminal proceedings, who are not accused persons, and who have no statutory rights of appeal.

[36] *Bryceland, Petr* 2003 SLT 54 at 56–57 per Lord Justice-General Cullen.

In other words, even if there are extraordinary or unforeseen circumstances, there is no other remedy provided by law, and equitable intervention would not conflict with statutory intention, the petitioner would still be expected to justify why the *nobile officium* should – and not merely could – be exercised.

There have been varying views on whether it is competent for a single judge to deal with a petition to the *nobile officium*. It seems to have been the view in earlier cases that it was not competent for the *nobile officium* to be exercised by a single judge.[37] Lord Ardwall said in *Lowson v HM Advocate* that a petition required to be dealt with by a quorum of three judges and cited authority in that regard, including *Slater & Skae* as "an authority of a very important kind, being a decision of the Lord Justice-Clerk [Macdonald]".[38]

More recently, Lord McCluskey stated in clear terms that "the *nobile officium* jurisdiction of the High Court ... of course cannot be exercised by a single judge",[39] although the contrary view was expressed by Lord Macfadyen:

> I am satisfied that it is competent for the petitioners to make the application which they now make in the form of a petition to the *nobile officium* of the High Court, and for that application to be heard by me sitting alone.[40]

The current position is perhaps best set out in *Express Newspapers plc, Petrs*.[41] The opinion of the Court, delivered by Lord Justice-General Rodger, noted that "it is established practice for petitions to the *nobile officium* to be presented to a court of three judges", but there "are signs also that it has not been the universal practice to place petitions and complaints for contempt of court before a court of three judges".[42] The Court's conclusion was that it is

---

[37] See *Lowson v HM Advocate* (1909) 2 SLT 329; and *Milne v McNicol* 1944 JC 151 at 152–53 per Lord Justice-Clerk Cooper.

[38] At 331–32 per Lord Ardwall; citing *Slater & Skae* (19 March 1899, unreported).

[39] *HM Advocate v Rae* 1992 SCCR 1 at 3 per Lord McCluskey.

[40] *BBC, Petrs (No 1)* 2000 JC 419 at 425 per Lord Macfadyen. This was, however, a case on contempt of court.

[41] 1999 JC 176.

[42] At 181 per Lord Justice-General Rodger.

for the High Court to determine the appropriate quorum to hear a petition to the *nobile officium*. However, that finding appears to be directed at petitions on contempt of court. Although it is unclear whether *Express Newspapers* can be taken as authority for the competency of a single judge hearing a petition to the *nobile officium* in cases other than those on contempt of court, it has at least been argued to be such.[43] Where an exercise of the *nobile officium* is subject to review in the High Court, it should be reviewed by a larger court.[44]

Where a bill of suspension is competent, it would usually be necessary to bring such a bill rather than petition the *nobile officium*. There are, however, instances of the Court exercising its discretion to "convert" proceedings to and from petitions to the *nobile officium* where competency has so required. The Court has both treated a bill of suspension as a petition to the *nobile officium*,[45] and treated a petition to the *nobile officium* as a bill of suspension.[46] The Court has also treated a petition to the *nobile officium* as a bail appeal.[47] Nevertheless, it goes without saying

---

[43] *BBC, Petrs (No 1)* 2000 JC 419 at 425; *BBC, Petrs (No 2)* 2000 JC 521 at 530 and 532. See also *Renton and Brown's Criminal Procedure* at paras 34-08 and 34-09, although the cases cited therein are largely concerned with contempt of court. In *HM Advocate v Bryceland* (HCJ, 8 Oct 2002, unreported, accessible at http://www.scotcourts.gov.uk/opinions/PAT0910.html), Lady Paton (at para [25]) interpreted *Express Newspapers* as confirming that "it is competent for a single judge in the High Court to hear an application to the *nobile officium*". As this position is not developed in the judgment, the issue would benefit from further clarification, particularly in the context of petitions to the *nobile officium* which are not concerned with contempt of court.

[44] See *Renton and Brown's Criminal Procedure* at para 34-07; and also *BBC, Petrs (No 2)* 2000 JC 521 at 532.

[45] *George Outram & Co Ltd v Lees* 1992 JC 17; *Reilly v HM Advocate* 1995 SLT 670. *Reilly* related to the service of an indictment at a bail address different from the normal place of residence – on domicile of citation considered in a petition to the *nobile officium*, see also *Hamid v Procurator Fiscal* [2012] HCJAC 101.

[46] *Ward v Brown* 2000 SLT 1355; *Crane v HM Advocate* 2006 JC 190. The High Court dealt with a petition to the *nobile officium* and bills of suspension together in *Robertson and Gough v HM Advocate* 2008 JC 146. For an instance of the Court of Session "converting" a petition to the *nobile officium* to a statutory petition, see *Stark's Trs, Petrs* 1932 SC 653.

[47] *Gilchrist, Petr* 1991 JC 160.

that it is advisable to invoke the correct remedy as circumstances dictate, rather than relying on the Court's discretion to convert proceedings. If a person does seek for an application to be treated as a petition to the *nobile officium* where the original form of application was incompetent, he may be required to make relevant and specific averments indicating how the *nobile officium* could properly be used in the circumstances of the case.[48]

By final word of preliminary comment, the European Court of Human Rights has indicated that the availability of the *nobile officium* could be regarded as an effective remedy for the purposes of Article 13 of the European Convention on Human Rights. Article 13 provides that: "Everyone whose rights and freedoms as set forth in this Convention are violated shall have an effective remedy before a national authority notwithstanding that the violation has been committed by persons acting in an official capacity." However, if for some reason recourse to the *nobile officium* is not available, then there can arise a violation of Article 13 of the Convention.[49]

The remainder of this chapter gives an overview of the various applications of the *nobile officium* of the High Court. As in the case of the *nobile officium* of the Court of Session, the headings under which cases are discussed are categorised primarily in the interests of manageability and structural coherence. They are not mutually exclusive, but where there is overlap a decision has been made as to the heading under which a case should most appropriately be discussed. Although the potential application of the jurisdiction is substantively wide, it should be noted that it is the professional responsibility of legal representatives to ensure that only stateable cases are presented to the *nobile officium*,[50] cautioning against the idea that the *nobile officium* should be petitioned speculatively in a last effort to secure redress, or be treated as a general extension of the appeal process.

---

[48] *Beck v HM Advocate* 2006 JC 178.

[49] *Mackay v United Kingdom* (2011) 53 EHRR 19. On point of the ECHR, see also *Burn, Petr* 2000 JC 403; and *ICL Plastics Ltd, Petr* 2005 SLT 675. See also p 249.

[50] *Telford v HM Advocate* 2012 SLT 911.

9.1 Statutory omissions

A statutory omission may be competently dealt with in the High Court of Justiciary where it is appropriate to criminal jurisdiction and the matter does not properly fall under the jurisdiction of another court.[51]

An example of the High Court exercising its *nobile officium* to supply a statutory omission is found in *Wan Ping Nam v Minister of Justice of the German Federal Republic*.[52] A seaman claiming to be a citizen of Hong Kong was suspected of having killed a fellow crew member on a vessel on the high seas off Islay. He was detained in custody on arrival at Greenock. The Government of the Federal Republic of Germany sought extradition of the suspect on the basis that the vessel was registered in Bremen. Section 10 of the Extradition Act 1870 provided that a fugitive criminal accused of an extraditable crime shall, if a foreign warrant for his arrest is duly authenticated and certain evidence produced, be committed to prison by a police magistrate. Section 11 provided that, if a police magistrate commits a fugitive criminal to prison, he shall inform him that he will not be surrendered until after the expiry of 15 days, and that he has a right to apply for a writ of *habeas corpus*. Section 16 provided that the Act shall be construed as if any sheriff or sheriff-substitute in Scotland were substituted for references to the "police magistrate" where appropriate.

Habeas corpus is not part of the law of Scotland and thus could not be granted by a Scottish court. However, on application by the suspect to the *nobile officium* of the High Court, it was held that it was the "plain intention" of the Extradition Act 1870 that relief should be available to persons committed to prison under section 10 and, accordingly, the Court had the power in exercise of its *nobile officium* to provide the means of giving effect to the

---

[51] See, eg, *Newland, Petr* 1994 JC 122, in which it was held that an alleged *casus improvisus* in the Prisoners and Criminal Proceedings (Scotland) Act 1993 properly fell within the jurisdiction of the Court of Session.

[52] 1972 JC 43.

intention of the legislature, and therefore to suspend the order of committal.

Lord Justice-General Emslie observed that "had the petitioner been committed to prison by a police magistrate in England, relief by way of application to the Court for a writ of *habeas corpus* would have been available to him", and that it "need hardly be said that [*habeas corpus*] does not run in Scotland and is wholly unknown to our law". Accordingly, the question was "whether this Court can and should, under its inherent power to prevent injustice, supply the apparent omission in the Act by affording a remedy to the petitioner". Being satisfied that this was an omission on the part of the statute, and that the plain intention of Parliament was that relief should be available to all persons committed under section 10, the Lord Justice-General expressed the view that:

> the circumstances of this case... are, on any view, extraordinary and we are satisfied that in the exercise of the *nobile officium* this Court may properly examine the allegation of injustice made by the petitioner, and suspend the order under which the petitioner is committed.[53]

In *Lloyds and Scottish Finance Ltd v HM Advocate*,[54] the Criminal Justice Act 1972 provided a means for true owners of forfeited property to come forward and vindicate their right; however the Act omitted to provide a comparable mechanism in Scotland. The Court exercised its *nobile officium* to ensure that the interests of a third party finance company which owned a forfeited car were nevertheless protected.

In *McKinlay v HM Advocate*,[55] the Court exercised its *nobile officium* to deal with an omission in the Prisoners and Criminal Proceedings (Scotland) Act 1993. Further, in *Campbell, Petr*,[56] the Court admitted an accused to bail where she did not fall under the relevant statutory provisions.

---

[53] At 47–48.
[54] 1974 JC 24.
[55] 1994 SCCR 261 (Note).
[56] 1990 JC 128.

9.2 Incompetency, unlawfulness and irregularity

The *nobile officium* has been used to challenge alleged incompetency, unlawfulness and irregularity[57] in decisions, orders and processes.

The *nobile officium* may be used to direct a sheriff to act in conformity with law or process. It may, for example, be used to direct the sheriff to prepare a stated case where he had refused to do so on point of relevancy, even though there had been the necessary compliance with statutory requirements, including the making of a timeous application.[58] It may also be used to direct a sheriff to state a case where the first application for the same had been refused due to non-compliance with a statutory provision, but where a second application had been made within the statutory time limit.[59] Where a sheriff adopted a practice of considering interim suspension in a manner for which there was no statutory authority, this was deemed incompetent. Whereas that incompetency may have been a ground for the Court exercising its *nobile officium* to recall the sheriff's refusal of interim suspension, the Court held that because the actions of the sheriff were incompetent, the petition was unnecessary.[60] The *nobile officium* has also been used in response to the sheriff having erred in his interpretation of statute and thereby liberating an accused.[61] Where a petition was made to the *nobile officium*

---

[57] It should be noted that under the Criminal Procedure (Scotland) Act 1995, s 300A, as inserted by the Criminal Proceedings etc (Reform) (Scotland) Act 2007, s 40, criminal courts have the power to excuse procedural irregularities. It is conceivable that some procedural matters which may previously have been amenable to redress by way of the *nobile officium* could now be disposed of via this statutory channel. See *Renton and Brown's Criminal Procedure* at para 2-01.2.

[58] *MacDougall, Petr* 1986 SCCR 128; *McTaggart, Petr* 1987 SCCR 638; *Crowe, Petr* 1994 SCCR 784; *Leonard, Petr* 1995 SCCR 39; *Reid, Petr* 1997 SLT 921. See also *Renton and Brown's Criminal Procedure* at para 33-03.1.

[59] *Singh, Petr* 1987 SLT 63.

[60] *Magee, Petr* 1996 JC 7.

[61] *HM Advocate v Keegan* 1981 SLT (Notes) 35. As noted at p 198, fn 84, the headnote in the case report appears to be incorrect – the accused was not admitted to bail as reported.

against a community service order imposed by the sheriff, but the Court held that a challenge to the competency of such an order should have been brought by way of bill of suspension and that resort to the *nobile officium* was incompetent, the Court treated the petition as though it was a bill of suspension and set aside the sheriff's order.[62]

The Court has entertained a petition from the Lord Advocate praying for the substitution of one offence for another where a sheriff had decided in relation to an offence not included in a particular statute. The sheriff found for the offence of "indecent exposure", which was not included in Schedule 1 to the Sex Offenders Act 1997. On the petition of the Lord Advocate, the Court exercised its *nobile officium* to declare the offence to be one of "shameless indecency" in accordance with the Act.[63]

A petition from an accused praying for the quashing of a conviction of, *inter alia*, "conspiracy" – a crime which was averred to be unknown to the law of Scotland – was refused as incompetent.[64] The accused had unsuccessfully appealed and unsuccessfully applied to the SCCRC. The Court took the view that the application to the SCCRC was a remedy which the petitioner had at his disposal, and which had been unsuccessful.[65]

---

[62] *Crane v HM Advocate* 2006 JC 190. See also *Ward v Brown* 2000 SLT 1355, in which a bill of suspension was treated as though it was a petition to the *nobile officium*. The case resulted in a sentence of imprisonment being quashed and the reduction in duration of a supervised attendance order.

[63] *Lord Advocate, Petr* 1998 JC 209.

[64] *Cochrane v HM Advocate* 2006 JC 135.

[65] See also *Harris v HM Advocate* 2010 SCL 241. The view has been taken elsewhere that the possibility of the SCCRC exercising its discretion in favour of an applicant cannot properly be seen as a "remedy" in the context of the scope and limits of the *nobile officium* – see *Akram v HM Advocate* 2009 SLT 805 at 810 per Lord Osborne. However, see also *McWilliam, Petr* 2002 SLT 972, in which the accused had yet to invoke the reference procedure to the SCCRC, that being regarded as "the appropriate first step before any *nobile officium* is exercised" (at 974). In other words, the Court in *McWilliam* was not saying that the possibility of reference to the SCCRC precluded exercise of the *nobile officium* by offering a "remedy", but was instead requiring that this avenue be pursued, leaving open the possibility for a petition to be brought thereafter should the SCCRC not convey the desired outcome. See also *Mitchell v HM Advocate* [2010] HCJAC 54.

It was held that the making of any error of fact or law could not be regarded as an unforeseen circumstance. In addition to the petition being refused as incompetent, it was observed that it would have been refused on the merits even had it been competent.[66]

An order of the High Court was held by exercise of the *nobile officium* to be *ultra vires* and void as effectively depriving an appellant of his rights under Article 6 of the European Convention on Human Rights.[67] A sentence imposed by the High Court was quashed where it had purported to quash a charge on appeal and impose a new sentence in relation to a charge which was not before the court.[68] In addition, an order of the trial judge in the High Court has been recalled when it purported to impose conditions whilst dispensing with reporting restrictions under section 169 of the Criminal Procedure (Scotland) Act 1975, there being no statutory authority for imposing those conditions.[69] An incompetent decision of second sift judges in the course of an attempted criminal appeal was also set aside by exercise of the *nobile officium*.[70]

In *Beattie, Petr*,[71] an accused had been sentenced to 16 years' imprisonment for various contraventions of the Misuse of Drugs Act 1971. On appeal, the High Court quashed the sentence and imposed a sentence of 14 years' imprisonment, holding that the trial judge had imposed an incompetent sentence in excess of the statutory maximum of 14 years. The accused petitioned the *nobile officium* averring that the High Court's sentence was

---

[66] For other petitions unsuccessfully objecting to the competency of decisions or orders of the sheriff, see *McDonald v HM Advocate* 2003 JC 60; *Wright v HM Advocate* 2005 JC 11; and *Newlands v HM Advocate* 2014 SCL 135.

[67] *Higson v Doherty* 2004 SCCR 63. No opinions were delivered by the Court.

[68] *Allan, Petr* 1993 JC 181.

[69] *Caledonian Newspapers Ltd, Petrs* 1995 JC 172.

[70] *Beggs, Petr* 2005 SLT 165. In *Megrahi, Petr* 2002 JC 38, the Court reserved opinion on the competency of a petition (refused on its merits) averring that there was no power in the High Court of Justiciary (Proceedings in the Netherlands) (United Nations) Order 1998 for a report to be sent by the trial judge to the Clerk of Justiciary giving an opinion on the case and on the grounds contained in a note of appeal.

[71] 1993 SLT 676.

oppressive and unjust in that it was incompetent: it sought to punish the petitioner twice over for one offence. The Court took the position that it was being asked to review the decision of the appeal court and to substitute its own view in its place, which was problematic in view of sections 262 and 281 of the Criminal Procedure (Scotland) Act 1975 which provided that interlocutors and sentences of the High Court shall be final and conclusive and not subject to review.[72] There were no extraordinary or unforeseen circumstances which would justify the Court exercising its *nobile officium*, and as such the petition was incompetent. Notable in this case is that, despite the general rule that the *nobile officium* may not be used in a manner which contradicts the express or implied meaning of statute, Lord Justice-General Hope suggested that extraordinary or unforeseen circumstances *could* justify such a contradiction:

> It had not been demonstrated that there is anything extraordinary or unforeseen in the circumstances of this case which would justify the exercise of the *nobile officium* in conflict with the intention of the Act, which is that decisions of the appeal court are final and not subject to review.[73]

Birrell v HM Advocate[74] was another case in which the petitioner was unsuccessful. An accused challenged a financial reporting order following his pleading guilty to charges of fraud and money laundering. It was averred that the order was incompetent inasmuch as the court had purported to adjourn proceedings in accordance with a non-existent provision in the Act of Adjournal (Criminal Procedure Rules) 1996, and the periods of adjournment exceeded a statutory time limit. The Court held that the validity of the decision was not affected by the erroneous reference to the non-existent provision, and moreover the alleged incompetency

---

[72] See also *Boyle, Petr (No 2)* 1993 SLT 1085 at 1090, where it was said that "[t]o a large extent ... it is for the High Court to determine the limits of its own jurisdiction, so long as this does not conflict with what Parliament has provided, either expressly or by necessary implication, in any enactment".

[73] At 678 per Lord Justice-General Hope.

[74] 2011 JC 27.

could have been added to the grounds of appeal in the original proceedings. The petitioner had not done so and had thus forgone an opportunity for challenge: "[t]hat omission cannot be corrected by a petition to the *nobile officium* which is a process of last resort to be used only in extraordinary or unforeseen circumstances and in the absence of any other remedy".[75] The Court refused the prayer of the petition.

In a case before the High Court, the trial judge sentenced an accused to life imprisonment for the murder of his wife after the jury had delivered its verdict and then left the bench, but without the prosecutor having moved for sentence. The accused petitioned the *nobile officium*, after his appeal against that decision was refused,[76] on the basis of irregularity in proceedings. The Court considered that it was "not in accordance with the ends of justice" that the Crown should be denied the opportunity to move for sentence, and exercised its *nobile officium* to quash the sentence which had been imposed and remit the case to the trial judge.[77]

Two separate attempts to challenge the order of a district court[78] were dismissed as incompetent.[79] Both related to orders made against keepers of dogs under the Civic Government (Scotland) Act 1982. Various averments were made between the two petitions, including a failure to give reasons, taking into account irrelevant factors and failing to take into account relevant factors. In neither case were there extraordinary or unforeseen circumstances warranting equitable intervention. In a third case concerning the keeping of dogs under the Act, it was said by Lord Coulsfield that the *nobile officium* may be appropriate for use where a district court failed to exercise its jurisdiction.[80]

---

[75] At 31 per Lord Malcolm.

[76] *Arthur v HM Advocate (No 1)* 2002 SCCR 796.

[77] *Arthur v HM Advocate (No 2)* 2003 SLT 90.

[78] District courts were replaced by justice of the peace courts: Criminal Proceedings etc (Reform) (Scotland) Act 2007, in particular ss 59 and 64.

[79] *MacPherson, Petrs* 1990 JC 5; *Black, Petr* 1991 SCCR 1.

[80] *City of Edinburgh District Council, Petrs* 1990 SCCR 511 at 518 per Lord Coulsfield.

The *nobile officium* has been successfully used to challenge the competency of an indictment. A dissolved partnership had been indicted, but the Court found that the indictment was incompetent on the basis that a dissolved partnership did not have continuing legal personality, and that an indictment should instead have been directed against the former partners as individuals. The Court granted declarator as such.[81] The *nobile officium* has also been competently petitioned with regard to alleged collusion between national authorities and a contention that the Lord Advocate was "turning a blind eye" to impropriety to the detriment of the accused.[82]

The *nobile officium* may provide support where an application for bail has been dealt with irregularly. The jurisdiction has been used to correct a sheriff's erroneous application of section 28(2) of the Criminal Procedure (Scotland) Act 1975 in failing to dispose of an application for bail within 24 hours of its presentation, or otherwise liberate the accused. The High Court ordered liberation in exercise of the *nobile officium*.[83]

There have been cases in which the Lord Advocate has petitioned the *nobile officium* for recall of an order granting bail.[84] The jurisdiction has been successfully petitioned by the Lord Advocate for recall of bail on the ground that it was incompetent for a single judge to admit to bail a person who

---

[81] *Balmer v HM Advocate* 2008 SLT 799.

[82] *Bennett v HM Advocate* 1995 SLT 510. The petition was refused on its merits.

[83] *Gibbons, Petr* 1988 JC 58. The 24-hour period within which a bail application must be disposed of only runs from the point at which the application is "presented" to the judge in question. Where a bail application had merely been lodged with the office of the sheriff clerk, the 24-hour period at no point began to run, and a subsequent petition to the *nobile officium* for liberation under the Criminal Procedure (Scotland) Act 1975, s 28(2) was refused: *Tin Fan Lau, Petr* 1986 SLT 535 (though see *Ritchie v Dickie* 1999 SC 593). See now the Criminal Procedure (Scotland) Act 1995, ss 22A and 23 (as amended).

[84] The headnote of *HM Advocate v Keegan* 1981 SLT (Notes) 35 states that the petition sought to have recalled an order made by the sheriff admitting the accused to bail. However, this appears to be incorrect, as the sheriff did not grant bail – he liberated the accused.

had been convicted of murder.[85] The power of the High Court to admit to bail a person charged with murder or treason has been said to be an "inherent power of the High Court" which "may be exercised only by a quorum of the High Court in exercise of its paramount authority".[86] It has itself been described as "equivalent or similar to the *nobile officium* of the Court of Session".[87]

There are two further cases on bail to which attention should be drawn. In each there had wrongly been an effective denial of bail, and a subsequent petition to the *nobile officium* was held incompetent. Strikingly, however, the Court still granted bail on the merits, notwithstanding the incompetency.

The first is *Gilchrist, Petr*,[88] in which an accused was charged on a summary complaint in the sheriff court and admitted to bail with the standard conditions, with an additional condition that he must not approach certain witnesses and houses. He thereafter applied to the sheriff court for review of the additional condition imposed under section 30(2) of the Criminal Procedure (Scotland) Act 1975. The sheriff refused the application as incompetent. Subsequently, the accused petitioned the *nobile officium* for review of his bail conditions. The Court held that the petition was incompetent because (upon a particular reading of section 299 of the Act) the petitioner had a statutory remedy open to him: the very application to the sheriff which the sheriff had refused. The sheriff erred in refusing the petition. Nevertheless, the Crown agreed that the present petition be treated as a bail appeal, and the Court, "[i]n order to avoid further expense and to afford the petitioner the remedy to which he appears to be entitled", treated the petition as a bail appeal and varied the conditions of the bail order.

---

[85] *HM Advocate v Renicks* 1999 SLT 407. See now the Criminal Procedure (Scotland) Act 1995, s 24 (as amended).

[86] *HM Advocate v Renicks* at 409.

[87] *Milne v McNicol* 1944 JC 151 at 153 per Lord Justice-Clerk Cooper. For a petition to the *nobile officium* for recall which was held to be incompetent, presented by the Lord Advocate, see *HM Advocate v Greene* 1976 SLT 120.

[88] 1991 JC 160.

In the second case, *Love, Petr*,[89] a pannel's bail application had been refused by the sheriff. The pannel then sought to appeal that refusal to the High Court as permitted by section 32(1) of the Criminal Procedure (Scotland) Act 1995. However, the Justiciary Office rejected the appeal as incompetent. The pannel therefore petitioned the *nobile officium* to challenge the refusal of bail. The Court regarded the petition to the *nobile officium* as incompetent on the basis that the Justiciary Office was wrong to reject the pannel's appeal, and as such the pannel was entitled to appeal to the High Court in terms of the Act. However, the Court recognised that the pannel had petitioned the *nobile officium* as he had no other means of applying for bail, and in order not to cause prejudice to the petitioner, it proceeded to deal with the petition on its merits. Despite holding that the petition was incompetent, the Court granted bail on the merits.

In both *Gilchrist* and *Love*, therefore, the Court entertained technically incompetent petitions for the granting of bail where a bail application had effectively been wrongly treated.

Additionally, there have been (not altogether successful) challenges to processes and proceedings relating to accused persons under the age of 18. In one case, a 15-year-old boy charged with murder and attempted murder petitioned the *nobile officium* averring that his transfer from one centre to another was contrary to the terms of a place of safety order, though the petition was refused.[90] Two petitions in which it was claimed that respective accused persons had been detained for more than 110 days by reference to section 101(2) of the Criminal Procedure (Scotland) Act 1975 failed, though neither on point of competency.[91]

Finally, it was held in *Draper, Petr* that, where a trial judge had been influenced by a completely erroneous view of the facts, this would "constitute the sort of manifest injustice which [the]

---

[89] 1998 JC 85.

[90] *B, Petr* 1993 SLT 455. See also *M, Petr* 1996 SLT 629.

[91] *Campbell, Petr* 1996 SLT 285 (which was successful only to the extent of confirming that the accused was entitled to liberation from a particular date); *X v HM Advocate* 1996 JC 129.

court would be entitled to rectify by application of the *nobile officium*", provided that it would not conflict with any express or implied statutory intention in so doing.[92]

9.3 Excessiveness and oppression

The *nobile officium* may be used to challenge otherwise competent decisions as excessive or oppressive.[93] An example of an excessive (though competent) sentence being quashed is in *Dickson, Petr*.[94] An accused was sentenced to two years' imprisonment and ordered to pay £16,000 in compensation, payable in instalments. He failed to pay that sum and was sentenced to 334 days' imprisonment. The Court held that it was unrealistic to expect the accused, in his circumstances (which included a period of unemployment), to have been able to pay that sum of money. The course adopted by the sheriff was excessive, and the order for imprisonment was quashed in exercise of the *nobile officium* and the case remitted to the sheriff for reduction or variation of the order.

In *Beglan, Petr*,[95] an accused had been convicted of embezzlement, was sentenced to nine months' imprisonment, and appealed against his sentence. He was granted interim liberation and later abandoned his appeal. The accused was anxious to "hand himself in" for his sentence to proceed as soon as possible, but repeated efforts on the part of his solicitors to take matters forward with the police and the Crown came to no avail. The accused therefore petitioned the *nobile officium* averring that the delay was oppressive and that, had the warrant

---

[92] *Draper, Petr (No 1)* 1996 SLT 617 at 622 per Lord Justice-Clerk Ross. See also *Draper, Petr (No 2)* 1997 SLT 815.

[93] For excessive sentences in the context of contempt of court in criminal proceedings, see pp 221–22.

[94] 2000 SCCR 617. See, similarly, *Fitchett v McFadyen* 2000 GWD 34-1312; and *Moscrop, Petr* 1999 GWD 16-758. For failure to establish excessiveness, see *Tulloch, Petr* 1999 GWD 31-1490. *Fitchett, Moscrop* and *Tulloch* each involved breach of a supervised attendance order.

[95] 2002 SLT 1175.

for his apprehension been promptly executed, his sentence would by that time have already been served. The Court noted that the accused was attempting to rebuild his life and that the inaction on the part of the authorities had put the accused in a position of anxiety for a year whilst he awaited the execution of his warrant. It therefore suspended the warrant and quashed the sentence on the basis that the authorities had acted oppressively.

Beglan was followed in a case in which a warrant for apprehension of the accused had failed to be executed 15 months after it was issued.[96] Even though the accused's solicitors had not tried to pursue the authorities in the manner that occurred in *Beglan*, the Court held that the delay on the part of the Crown was unreasonable and oppressive, and the circumstances were prejudicial and unfair to the accused in that, had the warrant been promptly executed, she would have already completed her sentence by the time of the petition. The Court therefore exercised its *nobile officium* to suspend the warrant.

It has been suggested, however, that mere administrative delay would not in itself justify exercise of the *nobile officium*, even where a petitioner averred inordinate delay on the part of the district court which had resulted in him being deprived of the advantage of a concurrent sentence.[97] There have also been unsuccessful attempts to challenge orders of forfeiture, essentially averring that the true owner had acted in good faith and had no control over the property used in the commission of an offence. These have failed on their merits, but not on point of competency.[98]

---

[96] *Waugh v HM Advocate* 2005 SLT 451.

[97] *Bradshaw, Petr* 1993 SCCR 94.

[98] *Woods, Petr* 1994 SLT 197; *Donald, Petr* 1996 JC 22; *Carroll, Petr* 1997 SLT 481. See also *Lloyds and Scottish Finance Ltd v HM Advocate* discussed at p 192, which concerned forfeiture in the context of a statutory omission. It is necessary to petition the *nobile officium* in the context of certain offences where the forfeited property is a vehicle, whereas there are now statutory channels for claiming other forfeited property: see the Proceeds of Crime (Scotland) Act 1995, ss 25–27; the Road Traffic Offenders Act 1988, s 33A; and *Renton and Brown's Criminal Procedure* paras 23-81, 23-82 and 23-94.

9.4 Bias, fairness and natural justice

The *nobile officium* has been invoked in the context of bias, fairness and natural justice. Petition may be competently made on the basis of an averment of bias on the part of a judge or doubts about the impartiality of proceedings.[99]

Petition was successfully made where an accused was denied an opportunity of making representations to a sheriff who ordered that a warrant for an alternative sentence of imprisonment should not be issued whilst the accused was in custody. The Court also found that there had been a failure to observe statutory procedure with regard to the accused.[100] It was held in *Hoekstra v HM Advocate (No 2)*[101] that where a judge who had heard an appeal could not properly be regarded as impartial, it would be necessary to treat his interlocutor as invalid and, there being no interlocutor which could be regarded as final and conclusive in terms of section 124(2) of the Criminal Procedure (Scotland) Act 1995, the appropriate course would be to set aside the purported interlocutor in exercise of the *nobile officium*.[102] The Court has also used its *nobile officium* to allow an accused to withdraw guilty pleas where questions over the impartiality of a judge were at issue,[103] and to review a decision to refuse leave to appeal where the judges sifting the appeal failed to provide adequate reasons.[104] A petition was unsuccessful where second sift judges refused an appeal and stated that they agreed with the reasons of the first judge, and

---

[99] *Mellors, Petr* 2003 SLT 479; *Bryceland, Petr* 2006 SCCR 291. These petitions were refused, but not on point of competency. For a borderline theatrical episode concerning the *nobile officium* and alleged bias or lack of impartiality on the part of judges, see *Robbie the Pict v HM Advocate* 2003 JC 78.

[100] *Nash, Petr* 1992 SLT 147. In *Houldsworth v HM Advocate* 2006 JC 174, a petition which complained *inter alia* of the denial of the right to an oral hearing was refused as unnecessary.

[101] 2000 JC 391.

[102] See *Renton and Brown's Criminal Procedure* at para 34-06.

[103] *Rimmer, Petr* 2002 SCCR 1. For a discussion of *Rimmer*, see *Kalyanjee v HM Advocate* 2014 SLT 740 at 752.

[104] *Akram v HM Advocate* 2009 SLT 805.

it was averred that reasons had not been given for the decision of the second sift judges.[105]

The *nobile officium* has been exercised to order the restoration of a legal aid certificate where an accused's legal aid was purportedly withdrawn by the sheriff under rule 164(1) of the Act of Adjournal (Consolidation) 1988, but without giving the accused an opportunity to be heard.[106] Similarly, the *nobile officium* was exercised to restore an accused's legal aid certificate purportedly withdrawn by the sheriff under rule 33.3(1)(a) of the Act of Adjournal (Criminal Procedure Rules) 1996 where the sheriff refused to hear representations from the accused's solicitor.[107] The jurisdiction was used to restore a legal aid certificate where a sheriff withdrew it after having suggested that he would do so if the accused persisted in making a bail application – his decision to withdraw the certificate was vitiated by taking into consideration the accused's intention to apply for bail.[108] In addition, directions for the withdrawal of legal aid under rule 33.3(1)(a) were recalled where one accused's refusal to explain to the solicitor his reason for failure to attend an intermediate diet was based on the explicit advice of his solicitor, and where the sheriff had, for various reasons, failed to reasonably exercise his discretion with regard to another accused.[109] The Court also exercised its *nobile officium* to restore a legal aid certificate where a sheriff had purported to retrospectively withdraw legal aid entitlement.[110]

Another aspect of fairness is the extent to which a jury may not be prejudiced. Where a juror was intimidated and upset by the accused staring at her, and made comments about this in the presence of other jurors, there were concerns that the whole jury might be prejudiced. The trial judge took the view that he was

---

[105] *McSorley, Petr* 2005 SCCR 508.
[106] *Lamont, Petr* 1995 SLT 566.
[107] *Ness, Petr* 1999 SLT 214. See also *Brannigan, Petr* 1999 SLT 679.
[108] *Anderson, Petr* 1998 SLT 101.
[109] *Shaw, Petr* 1999 SLT 215. See also *Potter, Petr* 1999 GWD 12-569.
[110] *Reid, Petr* 1999 SLT 212.

not entitled under the relevant statutory provision to discharge an entire jury. However, on the accused's petition to the *nobile officium*, the Court regarded the circumstances as extraordinary and unforeseen, and directed the judge to excuse the 15 jurors under that statutory provision and to select and empanel a further 15 jurors.[111]

In *McIntosh, Petr*,[112] a petition was successfully presented to the *nobile officium* for reversal of a decision which had refused to grant declarator that the Crown had no power to invite the court to make an assumption set out in a particular section of the Proceeds of Crime (Scotland) Act 1995. The Lord Advocate was seeking to act in a way that was incompatible with the accused's Convention rights by reference to the Scotland Act 1998. The Court granted the prayer of the petition and pronounced declarator that the Crown had no power to make said assumption.[113]

The *nobile officium* has, however, been unsuccessfully petitioned to incorporate a finding of the European Court of Human Rights (ECtHR) into domestic process so far as it affected a particular accused. In *Granger, Petr*,[114] the petitioner had been convicted of perjury in 1985 and, on subsequent application to the ECtHR, it was held that the refusal of legal aid for his appeal had been in breach of his Convention rights. The individual then requested the Secretary of State to remit the case back to the High Court in order to seek a quashing of the conviction, a request which was refused. He thereafter requested that the SCCRC examine his case with a view to its being referred back to the High Court, a request which was likewise refused. He therefore petitioned the *nobile officium* seeking for his conviction to be set aside in view of the ECtHR ruling. Lord Hardie considered the petition incompetent, as section 124(2) of the Criminal Procedure (Scotland) Act 1995 (as amended) prohibited review by any

---

[111] *Hughes, Petr* 1990 SLT 142.
[112] 2001 JC 78.
[113] However, the Crown's appeal to the Privy Council was successful: *McIntosh, Petr* 2001 SC (PC) 89.
[114] 2001 JC 183.

court of an interlocutor or sentence of the High Court, except where cases were referred to it by the SCCRC under the Act or where a case was appealed to the Judicial Committee of the Privy Council under the Scotland Act 1998.[115] The petitioner failed to bring himself within these exceptions and so the petition was incompetent and accordingly refused.

9.5 Errors

The *nobile officium* can be used to correct errors in course of criminal process. It has been used to correct an interlocutor of the High Court where the clerk of court had erroneously omitted to refer to leave being granted to bring a new prosecution, although it had been pronounced in open court and took effect as such.[116] The jurisdiction was also confirmed as competently used to replace a record copy indictment with a substitute indictment where the original had been inadvertently destroyed.[117]

In the unreported case of *McLellan v HM Advocate*,[118] the *nobile officium* was successfully petitioned to substitute a correct for an erroneous penalty. Eight penalty points – which was regarded as the minimum applicable – had been imposed for a road traffic offence. It was discovered after the appeal, however, that the minimum number of penalty points for the offence in question was only three. The High Court, in exercise of its *nobile officium*, quashed the decision of the appeal court and imposed three penalty points in place of the previous eight.

The Court confirmed that the *nobile officium* could be used to amend a complaint by inserting the correct name, address and

---

[115] It was nevertheless stated in the context of s 124(2) that "[i]t is conceivable that there could be extraordinary circumstances in which an appellant who was left without a remedy could invoke the *nobile officium*: for example, when by reason of a procedural mishap, his appeal was mistakenly refused": *Cobanoglu, Petr* 2012 SCL 604 at 609 per Lord Justice-Clerk Gill.

[116] *Heywood, Petr* 1998 SLT 1417. See also *Harris v HM Advocate* 2010 SCCR 50.

[117] *Bryceland, Petr* 2003 SLT 54.

[118] 4 Dec 1990, High Court of Justiciary.

date of birth of an accused following his brother's imitation of his identity throughout proceedings.[119]

9.6 Other procedural challenges

There have been challenges to decisions and exercises of discretion by way of the *nobile officium* regarding the production, availability or admission of evidence. In *Davies, Petr*,[120] the accused sought for a pair of gloves to be made available by the procurator fiscal to an expert for examination, to assist with the proper preparation of his defence. The procurator fiscal refused to make the gloves available, and the sheriff refused a motion seeking warrant for their examination. The accused successfully petitioned the *nobile officium* for the Court to grant warrant for their examination.

It was competent for a pannel to seek recovery of evidence by way of the *nobile officium* to assist with the preparation of his defence.[121] Likewise, it was competent to petition the Court to order a shorthand writer to produce notes of evidence taken during a trial, where the initial trial was deserted *pro loco et tempore* due to the illness of the accused, and a new indictment was served once the accused had recovered from illness.[122] The *nobile officium* has been used to grant warrant for a child victim of assault to be medically examined at the instance of the accused,[123] and it may also be used to challenge the validity of a search warrant.[124]

In *Windsor, Petr*,[125] the petitioner had been convicted of attempted murder. His appeal failed. Additional evidence was

---

[119] *Cox v Normand* 1992 SLT 412.

[120] 1973 SLT (Notes) 36.

[121] *McLeod v HM Advocate (No 2)* 1998 JC 67. The petition was refused on its merits. On a media entity attempting to use the *nobile officium* as a means of challenging a refusal by the Lord Advocate to make available copies of Crown productions, see *British Broadcasting Corporation, Applicants* 2012 SCL 347.

[122] *Muirhead, Petr* 1983 SLT 208. The petition was refused on its merits.

[123] *K, Petr* 1986 SCCR 709.

[124] *HM Advocate v Rae* 1992 SCCR 1.

[125] 1994 JC 41.

alleged to come to light thereafter, and on its strength the petitioner applied to the Secretary of State for Scotland for exercise of the royal prerogative of mercy or referral to the High Court for fresh consideration of the case. Those requests were declined. The petitioner thereafter presented a petition to the *nobile officium* praying for it to receive and consider the additional evidence with a view to quashing his conviction. Lord Justice-Clerk Ross noted that it had:

> been recognised that the court may exercise its *nobile officium* in order to alter or correct an order which has been pronounced by the court in the exercise of its appellate jurisdiction in cases where the court has exceeded its powers.[126]

However, there was no allegation that the court dismissing the appeal had exceeded its powers. The terms of the Criminal Procedure (Scotland) Act 1975 were such that the judgment of the High Court was final and conclusive when dismissing the appeal and affirming the verdict of the trial court. The only way in which the matter could be reopened was if the Secretary of State referred the case to the High Court under section 263 of the Criminal Procedure (Scotland) Act 1975, which he had declined to do. In addition, the Court did not accept the petitioner's averment that the emergence of new evidence constituted extraordinary and unforeseen circumstances, not least because there were provisions in the Act dealing with newly emerging evidence. Lord Justice-Clerk Ross regarded the case as similar to *McCallum, Petr*,[127] over which he also presided, where it was held that recourse to the Secretary of State was the only way to seek to have the Court consider new evidence.[128] The *nobile officium* was not available where Parliament had expressly provided a remedy, including when that remedy had been exhausted. The Court therefore dismissed the petition as incompetent.

---

[126] At 49 per Lord Justice-Clerk Ross.

[127] 1992 GWD 36-2099.

[128] An application could now be made to the SCCRC, established in 1999.

It was competent for the *nobile officium* to be petitioned for the destruction of evidence. A witness had appeared before a sheriff for precognition on oath with regard to a particular trial, and afterwards read over his recorded statement and signed it. He then requested that the procurator fiscal destroy the precognition. Unable to have that request satisfied, and averring that there was no other remedy available to him, he petitioned the *nobile officium* for the Court to ordain the Lord Advocate to produce the petitioner's precognition and to have it destroyed prior to the trial. The petition was refused on its merits.[129]

It was also competent to petition the *nobile officium* for the Court to ordain the Governor of HM Prison, Barlinnie, to make facilities available for the administration of sodium pentothal and methedrine, a so-called "truth drug", and for questioning the petitioner under those conditions as a means to him establishing his innocence. The Court was concerned about the implications this would have for the law of evidence and refused the petition on that basis, but there was no objection made on point of competency.[130]

The *nobile officium* has been used to admit an accused to bail for a mixture of more procedural[131] and substantive[132] reasons. The circumstances in which petitions have been made to this end have been varied, and the Court may attach conditions when exercising its *nobile officium* to admit a person to bail.[133] As with any petition to the *nobile officium*, one seeking admission to bail should, where possible, be made in conformance with relevant time limits. Where, for example, an accused sought to appeal against a refusal

---

[129] *Coll, Petr* 1977 JC 29.

[130] *Meehan v HM Advocate* 1970 JC 11.

[131] *Schiavone, Petr* 1992 SLT 1059.

[132] *Welsh, Petr* 1992 SLT 903. See also *Boyle, Petr* 1993 SCCR 251, in which the Court granted bail in exercise of the *nobile officium* where an accused had been in custody for around 15 months whilst various procedural intricacies were navigated, with a fresh diet having been adjourned to a later date. By contrast, the stage had not yet been reached in *McLeod, Petr* 1993 SCCR 601 when it would be appropriate to admit the accused to bail.

[133] As in *Y, Petr* 1995 SCCR 457.

to grant interim liberation out of time, his subsequent petition to the *nobile officium* for admission to bail was dismissed due to a failure to observe the statutory time limit.[134] The Court may, however, find justification for granting bail where the time limit has not been observed, such as in the event of an accused not being made aware of a refusal of bail in time to appeal, due to a misunderstanding between legal representatives.[135]

There have been unsuccessful, yet competent, petitions to the *nobile officium* with regard to witnesses. These have included a prospective Crown witness, who had absconded and was subsequently apprehended and detained in prison, petitioning for suspension and liberation.[136] In a partially unsuccessful petition, a complainer in relation to whom warrant for apprehension had been obtained prayed for the warrant to be quashed and his liberty granted. The petition was refused, but the Court downward adjusted the security for the complainer's appearance at future diets in accordance with his means.[137] By contrast, a petition was refused as incompetent where an essential defence witness was absent from trial and the accused moved the sheriff to desert *pro loco et tempore*. The sheriff refused to do so, and the accused petitioned the *nobile officium* for the High Court to discharge the trial in the sheriff court due to the absence of the essential witness. The Court held that the absence of a witness was not a sufficiently extraordinary and unforeseen circumstance to justify resort to the *nobile officium*, and that the accused had a remedy in proceeding to trial and, if convicted, appealing against the refusal of the sheriff to desert *pro loco et tempore*.[138]

---

[134] *Fenton, Petr* 1982 SLT 164. It is, however, unclear from the reported excerpt of the opinion whether the petition was incompetent, or whether it was competent but refused on its merits, for the Court stated that the petition was "not justified" and accordingly dismissed.

[135] *Scott, Petr* 1992 SCCR 102.

[136] *Stallworth v HM Advocate* 1978 SLT 93. See also *Gerrard, Petr* 1984 SLT 108.

[137] *Sargeant, Petr* 1990 SLT 286.

[138] *Wilson, Petr* 1992 SLT 145. The Court distinguished the case of *Vetters v HM Advocate* 1943 JC 138, as one in which, *inter alia*, no point of competency was taken. It regarded that case as concerning a petition to the *nobile officium*, though the case reports do not designate it as such.

Several cases have arisen with regard to solicitors' applications at the end of a trial for certification that the case had necessarily been one of exceptional length, complexity or difficulty for the purposes of legal aid fees. A solicitor's application for a certificate under article 13(2) of the Act of Adjournal (Criminal Legal Aid Fees) 1964 (as amended) was refused in *Heslin, Petr*.[139] The solicitor's petition to the *nobile officium* for review of that refusal was held to be incompetent on the basis that the trial judge had exercised his discretion as conferred by the provision in question.

Heslin was distinguished in *Rae, Petr*.[140] A solicitor petitioned the *nobile officium* to grant a certificate following its refusal by the trial judge. The Court adopted the view that in this case the trial judge had not at all exercised his discretion on the application, and that this was exceptional and constituted oppression resulting in injustice. The case was therefore distinguishable as the trial judge must actually have exercised his discretion. The Court therefore remitted to the trial judge to dispose of the application on its merits.

Where an application for certification was sought with regard to a trial which never took place and the application was refused as incompetent, the Court in a petition to its *nobile officium* declined to regard the lack of provision for those circumstances in the Act of Adjournal as one of omission due to oversight, nor that the circumstances were extraordinary or unforeseen. The petition was refused, even though the Court expressed a hope that certain proposed amendments to the Act of Adjournal might be implemented.[141]

Where the conduct of a solicitor had in part resulted in the exceptional length of a trial, and the sheriff refused an application for certification on that basis, the Court – noting both *Heslin* and *Rae* – regarded the sheriff as having exercised her discretion in the application, and refused a petition to the *nobile officium*

---

[139] 1973 SLT (Notes) 56.
[140] 1982 SLT 233.
[141] *Harper, Petr* 1982 SLT 232.

as incompetent.[142] Remaining with the topic of legal aid, a stipendiary magistrate had legitimately exercised his discretion to refuse legal aid by taking all relevant factors into consideration. The High Court refused a petition for recall of the decision to refuse legal aid even where it regarded the refusal of legal aid as wrong in the circumstances.[143]

Several cases have arisen with regard to abandonment of appeals. In *Ferguson v HM Advocate*,[144] an accused lodged a note of application for leave to appeal against a sentence of 21 months' imprisonment in terms of section 233 of the Criminal Procedure (Scotland) Act 1975. Section 244 provided a mechanism for abandoning the application; however, the accused did not take advantage of this. On the morning of the trial, he instructed counsel to abandon the application. Counsel moved the Court for leave to abandon, but the Court refused to do so and increased the accused's sentence to four years' imprisonment. The accused petitioned the *nobile officium* praying for recall of the sentence as incompetent, oppressive and unfair. The Court considered that the circumstances did not fall within the category of extraordinary or unforeseen occurrences. Although that alone would be a ground for dismissing the petition, the Court articulated the further point that, once a case had called (as this case had), the Court became "master of the procedure".[145] Any motion made thereafter fell to be dispensed with in terms of the Court's discretion. The statutory mechanism had not been utilised, and as such the petition was dismissed. *Ferguson* was later regarded as having changed the principle of law that an appellant was entitled to abandon his appeal at any time up to the point when his argument was tendered to the court.[146]

---

[142] *Mullane, Petr* 1990 SLT 673.
[143] *McLachlan, Petr* 1987 SCCR 195.
[144] 1980 JC 27.
[145] At 30 per Lord Justice-Clerk Wheatley.
[146] See *Hendry v HM Advocate* 2006 JC 129 at 132 per Lord Justice-Clerk Gill.

Where an accused sought to withdraw a notice of abandonment by petition to the *nobile officium*, it was held that the accused had utilised statutory machinery to abandon his appeal and finality attached to the decision to abandon.[147] However, the abandonment of an appeal has not prevented the Court from reviving or reinstating the appeal in other circumstances. Where an accused abandoned an appeal without taking legal advice, but apparently relying on the advice of his mother, the Court was persuaded that the circumstances were sufficiently extraordinary and unforeseen to permit review of the excessive sentence against which appeal was originally sought, even though there was no statutory means of reviewing the sentence post-abandonment.[148] Likewise, where an accused had abandoned an appeal on the advice of his solicitor, though without being advised that he was entitled to obtain a second opinion or to represent himself, the Court regarded these circumstances as sufficiently exceptional and unforeseen in which to allow reinstatement of the appeal, adding that this did not conflict with statute and that it was "in the interests of justice" to reinstate the appeal.[149] In *Manson, Petr*,[150] an accused who was found guilty of certain charges sought leave to pursue a second appeal out of time, his first appeal having been dismissed for want of insistence. The Court was unpersuaded by the accused's reasons for failure to appear at the hearing of the first appeal, and his petition to the *nobile officium* was accordingly dismissed.

---

[147] *Young, Petr* 1994 SLT 269.
[148] *Mathieson, Petr* 1980 SLT (Notes) 74.
[149] *McIntosh, Petr* 1995 SLT 796. An apparently contrary position was taken in *Mitchell v HM Advocate* [2010] HCJAC 54, where Lord Justice-Clerk Gill stated that, where a proposed ground of appeal had been formally abandoned on senior counsel's advice, "[t]he *nobile officium* cannot be invoked to allow the reinstatement of that ground of appeal on the basis that the advice was erroneous" (at para [15]). On the requirement to invoke the review proceedings of the SCCRC prior to seeking exercise of the *nobile officium*, and on the limits of extraordinary circumstances in this context, see *McWilliam, Petr* 2002 SLT 972, and also p 194, fn 65.
[150] 1991 SLT 96.

In *McGregor, Petr*,[151] it was considered incompetent for an offender to make an ordinary appeal against a sheriff's decision to revoke a supervised attendance order and impose a sentence of three months' imprisonment. The Court was satisfied that a petition to the *nobile officium* was a competent and appropriate way of reviewing the sentence as though it had been an appeal under the relevant statutory provision. The "appeal" was successful.

The *nobile officium* has received petitions in response to, or in prevention of, miscarriages of justice. In the case of *McCloy, Petr*,[152] a boy had been charged along with two others of forcing open lockfast cars and stealing items therefrom. He was convicted despite pleading not guilty. He asked for a stated case, with the magistrate explaining that he believed the evidence of one of the co-accused who had pleaded guilty. However, that co-accused had in fact not given evidence. The accused was prevented from appealing by bill of suspension due to section 68(2) of the Summary Jurisdiction (Scotland) Act 1954 and therefore petitioned the *nobile officium*. Counsel for the petitioner, the Lord Advocate and the police fiscal (the case had originally been heard in the Central Police Court) agreed that there had been a manifest miscarriage of justice, and the Court, finding the circumstances to be special and there being no other remedy available to the petitioner, granted the prayer of the petition by quashing the conviction.

The case of *Anderson v HM Advocate* was an unsuccessful attempt to allege a miscarriage of justice on the basis that the sheriff had failed in his appreciation of the evidence in his preparation of a stated case.[153] The petition failed on a lack of extraordinary or unforeseen circumstances, and was in any event rendered incompetent by the existence of a statutory remedy which had been unsuccessfully utilised.

---

[151] 1999 SLT 676.

[152] *McCloy, Petr* 1971 SLT (Notes) 32. See also *Anderson v HM Advocate* 1974 SLT 239 at 241–42 per Lord Justice-General Emslie.

[153] 1974 SLT 239. See also *Renton and Brown's Criminal Procedure* at para 31-31.

Some final miscellaneous procedural matters fall for consideration. An unfortunate situation arose in *Strock, Petr*,[154] in which a petition was made to the *nobile officium* upon bad directions by the court administration. A pannel sought return of over £14,000 belonging to him under section 270(2) of the Criminal Procedure (Scotland) Act 1975. His solicitors applied to the Clerk of Justiciary for release of the money under section 270(2). The Justiciary Office replied by letter that the provisions of section 270 would not apply in the pannel's case, and suggested that the only way to proceed was by the *nobile officium*. The pannel therefore petitioned the *nobile officium*, however the Court held that section 270 did apply to the petitioner, and accordingly the petition was incompetent because he had at his disposal another remedy or procedure whereby the money could be recovered. This would not be the last case in which erroneous directions were given by the court administration,[155] though in *Love* the Court ultimately entertained the matter in question. The decision in *Strock* is understandable from the perspective of the Court not permitting the *nobile officium* to be used where there exists a statutory remedy for utilisation – thus upholding one of the central principles of the *nobile officium* as a remedy of last resort. However, questions arise when a petitioner bears the burden of taking inappropriate or incorrect action on the basis of representations made by the court administration. There is at least a case for arguing that the equitable nature of the *nobile officium* would justify a more lenient approach to a petitioner in these circumstances, and the Court could conceivably have converted proceedings into an application under section 270(2).[156]

---

[154] 1996 JC 125.

[155] See also *Love, Petr* 1998 JC 85; and, in the Court of Session, *Institute of Chartered Accountants of Scotland, Petrs* 2002 SLT 921.

[156] There was already authority for the High Court treating a petition to the *nobile officium* as a bail appeal: *Gilchrist, Petr* 1991 JC 160. It would later go on to treat a petition to the *nobile officium* as a bill of suspension: *Ward v Brown* 2000 SLT 1355; *Crane v HM Advocate* 2006 JC 190. There was also authority in the Court of Session for the effective conversion of a petition to the *nobile officium* to a statutory application: *Stark's Trs, Petrs* 1932 SC 653.

The Court opined in *Clarke v Fraser*[157] that a petition to the *nobile officium* may have been a way of dealing with a situation in which a district court was unable to properly convene due to heavy snowfall preventing the justice, clerk and procurator fiscal from reaching the court, and the justice and the clerk subsequently purporting to conduct and adjourn proceedings by telephone. The Court did not elaborate, however, on how the *nobile officium* might be used in this scenario.

The *nobile officium* demonstrated capacity for application in the area of extradition and foreign affairs. The jurisdiction could potentially be used to challenge removal from the jurisdiction on fear of being tortured or killed in a foreign jurisdiction;[158] however this would nowadays more likely be pursued on human rights grounds. It was competent for a foreign citizen to petition the *nobile officium* in application for discharge from commitment for extradition under section 11(3) of the Extradition Act 1989;[159] however, a petition averring that the status of a person subject to an extradition order had changed, rendering the application for extradition invalid, was dismissed as incompetent and an abuse of process.[160]

The *nobile officium* appears to have been used to remand an accused suffering from a mental disorder at a state hospital, at the accused's own instance.[161] The statutory power of the Court to exclude persons from proceedings and to prohibit publication relating to proceedings, in the context of offenders rendering assistance to investigations and prosecutions, extends to proceedings under a petition to the *nobile officium*.[162] It was confirmed that the refusal by a single judge to grant warrant for service of a petition to the *nobile officium* is not susceptible to appeal.[163]

---

[157] 2002 SLT 745.

[158] *Haimovici, Petr* 1953 SLT (Notes) 49.

[159] *Triplis, Petr* 1998 SLT 186. The petition was refused on its merits.

[160] *La Torre v Lord Advocate and Scottish Ministers* 2008 JC 72.

[161] *Johnstone v HM Advocate* 2013 SLT 1115 at 1117.

[162] Police, Public Order and Criminal Justice (Scotland) Act 2006, ss 93 and 96.

[163] *Telford v HM Advocate* 2012 SLT 911 at 913 per Lord Carloway.

9.7 Contempt of court

The *nobile officium* may be competently invoked to challenge a finding of contempt of court in criminal proceedings.[164] Whilst this may also be capable of achievement by bringing a bill of suspension,[165] it is not always competent to do so. For example, section 130 of the Criminal Procedure (Scotland) Act 1995 provides that it shall not be competent to appeal to the High Court by bill of suspension against any conviction, sentence, judgment or order pronounced in proceedings on indictment in the sheriff court.[166] It had already been confirmed that a petition to the *nobile officium* is the only route by which appeals in solemn criminal proceedings in cases of contempt of court may be remedied.[167] Nevertheless, as a bill of suspension is only competent in relation to inferior courts, the *nobile officium* is the appropriate route for challenging a finding of contempt in the High Court.[168] It should be noted that even though the *nobile officium* is typically capable of invocation only where there are extraordinary or unforeseen circumstances, the jurisdiction is, in the circumstances outlined, a standard means of appealing against a sentence for contempt of court. As

[164] For contempt of court in civil proceedings, see Section 8.3. Petitions regarding contempt of court in civil proceedings should be brought in the Court of Session; eg, in *Cordiner, Petr* 1973 JC 16, the High Court held that it was "wholly incompetent" to petition its *nobile officium* with regard to contempt of court in an action of divorce in the Court of Session, for which a sentence of three years' imprisonment had been imposed.

[165] *Mayer v HM Advocate* 2005 JC 121 at 134.

[166] See also *George Outram & Co Ltd v Lees* 1992 JC 17.

[167] *Report of the Committee on Contempt of Court* (Cmnd 5794, 1974) ("Phillimore Report"). This view was confirmed in *Express Newspapers plc, Petrs* 1999 JC 176 at 180. The Court noted in that case that Parliament had not chosen to substitute any statutory procedure for the *nobile officium* as a means of appealing in such cases when it came to enact the Contempt of Court Act 1981, even although it would have been aware of the recommendation that such appeals be taken by note of appeal. The Court also noted that the position had not been changed in subsequent criminal procedure legislation.

[168] See *Wylie v HM Advocate* 1966 SLT 149; and *George Outram & Co Ltd v Lees* 1992 JC 17.

noted by the Court, "[o]ne might hesitate to describe th[at] situation ... as 'unforeseen'".[169]

In *Kemp, Petrs*,[170] a trial judge had found newspaper editors guilty of contempt of court, but issued admonitions. The relevant newspaper entities petitioned the *nobile officium* for recall of the findings by the trial judge that they were guilty of contempt. The High Court was persuaded that contempt had not been committed, not least because the articles in question were simple narratives of fact. The Court exercised its *nobile officium* to recall the findings of the trial judge that the petitioners were in contempt, and quashed the admonitions imposed on each of the petitioners.

Similarly, the *nobile officium* was exercised in *Cox and Griffiths, Petrs*[171] to quash a finding of contempt. A newspaper had reported that a number of high risk prisoners were being moved from a prison under armed police guard. The following week, most of those prisoners appeared for trial in the High Court. Prior to the empanelling of the jury, counsel for one of the pannels submitted that the newspaper article amounted to contempt of court under the strict liability rule in the Contempt of Court Act 1981. The trial judge summoned the duty editor of the newspaper and the author of the article, found them in contempt and imposed fines. The High Court held that the threshold for the application of strict liability had not been satisfied, and quashed the finding of contempt.

In *Adams, Petr*,[172] the news editor of a radio programme had been fined £20,000 for contempt of court. Upon the editor's petition to the *nobile officium*, the Court regarded the trial judge as having misunderstood the degree of culpability attaching to the editor, and whilst leaving the finding of contempt in place – as accepted by the petitioner – found the penalty which had

---

[169] *Express Newspapers plc, Petrs* 1999 JC 176 at 180.

[170] 1982 JC 29.

[171] 2002 SLT 745.

[172] 1987 SCCR 650.

been imposed to be unjustifiable and accordingly quashed the penalty.[173]

In addition to the *nobile officium* being capable of competent invocation to quash a finding of contempt of court, it has also been competently petitioned to *obtain* a finding of contempt, and to prevent or restrain the future publication or broadcast of material. An example of a successful petition in that regard is found in *Atkins v London Weekend Television*,[174] in which a television programme had broadcast photographs of a woman who was awaiting trial for assaulting a child (who later died) to the danger of her life. These were broadcast the day before the trial, along with photographs of the victim and Edinburgh Sheriff Court where the trial was due to take place. The accused, who had pleaded not guilty, presented a motion to adjourn the trial diet to a later date, and this was granted by the sheriff. The diet was not called on the appointed date and the indictment fell. The accused petitioned the *nobile officium* to prohibit the broadcaster from broadcasting any programme calculated to prejudice the future trial of the petitioner. The Court was satisfied that the way in which the programme covered the petitioner's impending trial, and possible connotations of wrongdoing by discussing the impending trial in the context of other controversial cases, was highly likely to prejudice the petitioner's prospects of a fair and impartial trial. The programme's coverage of the case constituted a material interference with the due and proper administration of criminal justice. The Court found the broadcast in contempt of court, and granted the prayer of the petition in addition to imposing fines on the company, its managing director, the editor and producer.

The *nobile officium* may also be exercised to prohibit the broadcast of a programme where there is more than a minimal risk of prejudice to the trial of accused persons, even where

---

[173] For an unsuccessful, though competent, petition to the *nobile officium* by newspaper entities found in contempt of court, see *Scottish Daily Record and Sunday Mail Ltd v Thomson* 2009 JC 175.

[174] 1978 JC 48.

the programme would not formally constitute contempt of court.[175]

Section 4(2) of the Contempt of Court Act 1981 provides that a court may order that the publication of any proceedings be postponed for such period as the court thinks necessary, where it appears necessary for avoiding a substantial risk of prejudice to the administration of justice. An order of that kind was made in proceedings leading to *Scottish Daily Record and Sunday Mail Ltd, Petrs*.[176] Certain media entities sought recall or variation of that order from a different trial judge, but this was refused as incompetent. The media entities then petitioned the *nobile officium* for recall or variation of the original order (but not the refusal of recall). The Court held that this failure to challenge the refusal of recall was fatal, as the petitioners had not availed themselves of an available remedy. Section 4(2) of the Act did not, in the view of the Court, prevent a court from reviewing the terms of an order made under that section, thus a remedial course was available. The petition was therefore dismissed as incompetent. Nevertheless, an order made under section 4(2) may be recalled by petition to the *nobile officium*.[177]

An example of an unsuccessful attempt to obtain a finding of contempt by petition to the *nobile officium* is furnished in *Megrahi v Times Newspapers*.[178] Abdelbaset al-Megrahi and another prayed for a finding that a newspaper publisher, its editor and a journalist be found in contempt for a particular article and editorial published in *The Sunday Times* newspaper. The Court dismissed the petition on several grounds, but not on point of competency.

Another petition concerning al-Megrahi was presented by the BBC and others for the Court to give its consent to their broadcasting proceedings of the Lockerbie trial from the special sitting of the High Court in the Netherlands. The petition was

---

[175] *Muir v British Broadcasting Corporation* 1997 SLT 425.
[176] 1999 SLT 624.
[177] *BBC, Petrs (No 3)* 2002 JC 27.
[178] 2000 JC 22.

refused, but the Court was satisfied that it was competently presented.[179]

Cases on contempt of court need not, of course, involve broadcast or print media. A finding of contempt was recalled in *Blair-Wilson, Petr*,[180] in which a sheriff had found a solicitor in contempt for his alleged conduct during a sheriff and jury trial. The solicitor petitioned the *nobile officium* for recall of the finding of contempt, and the Court agreed that whilst a sheriff was entitled to find a solicitor in contempt, there was nothing justifying such a finding in the present case, and the sheriff had acted inappropriately. The Court therefore granted recall.

A finding of contempt was successfully quashed in *Mayer v HM Advocate*,[181] in which a member of the Faculty of Advocates petitioned the *nobile officium*. The Court took the view that the procedures adopted in the trial court were flawed, thus granting the prayer of the petition and remitting to a different judge to consider the issue of the petitioner's disputed contempt. The *nobile officium* has also been used to set aside a finding of contempt where a sheriff had failed to follow certain procedural safeguards.[182]

In addition, the *nobile officium* has been used to quash a sentence for contempt which, even though it was the statutory maximum, was considered by the Court to be excessive in the circumstances, with the Court substituting a reduced sentence.[183] Sentences imposed for contempt have also been reduced on the ground that they were excessive,[184] and the jurisdiction has been

---

[179] *BBC, Petrs (No 1)* 2000 JC 419 at 425 per Lord Macfadyen. See also *BBC, Petrs (No 2)* 2000 JC 521.

[180] 1997 SLT 621.

[181] 2005 JC 121.

[182] *Martin v HM Advocate* [2014] HCJAC 15.

[183] *Cowan v HM Advocate* 2009 SLT 434. Though see a suggestion that it might not necessarily follow that the Court can exercise its *nobile officium* to take upon itself a statutory function in substituting a shorter sentence in place of a quashed sentence: *Flynn v HM Advocate* 2003 JC 153 at 177–78 per Lord Justice-General Cullen.

[184] *Smith, Petr* 1987 SCCR 726; *McInally, Petr* 1993 SCCR 212; *Gallagher, Petr* 1996 SCCR 833.

used to quash an excessive sentence and substitute an admonition in its place.[185] Some petitions of this kind have been refused on their merits.[186]

Finally, as noted, the Court has the discretionary power to "convert" proceedings to or from those under its *nobile officium*. In one example of this with regard to contempt of court,[187] persons found guilty of the offence brought a bill of suspension in the High Court. This was held to be incompetent by virtue of section 230 of the Criminal Procedure (Scotland) Act 1975. However, the Court treated proceedings as though they were a petition to the *nobile officium*, and on that basis recalled the finding of contempt and quashed the fines which had been imposed. In this way, the substantive crave of the bill was satisfied.

---

[185] *C v HM Advocate* 2011 SLT 22.

[186] *McNeilage, Petr* 1999 SCCR 471. For cases in which petitions presented by individuals against findings of contempt of court were held competent, though refused on their merits, see *Wylie v HM Advocate* 1966 SLT 149; *Robertson and Gough v HM Advocate* 2008 JC 146; *Haney v HM Advocate* [2012] HCJAC 144; *Bowie v Procurator Fiscal* [2014] HCJAC 65; and *Hood v HM Advocate* [2014] HCJAC 85.

[187] *George Outram & Co Ltd v Lees* 1992 JC 17.

CHAPTER 10

LIMITATIONS

10.1 Scope of the *nobile officium*

The general scope of the *nobile officium* was considered in the introduction, and has been more specifically refined through the substantive chapters. Some additional observations will be made on the scope of the *nobile officium* in the context of the parameters of, and limitations on, the jurisdiction.

It is important to note the discretionary nature of the *nobile officium*. Notwithstanding the discussion below on precedent,[1] the *nobile officium* cannot be petitioned as of right. The court is not bound to decide on petitions in the same manner as in previous cases. It has been stated that "[a]n application for the exercise of the *nobile officium* is never granted as matter of course; it is always necessary to show cause",[2] and more recently that "[b]efore the exercise of the discretion can even be considered, a clear *prima facie* case must be set out. Without this, an application is incompetent."[3]

It has been said that the *nobile officium* should not be used to provide escape from a difficult situation,[4] and that in general the jurisdiction is not to be used to correct a blunder.[5] However, there is no categorical exclusion of the potential for the court to correct a blunder. Reference has been made to "a general class of case in which the Court, in the exercise of its *nobile officium*, is in use to correct blunders or errors that have been made in carrying out

---

[1] See Section 10.5.
[2] *Gibson's Trs, Petrs* 1933 SC 190 at 210 per Lord Anderson.
[3] *La Torre v Lord Advocate and Scottish Ministers* 2008 JC 72 at 74 per Lord Nimmo Smith.
[4] David M Walker, *The Law of Civil Remedies in Scotland* (1974, W Green) at 1195.
[5] See *Tod v Anderson* (1869) 7 M 412 at 415.

the procedure of the Bankruptcy Acts".[6] There would, however, typically require to be some additional reason for the court's intervention, beyond the mere correction of an error. In the field of bankruptcy, for example, the Court of Session has equitably interposed in allowing for the correction of errors not necessarily to rescue the erring petitioner for his own sake, but rather to protect the interests of creditors who may be affected by the error in question.[7] Consider, for example, the risk posed to the interests of creditors where an error is made in a statutory notice relating to a sequestration.

Failure to comply with procedure may not be reason enough for equitable intervention. Where a person has inadvertently failed to comply with a statutory timetable, they cannot seek to rely on the *nobile officium* to excuse that failure.[8] Nor may the jurisdiction be invoked to allow an appeal to be received late where there has been a failure to obtemper provisions in the sheriff court rules.[9]

As such, the court may exercise its *nobile officium* to correct a blunder, but it may depend on the nature and extent of the interests which stand to be impaired, and the gravity of that impairment, as to whether the court is prepared to intervene.[10] Where a person has failed to avail himself of a statutory remedy as a result of the incompetence of his solicitors, his remedy is to seek redress against the solicitors who were negligent.[11] The jurisdiction is not to be "used as a mere cloak for incompetence on the part of the applicant's representatives".[12]

---

[6] *White Cross Insurance Association, Petrs* 1924 SC 372 at 375 per Lord Anderson. A number of cases in which *per incuriam* errors and omissions were cured by exercise of the *nobile officium* are discussed in Chapter 4.

[7] *McCosh, Petr* (1898) 25 R 1019 at 1020 per Lord President Robertson.

[8] *The Royal Bank of Scotland plc v Clydebank District Council* 1992 SLT 356 at 365 per Lord McCluskey. See, however, *HM Advocate, Petr* 1990 JC 281.

[9] *GAS Construction Co Ltd v Schrader* 1992 SLT 505.

[10] See generally *Tod v Anderson* (1869) 7 M 412.

[11] *Barlow v City Plumbing Supplies Holdings Ltd* [2009] CSOH 5 at para [16] per Lord Hardie.

[12] *Maitland, Petr* 1961 SC 291 at 293 per Lord President Clyde. See also *Berry, Petr* 1985 JC 59; *Connolly, Petr* 1997 SLT 689; and *Ryan, Petr* 2002 SLT 275. See, however, *Scott, Petr* 1992 SCCR 102. The petition in *Fraser, Petr* 1950 SLT (Notes) 33 was competent though refused on its merits.

The *nobile officium* cannot be used to recall the words of a judicial opinion,[13] and it cannot generally be exercised to review the merits of a decision taken by the court under statutory provisions for appeal.[14] It has also been said that the *nobile officium* cannot be used to authorise an appeal marked to the sheriff to be subsequently marked by the sheriff to the Court of Session, in lieu of that appeal to the sheriff.[15]

The question of whether any of these limitations are binding on the courts, or whether they are undertaken on a voluntary basis, is an open one.[16] Are the various limitations articulated by the courts a reflection of their perceived lack of authority to act where, for example, an application of the *nobile officium* might conflict with implied statutory intention, or where another remedy exists? Are these limitations expressions of principle about how the courts conceive the doctrinal basis of the jurisdiction to fit into the wider law and legal system? Are they driven, in whole or in part, by a desire to prevent the floodgates from opening, and by ensuring that relatively high thresholds must routinely be met? Lord Sands was of the bold view that "there is no constitutional authority that can declare an exercise of the *nobile officium* invalid as beyond the lawful authority of the Court", though he qualified this by saying that "far from encouraging laxity", it prescribed "extreme caution in the exercise of powers so uncircumscribed".[17] It appears that, over time, the courts have become increasingly aware of the doctrinal and perhaps practical need to ensure that the *nobile officium* is not used too readily or freely, and gone are the days when the jurisdiction could be used as a pretext for quasi-legislation or the imposition of penalties.[18] The emphasis is now firmly on judicial self-restraint.

---

[13] *Thomson, Petr* 1999 GWD 23-1087.

[14] See *Perrie, Petr* 1992 SLT 655 at 658 per Lord Justice-General Hope.

[15] *J & J Fraser v Smith* 1937 SC 667 at 672 per Lord Mackay.

[16] See also Stephen Thomson, "The *nobile officium* in civil jurisdiction: an outline of equitable gap-filling in Scotland" (2014) 29 Tulane European & Civil Law Forum 125 at 140–142.

[17] *Gibson's Trs, Petrs* 1933 SC 190 at 211 per Lord Sands.

[18] See pp 11–12.

In the context of general scope, it is useful to consider the potential ambit of the jurisdiction with an example of a misconceived application. In *Pringle, Petr*,[19] a person sought an order that he was not required to pay the community charge which he alleged was in violation of the Treaty of Union 1707. It was held that the *nobile officium* could not be invoked when to do so would override the express provision of a statute, which was in this case the Abolition of Domestic Rates etc (Scotland) Act 1987. Although the Court did not state as much, this avenue of challenge must surely have been doomed to fail. It was noted that the petitioner did not seek a declaration that the Act was invalid, that he could not utilise the appellate machinery under the Act itself to obtain relief, and that it would not be open to him to raise an action of declarator inasmuch as he accepted that the Act had the force of law. However, it is difficult to conceive of how the *nobile officium* could be used by a person to obtain relief from a statutory obligation to pay tax. As a petition to the *nobile officium* is a supplication of equitable jurisdiction, any resultant decision of the Court is not binding in future cases in the same way that a decision under ordinary jurisdiction would be. A decision which granted relief to the petitioner from payment of the community charge would not relieve other persons who were also liable for payment. Unless the petitioner could demonstrate some exceptional circumstances or special reason why he should be relieved of liability, there is surely no equitable basis for holding that one taxpayer should be relieved of his liability to pay the community charge, whilst others may not. In short, this was an ill-conceived attempt to mobilise the *nobile officium*, with a failure to appreciate its scope and nature.

10.2 Extraordinary or unforeseen circumstances

Lord Justice-General Emslie described the existence of extraordinary or unforeseen circumstances as "the primary

---

[19] 1991 SLT 330.

justification for the exercise of the *nobile officium*".[20] That is a more accurate statement of the law than that the *nobile officium* can "only" be exercised where there are extraordinary or unforeseen circumstances.[21] The exceptional nature of the jurisdiction has been repeatedly emphasised,[22] and there is a fairly consistent trend in the case law indicating that the existence of such circumstances is, if not a prerequisite for the exercise of the jurisdiction, then certainly a significantly encouraging factor.[23] In several cases it has been said that there is nothing so extraordinary or unforeseen as to justify exercise of the jurisdiction.[24] The principal utility of the *nobile officium* is, indeed, precisely to deal with the emergence of circumstances or factors which are exceptional, unforeseen, unusual or otherwise special. Lord President Hope neatly stated that "[t]he power may be exercised in highly special or unforeseen circumstances to prevent injustice and oppression".[25]

---

[20] *Anderson v HM Advocate* 1974 SLT 239 at 240.

[21] *Anderson v HM Advocate* at 240 per Lord Justice-General Emslie; *Birrell v HM Advocate* 2011 JC 27 at 31 per Lord Malcolm.

[22] James Avon Clyde, "Translator's Note" in Sir Thomas Craig of Riccarton, *The Jus Feudale* (1934, William Hodge) vol 1 at xxii; *B's Executor v Keeper of the Registers and Records of Scotland* 1935 SC 745 at 752 per Lord Anderson; *Coles, Petr* 1951 SC 608 at 615 per Lord Mackay; *MacPherson, Petrs* 1990 JC 5 at 13 per Lord Justice-General Hope; *McWilliam, Petr* 2002 SLT 972 at 973 per Lord Hamilton; *Anderson v Shetland Islands Council* [2014] CSIH 73 at para [12] per Lord Brodie. The *nobile officium* was described by Lord Justice-General Clyde as "unusual but well recognised" (*Wylie v HM Advocate* 1966 SLT 149 at 151).

[23] See, eg, *Macpherson, Petrs* 1990 JC 5 at 12 per Lord Justice-General Hope; *Windsor, Petr* 1994 JC 41 at 54 per Lord Sutherland; *Newland, Petr* 1994 JC 122 at 126 per Lord Justice-General Hope; *McIntosh, Petr* 1995 SLT 796 at 798; *Cooney v HM Advocate* 1999 GWD 28-1322; and *Birrell v HM Advocate* 2011 JC 27 at 31 per Lord Malcolm. The converse also applies, with a failure to demonstrate extraordinary or unforeseen circumstances having proved problematic or discouraging in a number of petitions – see, eg, *Anderson v HM Advocate* 1974 SLT 239; *HM Advocate v Greene* 1976 SLT 120; *Ferguson v HM Advocate* 1980 JC 27; *Harper, Petr* 1982 SLT 232; and *Manson, Petr* 1991 SLT 96.

[24] For some examples of this, see *MacPherson, Petrs* 1990 JC 5 at 14 per Lord Justice-General Hope; and *M v Kennedy* 1995 SC 61 at 66.

[25] *R v Kennedy* 1993 SC 417 at 421 per Lord President Hope.

There are, however, instances of recurring petitions to the *nobile officium* in particular areas which are less easily considered to involve extraordinary or unforeseen circumstances. A notable example is in the area of contempt of court, where resort to the *nobile officium* is a standard way of challenging findings of contempt in both civil and criminal proceedings. Accordingly, the criterion of extraordinary or unforeseen circumstances is more correctly considered a general rule than an absolute. Also relevant in this regard is the role of precedent in the *nobile officium* jurisprudence, generating themes, patterns and recurring instances of successful petition.[26] Nevertheless, demonstration of extraordinary or unforeseen circumstances will often substantially improve the prospects of a petition to the *nobile officium*.

What qualifies as an extraordinary or unforeseen circumstance must be determined on a case-by-case basis. It has been said that what is meant by "extraordinary or unforeseen" in a statutory context is that "the circumstances which have arisen are of a kind which has not been anticipated by the makers of the legislative framework within which the court must otherwise operate".[27] However, the *nobile officium* does not always operate in relation to a statutory framework, and as such what is extraordinary or unforeseen may be broader in other contexts.

10.3 Relationship with statute

It has been stated that the *nobile officium* "ought never to be at variance with the law".[28] In this vein, it is generally a bar to the

---

[26] On precedent, see Section 10.5.

[27] *La Torre v Lord Advocate and Scottish Ministers* 2008 JC 72 at 74 per Lord Nimmo Smith. See also *MacPherson, Petrs* 1990 JC 5 at 12 per Lord Justice-General Hope. In the context of the *nobile officium* of the High Court, see also Moncreiff, *Law of Review in Criminal Cases* at 264.

[28] *Graham v Graham* 1780 Mor 8934. For an interesting statement to this effect with regard to the *nobile officium* of the General Assembly, see William Mair, *A Digest of Laws and Decisions Ecclesiastical and Civil* (William Blackwood, 1887) at 45. McNeill wrote of "the principle that the equitable power of the king should be exercized only where the common law was deficient and in such a way as not to impinge on it" – *Jurisdiction of the Scottish Privy Council* at 101. See also McNeill at 68.

competency of a petition where an exercise of the *nobile officium* would conflict with statute. It has been stated that the jurisdiction "may never be invoked when to do so would conflict with statutory intention".[29] To do so would both constitute a conflict with legislative intention, and involve an application of equitable jurisdiction where there is an existing legal provision.[30]

The rule against conflict with statute takes on several dimensions. Most straightforwardly, the *nobile officium* cannot be competently used in a way which would override[31] or conflict with[32] the express provision of a statute, or express statutory intention. This has been described as beyond the court's jurisdiction.[33] The court may neither use the *nobile officium* to supersede a statutory provision[34] or to substitute a new provision in its place.[35] It could not, for example, use the jurisdiction to recall an interlocutor allowing proof in contravention of a statutory finality provision.[36] This would also in general preclude the *nobile officium* being used to extend a statutory time

---

[29] *Perrie, Petr* 1992 SLT 655 at 657 per Lord Justice-General Hope.

[30] This feeds into the potential availability of other remedies – see Section 10.4.

[31] *Adair v Colville & Sons* 1922 SC 672 at 677 per Lord Justice-Clerk Scott Dickson; *Liquidator of Nairn Public Hall, Petrs* 1946 SC 395 at 397 per Lord Justice-Clerk Cooper; *Humphries v X and Y* 1982 SC 79 at 83 per Lord President Emslie; *MacPherson, Petrs* 1990 JC 5 at 12 per Lord Justice-General Hope; *Pringle, Petr* 1991 SLT 330 at 332 per Lord President Hope; *Connolly, Petr* 1997 SLT 689.

[32] *B's Executor v Keeper of the Registers and Records of Scotland* 1935 SC 745 at 752 per Lord Anderson; *McLaughlin, Petr* 1965 SC 243 at 245 per Lord President Clyde; *Anderson v HM Advocate* 1974 SLT 239 at 240 per Lord Justice-General Emslie; *Berry, Petr* 1985 JC 59; *MacPherson, Petrs* 1990 JC 5 at 12 per Lord Justice-General Hope; *Windsor, Petr* 1994 JC 41 at 54 per Lord Sutherland; *McIntosh, Petr* 1995 SLT 796 at 798 per Lord Justice-General Hope. See also *Tennent's Judicial Factor v Tennent* 1954 SC 215 at 225 per Lord President Cooper.

[33] *Adair v Colville & Sons* 1922 SC 672 at 678 per Lord Hunter.

[34] *MacGown v Cramb* (1897) 24 R 481 at 482 per Lord Adam. These comments were endorsed in *Adair v Colville & Sons* at 677 per Lord Justice-Clerk Scott Dickson.

[35] *Alexander Henderson Ltd, Petrs* 1967 SLT (Notes) 17 at 18 per Lord President Clyde.

[36] *MacGown v Cramb* (1897) 24 R 481.

limit[37] or to excuse a failure to comply with sheriff court rules.[38] It was said that in the absence of a statutory provision excusing non-compliance with a statutory timetable, non-compliance was "fatal" and the *nobile officium* "should not be regarded as the kiss of life in such circumstances".[39]

The court has also held that an exercise of the *nobile officium* cannot conflict with *implied* statutory provision or intention,[40] nor can it be used to circumvent a statutory provision.[41] It has been held that the court cannot direct a person to do something contrary to his statutory duty,[42] though in exceptional circumstances it reserves the power to do so.[43]

This kind of restriction also operates in the other direction: it may not be used to extend the scope of a statutory provision.[44]

---

[37] See *The Royal Bank of Scotland plc v Clydebank District Council* 1992 SLT 356 at 365 per Lord McCluskey; *Connolly, Petr* 1997 SLT 689; and *Ryan, Petr* 2002 SLT 275 (in relation to *Ryan*, see now the Criminal Procedure (Scotland) Act 1995, ss 107(9A), 180(9A) and 187(8A)). See also, however, *Berry, Petr* 1985 JC 59; *HM Advocate, Petr* 1990 JC 281; *HM Advocate, Petr* 1994 SCCR 136 at 139; and *Strang v HM Advocate* 2006 JC 100. An application for extension of time may have to show a "procedural vice or inherent irregularity of the fundamental and extraordinary kind which might make a decision of the High Court amenable to the jurisdiction of the *nobile officium*": *Cobanoglu, Petr* 2012 SCL 604 at 612.

[38] *GAS Construction Co Ltd v Schrader* 1992 SLT 505.

[39] *Fenton, Petr* 1982 SLT 164 at 164.

[40] *B's Executor v Keeper of the Registers and Records of Scotland* 1935 SC 745; *Anderson v HM Advocate* 1974 SLT 239 at 240 per Lord Justice-General Emslie; *Humphries v X and Y* 1982 SC 79 at 83 per Lord President Emslie; *Berry, Petr* 1985 JC 59; *MacPherson, Petrs* 1990 JC 5 at 12 per Lord Justice-General Hope; *Windsor, Petr* 1994 JC 41 at 54 per Lord Sutherland. For concern expressed about the Court potentially acting contrary to the spirit of a statute in exercise of its *nobile officium*, see *Tod v Anderson* (1869) 7 M 412 at 413–14 per Lord Justice-Clerk Patton.

[41] *London and Clydeside Estates Ltd v Aberdeen District Council* 1980 SC (HL) 1 at 36 per Lord Fraser of Tullybelton; *Connolly, Petr* 1997 SLT 689 at 690 per Lord Justice-General Rodger; *West Lothian Council v McG* 2002 SC 411 at 425 per Lord Justice-Clerk Gill.

[42] *B's Executor v Keeper of the Registers and Records of Scotland* 1935 SC 745.

[43] See *B's Executor* at 750 per Lord Justice-Clerk Aitchison.

[44] *Maitland, Petr* 1961 SC 291 at 293 per Lord President Clyde; *Humphries v X and Y* 1982 SC 79 at 83 per Lord President Emslie; *Jamieson, Petrs* 1997 SC 195 at 199 per Lord Kirkwood. See also *Thomson v Principal Reporter, Scottish Children's Reporter Administration* 1998 SC 848.

This could be argued to be tantamount to acting contrary to statute, by extending the scope of statutory intention. This was illuminated by Lord Justice-Clerk Thomson in *Smart v Registrar General for Scotland*:

> The *nobile officium* cannot be used to extend the scope of Acts of Parliament. Where the intention of a statute is clear but the machinery required for carrying out that intention is lacking, the *nobile officium* can, under special circumstances, be invoked to provide the necessary machinery, but in the present case it seems to me that the intention of the statute is clear and the machinery for carrying out that intention in Scottish matters is provided.[45]

It was stated in *Adair v Colville & Sons* that the *nobile officium* could not be used to "interfere with the provisions of an Act of Parliament, and either supplement them or derogate from them".[46] This would also prevent the court from imposing additional requirements to those found in statute. The jurisdiction would neither be competently used to put a person in a better position than that to which he is entitled under the statutory framework,[47] as this would be an extension of the protection offered by that framework or could potentially undermine it. In *Crichton-Stuart's Tutrix, Petr*,[48] for example, it was held that the Court could not exercise its *nobile officium* to extend the scope of a statutory provision by communicating a special statutory right to persons other than those for whom the statutory right was created. Likewise, it was stated that it could not be invoked to "give a remedy to someone other than the parties to whom Parliament has chosen to give a remedy".[49] Lord Cullen explained that:

> the Court is invited, under the guise of an exercise of its *nobile officium*, to contravene an express provision of its statutory jurisdiction....

---

[45] *Smart v Registrar General for Scotland* 1954 SC 81 at 85 per Lord Justice-Clerk Thomson.

[46] 1922 SC 672 at 678 per Lord Ormidale. See also *Maitland, Petr* 1961 SC 291 at 293 per Lord President Clyde.

[47] See *Campbell, Petr* (1890) 18 R 149 at 152 per Lord McLaren.

[48] 1921 SC 840.

[49] *Maitland, Petr* 1961 SC 291 at 293 per Lord President Clyde.

[T]he *nobile officium* does not include a legislative power to alter statutes in the way the petition proposes.[50]

In addition to the *nobile officium* being unavailable for the extension of statutory provisions, it is neither for the jurisdiction to extend the Rules of Court.[51]

Notwithstanding these restrictions, there is a limited class of cases in which the courts have effectively assented to acting contrary to the letter of statute or extending a statutory provision. This would not be a regular use of the *nobile officium*, but the following cases are nevertheless evidence of the jurisdiction being used to that effect. This is seen primarily in relation to statutory time limits, with the *nobile officium* having been used in both the Court of Session[52] and the High Court[53] for the actual or effective extension of time limits.

One statement on this matter from the Court of Session was made by Lord President Hope in *Wright v Tennent Caledonian Breweries Ltd*, in which a person whose estate had been sequestrated was unable to meet a statutory deadline for seeking recall of sequestration due to circumstances which were effectively beyond her control:

> The problem which has arisen in the present case is that, while the petitioner seeks a recall under the statute, she has been deprived of that remedy because she was unable to meet the statutory time limit for bringing the application. This is due to the unforeseen circumstance, for which the Act makes no provision, that the period between the date of sequestration as defined by s 12(4)(b) and the date when sequestration was in fact awarded was more than 10 weeks.

---

[50] *Crichton-Stuart's Tutrix, Petr* at 846 per Lord Cullen. See also *Hunter v Secretary of State for Scotland* 1994 SCLR 479. As noted at p 141, fn 20, it is not for the courts to assume a legislative function in filling lacunae or omissions – see, eg, *A v B* (1848) 11 D 101 at 109 per Lord Jeffrey; *Hatcher v Harrower* 2011 JC 90 at 93 per Lord Bonomy; and *HM Advocate v Harris (No 2)* 2011 JC 125 at 134 per Lord Justice-General Hamilton.

[51] *Jamieson, Petrs* 1997 SC 195.

[52] *Banff County Road Trs, Petrs* (1881) 9 R 20; *Liquidator of the Clyde Marine Insurance Co Ltd, Petr* 1921 SC 472; *Kippen's Tr, Petr* 1966 SC 3; *Humphries v X and Y* 1982 SC 79.

[53] *HM Advocate, Petr* 1990 JC 281; *Scott, Petr* 1992 SCCR 102.

> It seems to me that it would be appropriate to extend the time for the presentation of the petition for recall by a suitable period on the ground that compliance with the statutory timetable was impossible, provided always that we were persuaded that the petitioner has reasonable grounds for seeking a recall. So I would not be willing to dismiss the petition on the ground that it is incompetent. I think that this is the kind of case where the inherent equitable jurisdiction of the Court of Session may be exercised to make good the situation which has occurred.[54]

The reasoning here was that the statute made no provision for this length of time between the date of sequestration and the date when sequestration was actually awarded, and that the Court would be providing for this unforeseen circumstance. However, it is plainly stated in the judgment that the *nobile officium* was being used "to extend the time" limit where compliance with the statutory timetable was impossible. In other words, the Court used the *nobile officium* contrary to the strict letter (though not necessarily the spirit) of the statute by extending the prescribed time limit.

There are some other cases appropriate for consideration at this juncture. One is a case in the Court of Session in which the very point of exercising the *nobile officium* was to circumvent a statutory requirement. That was the case of *Roberts, Petrs*,[55] in which a statutory requirement for a bankrupt to take an oath or declaration was dispensed with on the ground that he had become insane. Lord President Balfour said the following:

> The bankrupt has satisfied all the requirements of the statute, in so far as it is possible for a man mentally afflicted to do so. The sequestration was awarded as far back as 1894, and all the known estate has been got in and divided among the creditors, including certain estate which accrued to the bankrupt after the sequestration. In these circumstances the alternatives are either that the bankrupt shall never get his discharge, or that someone else shall make the declaration or oath required by section 147 of the Bankruptcy Act of 1856, in place of

---

[54] 1991 SLT 823 at 825–26 per Lord President Hope. The petition was unsuccessful for other reasons.

[55] (1901) 3 F 779. For discussion of this case, see p 114.

him, or that the Court should in the very special circumstances of the case dispense with that declaration or oath.[56]

Lord Adam went on to say that:

> The bankrupt here has, so far as any third party can find out, made a full and fair disclosure of his estate, and all that the Act still requires is a declaration or oath by the bankrupt that he has made a full and fair disclosure, and has not made any secret arrangements with his creditors. Now, the bankrupt here is in a state of mind which makes it impossible for him to make such a declaration, and the question is whether we should in these circumstances dispense with the declaration required by the statute, or whether someone else should make the declaration for him. It seems to me preferable that the declaration should be dispensed with rather than that it should be made by a person not specified by the Act, and who, in a hundred cases out of a hundred and one, would know nothing about it. I think that would be a greater and unnecessary exercise of the *nobile officium*, and I agree that we ought in the present circumstances to dispense with the declaration.[57]

Although this decision might be justified on the basis that it would presumably have been the intention of Parliament that a person in the situation of the insane bankrupt ought not to be denied discharge by reason of an effective inability to make the statutory declaration, this would of course be a presumption, and no reasoning to that effect was put forward by the Court. Instead, the Court exercised its *nobile officium* to disapply a statutory provision because it regarded it as equitable to do so. The decision as applied to the facts of the case might not be substantively controversial, but the underlying principle is quite powerful.

In another case before the Court of Session, *Brown v Middlemas of Kelso Ltd*,[58] it was held that it would be inappropriate to exercise the *nobile officium* to extend a statutory time limit. However, it is evident from the judgment of Lord Justice-Clerk Ross that this was not a blanket prohibition on any such possibility, rather the petitioner had failed to present a

---

[56] At 781 per Lord President Balfour.

[57] At 781 per Lord Adam.

[58] 1994 SC 401.

sufficiently compelling case for the jurisdiction to be exercised in this way:

> We are satisfied that the present case is not one where it would be appropriate for us to exercise our equitable powers. In the absence of any reasonable explanation for the failure to lodge a petition for recall timeously, it would be inappropriate for this court in effect to extend the time within which an application could be made to recall the sequestration. Parliament has laid down time-limits within which such an application must be made, and Parliament has not made any provision for these time-limits being extended. In these circumstances it would be quite wrong for this court effectively to extend the time-limits. We would to all intents and purposes be supplementing the statutory procedure by amending the statute. There is no *casus improvisus* in this statute and it would be wrong for this court to extend the operation of the statute beyond what had been enacted by Parliament. As already indicated the present case is plainly different to *Wright v. Tennent Caledonian Breweries Ltd*. Since the petitioner has not been able to say any more than that the petition for recall of sequestration was not lodged within the time-limit laid down by Parliament, we are satisfied that the petitioner has not made out any case which would justify this court in exercising its *nobile officium* in the manner proposed.[59]

In *Macdonald, Petrs*,[60] the *nobile officium* was exercised to appoint a meeting of creditors in a sequestration more than double the number of days in advance of the statutory maximum. A meeting had previously been appointed to be held at Lochmaddy on North Uist; however the relevant documents were not received there until one week after the date of the intended meeting due to adverse winds. The increased advance notice of the meeting was therefore intended to avoid a repeat of such communications problems. This may be interpreted as equitable intervention for the facilitation of a statutory procedure, but it still involves the Court using its *nobile officium* to disapply a statutory time limit and apply what is viewed as a more equitable time requirement. In short, it goes against the letter of an express provision in the statute.

---

[59] At 405 per Lord Justice-Clerk Ross.
[60] (1861) 23 D 719.

It was indicated in a case before the High Court that the *nobile officium* can, in special circumstances, be used contrary to statutory intention:

> It had not been demonstrated that there is anything extraordinary or unforeseen in the circumstances of this case which would justify the exercise of the *nobile officium* in conflict with the intention of the Act, which is that decisions of the appeal court are final and not subject to review.[61]

In other words, conditions of this kind might be satisfied in a special case. These cases might fall under the general scope of the idea of a statutory omission, whereby the volition for equitable intervention is to supply the machinery for giving effect to a statutory framework.[62] However, firm conclusions cannot necessarily be drawn, and there is at least a significant element of inference and presumption about statutory intention when the courts intervene in this way. The courts also define what does and does not constitute conflict with statutory provisions on a case-by-case basis,[63] and not always in a predictable manner. Although the few instances in which time limits have been extended might be deemed fair, just or apt in the circumstances, and whilst one would not seek to overstate the point, such cases are a challenge to any blanket rule that the *nobile officium* cannot be used contrary to an express statutory provision.

A final point on the relationship between the *nobile officium* and statute is illustrated by the case of *Campbell, Petr*.[64] A building society had been dissolved by an instrument of dissolution. At that date, the building society was infeft in certain heritable subjects, and the trustee of the society had sold the subjects on to a third party, as authorised by the instrument of dissolution. The purchaser objected, however, that the trustee was unable to give valid title inasmuch as a dissolved company could not grant

[61] *Beattie, Petr* 1993 SLT 676 at 678 per Lord Justice-General Hope.
[62] See *Abel v Watt* (1883) 11 R 149 at 151 per Lord President Inglis.
[63] See, eg, *Humphries v X and Y* 1982 SC 79 at 83–84 per Lord President Emslie.
[64] (1890) 18 R 149.

a conveyance of the subjects. The trustee petitioned the Court to authorise and empower him to execute and deliver the necessary dispositions and conveyances, without completing a feudal title in his person.

The Court refused the petition. Lord President Inglis explained that the office of trustee was in this case entirely statutory. The statute must either have given the trustee the power to sell and dispose of the subjects without making up a feudal title in his own person, or it had withheld that power. In the former case, the intervention of the Court was unnecessary, whilst in the latter case the Court had no jurisdiction to "dispense with the ordinary forms of conveyancing in the case of dissolved companies of this kind".[65] In other words, the petitioner:

> either has a good title to convey, and in that case he does not need our authority, or he has not a good title to convey, and in that case we are not in a position to give him a good title.[66]

To give the petitioner a good title would in essence be a circumvention of statute.[67] This case demonstrates reluctance on the part of the Court to extend the scope of a statutory provision, and rather than being a case for the *nobile officium*, it was one based on statutory construction.[68] It is a reminder that, subject to the limited qualifications outlined above, the Court is cautious about how an exercise of the *nobile officium* integrates with the relevant statutory framework.

10.4   No other remedy available

The *nobile officium* is regarded as a process of last resort.[69] This is in line with the *raison d'être* of the jurisdiction as a procedural mechanism for obtaining a remedy where no other process can yield one. The general rule is therefore that the *nobile officium*

---

[65]   At 151 per Lord President Inglis.
[66]   At 152 per Lord Kinnear.
[67]   See *Campbell, Petr* at 152 per Lord McLaren.
[68]   *Campbell, Petr* at 151 per Lord President Inglis.
[69]   *Birrell v HM Advocate* 2011 JC 27 at 31 per Lord Malcolm.

may be competently invoked only where there is no other remedy available to the petitioner.[70]

The intending petitioner would be expected to have availed himself of other available remedies,[71] and this would include both statutory and non-statutory remedies.[72] Where there is another remedy available, it will generally be incompetent to petition the *nobile officium* regardless of whether or not resort has been made to that remedy.[73] That includes the remedy which was available but which was not pursued and which is no longer available.[74] It has been said that resort should be had to the alternative remedy even where it is a "more cumbrous and expensive way" of addressing the issue at hand.[75]

It is not permissible for the *nobile officium* to be petitioned as an attempt to present under a different guise an alternative

---

[70] *McCallum v McCallum* (1893) 20 R 293 at 294 per Lord Adam; *Central Motor Engineering Co v Gibbs* 1917 SC 490; *Cunningham v Cunningham* 1928 SC 790 at 795 and 797 per Lord Justice-Clerk Alness and Lord Ormidale, respectively; *Gibson's Trs, Petrs* 1933 SC 190 at 216 per Lord Blackburn; *B's Executor v Keeper of the Registers and Records of Scotland* 1935 SC 745 at 752 per Lord Anderson; *Glasgow Magdalene Institution, Petrs* 1964 SC 227 at 229 per Lord President Clyde; *Cordiner, Petr* 1973 JC 16 at 18 per Lord Justice-General Emslie; *Anderson v HM Advocate* 1974 SLT 239 at 240 per Lord Justice-General Emslie; *London and Clydeside Estates Ltd v Aberdeen District Council* 1980 SC (HL) 1 at 45; *Evans v HM Advocate* 1992 SLT 401; *Clayton, Petr* 1992 SLT 404; *Perrie, Petr* 1992 SLT 655 at 658 per Lord Justice-General Hope; *Windsor, Petr* 1994 JC 41 at 53–54 per Lord Sutherland; *M v Kennedy* 1995 SC 61; *Strock, Petr* 1996 JC 125; *Drummond, Petr* 1998 SLT 757; *La Torre v Lord Advocate and Scottish Ministers* 2008 JC 72 at 74 per Lord Nimmo Smith; *Paterson v HM Advocate* 2008 JC 230; *Birrell v HM Advocate* 2011 JC 27 at 31 per Lord Malcolm. See also *British Broadcasting Corporation, Applicants* 2012 SCL 347; and see further Stair, IV, 3, 1; Erskine, *Institute*, I, III, 22; Bankton, *Institute*, IV, 7, 24; *Stair Memorial Encyclopaedia*, Civil Jurisdiction, vol 4 at para 4; and *Dunedin Encyclopaedia*, vol X at 326.

[71] *Scottish Daily Record and Sunday Mail Ltd, Petrs* 1999 SLT 624 at 628 per Lord McCluskey.

[72] In the area of trusts, for example, the *nobile officium* will in general not be available (or necessary) where the trust deed or statute makes adequate provision – see Chapter 2.

[73] *Anderson v Shetland Islands Council* [2014] CSIH 73 at para [12] per Lord Brodie.

[74] *Cobanoglu, Petr* 2012 SCL 604 at 610 per Lord Clarke.

[75] *Anderson, Petrs* (1884) 11 R 405 at 407 per Lord Craighill.

process (such as a reclaiming motion) which had previously failed.[76] The condition that there should be "no other remedy or procedure ... provided by the law"[77] does not cover the "remedy exhausted and procedure fully followed but without success. This would convert the *nobile officium* into an ultimate appeal of last resort in every case, and it is plainly not that".[78] That the petitioner had in that case unsuccessfully made use of available remedies meant that "an essential precondition for the application of the *nobile officium* is accordingly wanting, so that the petition is incompetent and must be dismissed".[79]

There may be a tension in this area between the existence or otherwise of a prescribed mode of appeal. For example, it was suggested in *MacPherson, Petrs* that it was problematic for a petition to the *nobile officium* that Parliament had provided no right of appeal with regard to a particular complaint.[80] However, might not a mode of appeal have the opposite effect in some cases, so that it can be said that there was a remedy open to the petitioner, and that this would militate against the prospects of a petition to the *nobile officium*? As noted, it is not decisive *whether* the intending petitioner has resorted to an alternative remedy – rather, it is decisive that there *is* an alternative remedy. What may be even more decisive is whether, in the circumstances, there are sufficiently exceptional or unforeseen circumstances justifying equitable intervention.

A statement of the general principle was made by Lord Skerrington in *Central Motor Engineering Co v Gibbs*:

> I do not think that it is legitimate to ask the Court to exercise its *nobile officium* unless it is made clear that there is no other remedy open to

---

[76] *Anderson v Shetland Islands Council* [2014] CSIH 73 at para [12].

[77] *Perrie, Petr* 1992 SLT 655 at 658 per Lord Justice-General Hope.

[78] *Windsor, Petr* 1994 JC 41 at 53 per Lord Murray. The description of the *nobile officium* by Lord Mackay as "the ultimate appeal" should not be taken literally: *Craig & Co Ltd, Petrs* 1946 SC 19 at 22.

[79] *Windsor, Petr* 1994 JC 41 at 53 per Lord Murray.

[80] See *MacPherson, Petrs* 1990 JC 5 at 14 per Lord Justice-General Hope. See also *Berry, Petr* 1985 JC 59; and *Perrie, Petr* 1992 SLT 655 at 658 per Lord Justice-General Hope.

the petitioners. An excellent illustration of a case in which the *nobile officium* is properly exercised in bankruptcy law is where, in peculiar circumstances, justice requires that a certain sequestration should be declared at an end. Now, apart from the *nobile officium*, I know of no legal remedy that could be obtained in such cases.[81]

Lord Justice-Clerk Cooper supported that view in *Craig & Co Ltd, Petrs*,[82] and in the same case Lord Mackay took the position that it favoured an exercise of the *nobile officium* that he could not see how a particular state of affairs could be resolved within the parameters of the statute in question.[83]

In a more recent example, a petition to the *nobile officium* was deemed incompetent on the basis that the petitioners' prayer was capable of being made the subject of a statutory appeal to the sheriff. That alone was sufficient to exclude recourse to the *nobile officium*, and there was nothing extraordinary to justify such recourse.[84]

The general rule that there should be no other remedy available applies in both the Court of Session and the High Court. For example, it was held that a petition to the *nobile officium* was incompetent because an alternative remedy was open to the petitioner in the form of applying to the High Court for an extension of time in which to lodge an appeal against sentence.[85] However, there is an exceptional case of the High Court deeming a petition to the *nobile officium* incompetent on the basis that a statutory remedy was available, but nevertheless granting the substantive prayer on its merits.[86]

Where a petition to the *nobile officium* is presented alongside another instance of process, this will likely taint the competency of the petition to the *nobile officium* on the basis that another

---

[81] 1917 SC 490 at 493 per Lord Skerrington.

[82] 1946 SC 19 at 22 per Lord Justice-Clerk Cooper.

[83] At 23 per Lord Mackay.

[84] *M v Kennedy* 1995 SC 61.

[85] *Clayton, Petr* 1992 SLT 404. See also *Cordiner, Petr* 1973 JC 16 at 18 per Lord Justice-General Emslie; and *Paterson v HM Advocate* 2008 JC 230.

[86] *Love, Petr* 1998 JC 85. See also *Gilchrist, Petr* 1991 JC 160. See pp 199–200 and 215.

remedy is available. In *Paterson v HM Advocate*,[87] for example, a petition to the *nobile officium* was presented alongside a bill of advocation. The Court held that the bill of advocation was the appropriate means by which to address the issue, and so the petition to the *nobile officium* would accordingly be incompetent. If the alternative is not found to render the petition to the *nobile officium* incompetent, it will at least be unnecessary.[88]

10.5 Precedent

There is a fundamental tension in the relationship between the *nobile officium* and precedent. In concept, an exercise of the *nobile officium* should neither require nor create a precedent, as it is an instance of equitable adjudication rather than strict legal adjudication. It should be unnecessary to cite prior instances in which the *nobile officium* has been exercised in support of a petition to the jurisdiction, and there should be little expectation that a successful petition would serve as a precedent in future cases.

Although the idea of the *nobile officium* is supplication of an equitable jurisdiction which should be justified primarily by reference to the demands of justice, the courts have in many instances imposed precedential requirements. Whilst a student textbook from 1896 described the *nobile officium* as apt for application where there was no legal authority,[89] Aeneas Mackay wrote in the 1870s that the "tendency in recent times has been to restrict its use to cases in which there is a direct precedent or, at least, an analogous decision".[90] The *Dunedin Encyclopaedia* noted in 1930 that the Court would then seldom supply omissions in statutes or deeds (such as in trusts) unless there was a precedent or analogous case, and the "safe course" for the practitioner would be to assume that it is doubtful whether the *nobile officium*

---

[87] 2008 JC 230.
[88] *Langlands v Manson* 1962 SC 493.
[89] Morton, *Manual of the Law of Scotland* at 14.
[90] Mackay, *The Practice of the Court of Session*, vol 1 at 209.

would be exercised unless it had been before.[91] Lord Cooper of Culross wrote in 1958 that the "modern tendency" was to confine the exercise of the *nobile officium* "within the range of past precedents".[92] Likewise, T B Smith wrote in 1962 that "the Court of Session, in exercising [the *nobile officium*], has become restricted by adherence to precedents, and has thus tended to surrender (perhaps not irrevocably) much of the initiative it claimed in the past".[93]

The reality is that the courts' treatment of precedent lies somewhere between the extremes of an absolute requirement for prior authority and a carefree attitude to the existence or otherwise of precedent. This tentative middle ground is seen in *Central Motor Engineering Co v Gibbs*:

> I should be slow to set limits to what can be done by this Court in the exercise of its *nobile officium*. I will only say that no case has been cited which is a warrant for our doing what is here asked. It is an unprecedented application. And, although Mr Sandeman was successful in citing cases where the Court had, in the exercise of its *nobile officium*, declared sequestration proceedings to be at an end, he was unable to produce any authority for a petition in the terms we have before us.[94]

Lord President Cooper stated:

> I am not prepared to set any limits to what the Court might in special circumstances do in the exercise of the *nobile officium* by way of giving retrospective sanction to *ultra vires* acts of administration by trustees; but we are not in use to expand the *nobile officium* beyond its accepted limits.[95]

---

[91] *Dunedin Encyclopaedia*, vol X at 326.

[92] Lord Cooper of Culross, "The Central Courts after 1532" at 345. A Mackenzie Stuart wrote of "precedents" in the *nobile officium* jurisprudence on trusts: *The Nobile Officium and Trust Administration* at 1.

[93] Smith, *A Short Commentary* at 45.

[94] 1917 SC 490 at 493 per Lord Mackenzie.

[95] *Horne's Trs, Petrs* 1952 SC 70 at 72 per Lord President Cooper. Lord Neaves stated that he did "not wish to put strict limits on the *nobile officium*, where its exercise would be reasonable and beneficial": *Tod v Anderson* (1869) 7 M 412 at 415. Lord President Emslie stated that the limits of the *nobile officium* are "well understood" and "will not be extended": *Humphries v X and Y* 1982 SC 79 at 82–83.

The rough picture was also captured in *The Royal Bank of Scotland plc v Gillies*:

> Although the court tends to limit the exercise of its jurisdiction under the *nobile officium* to cases in which the power has already been exercised, it is neither possible nor desirable to define exhaustively or comprehensively all the circumstances in which resort may be had to the *nobile officium*.[96]

Similarly, it was stated in *Institute of Chartered Accountants of Scotland, Petrs* that:

> The court has repeatedly emphasised that the limits of the *nobile officium* will not be extended, or (at the very least) that the court tends to limit the exercise of its jurisdiction under the *nobile officium* to cases in which the power has already been exercised. The concern to limit the application of *nobile officium* jurisdiction, and to achieve consistency in its application, is in my view entirely justified.[97]

It is perhaps surprising that the courts have been so attentive to precedent in exercise of a jurisdiction which should, in concept, operate outside the normal parameters of precedent. In some cases there is a consideration of principle and precedent, implying either that principle alone might not be sufficient, or that principle and precedent operate as distinct legitimators for equitable intervention. In *The Royal Bank of Scotland plc v Gillies*, the authorities cited were said to be not "precisely in point", so that the question of whether to resort to the *nobile officium* could "only be determined upon general principles".[98]

This idea is seen elsewhere. It was said in one case that there was "precedent enough, as well as principle, for this proceeding",[99] and in another that "[t]here is no precedent for the course we are asked here to follow, and there are many reasons

---

[96] *The Royal Bank of Scotland plc v Gillies* 1987 SLT 54 at 55 per Lord Justice-Clerk Ross.

[97] *Institute of Chartered Accountants of Scotland, Petrs* 2002 SLT 921 at 924 per Lord Menzies.

[98] At 55 per Lord Justice-Clerk Ross.

[99] *Morison's Tutors, Petrs* (1857) 19 D 493 at 494 per Lord President McNeill.

against it".[100] Lord Adam was "not aware of any precedent or principle" for persons seeking authority from the court to sell property in particular circumstances,[101] whilst Lord Justice-General Hope stated that:

> No precedent has been cited to us for the exercise of the power in these circumstances, and it would be contrary to principle for us to grant such an order on the ground that the appeal court had erred in refusing to hear the evidence.[102]

There are instances of courts searching for authority, or being influenced by it, in considering whether or not to exercise the *nobile officium*. It was stated that a particular petition was "certainly without precedent, unless the case of *Coat's Trs* can be prayed in aid",[103] and elsewhere the court thought itself "warranted in granting [the power to borrow] by the case of the *Prime Gilt Box*".[104] Lord President Clyde referred to "authority to cover the exercise of the *nobile officium*, in the direction in which the petition prays us to use it",[105] whilst Lord Morison said in the same case that "[t]he authorities to which we were referred amply justify, in my opinion, the exercise of the powers craved in this note".[106] Lord President Robertson approved of a petition as falling within a particular class of cases,[107] and Lord Mackay set out to consider "the precedents on the bounds of our *officium*" before citing a number of authorities.[108] Lord President Clyde stated that a particular case in which there had been an exercise of the *nobile officium*, which had been cited as an authority by counsel, "cannot in future be regarded as a precedent for other

---

[100] *Maclean, Petr* (1895) 3 SLT 74.

[101] *Campbell, Petr* (1890) 18 R 149 at 151–52 per Lord Adam.

[102] *Perrie, Petr* 1992 SLT 655 at 658 per Lord Justice-General Hope.

[103] *Hall's Trs v McArthur* 1918 SC 646 at 649–50 per Lord Johnston.

[104] *Anderson's Trs, Petrs* 1921 SC 315 at 323 per Lord Ormidale.

[105] *Frew's Trs, Petrs* 1932 SC 501 at 503 per Lord President Clyde.

[106] *Frew's Trs, Petrs* at 504 per Lord Morison. See p 246 on the comments of Lord Blackburn, who went further, in the same case.

[107] *McCosh, Petr* (1898) 25 R 1019 at 1020 per Lord President Robertson.

[108] *Stewart v Brown's Trs* 1941 SC 300 at 307 per Lord Mackay.

cases",[109] indicating that it could and perhaps would have been a precedent had it not been for the lack of opinions expressed in the case. More recently, it had "never been suggested in any discussion of the subject of which we are aware that mere administrative delay will in itself justify the exercise"[110] of the *nobile officium*, an apparent search for authority.

On quite practical grounds it was stated by Lord Hunter that:

> I know of no case where such an application has ever been granted. It is not suggested that there ever has been such an application entertained. In my opinion it would be a very bad practice to innovate on recognised procedure and introduce such a form of application as that before us, because it appears to me that it would lead to this, that, whenever a person had a petitory right but thought it better to appeal to the *nobile officium*, he might do so.[111]

In *White Cross Insurance Association, Petrs*, Lord Anderson began his opinion from the point of authority, apparently satisfied that the existence of precedent was the starting point, rather than an express consideration of the principle of the case:

> This is an example of a general class of case in which the Court, in exercise of the *nobile officium*, is in use to correct blunders or errors that have been made in carrying out the procedure of the Bankruptcy Acts. Cases in the books show that other errors have been rectified by the Court .... The particular error in this case is familiar ... There is no doubt, on the authorities to which [counsel for the petitioner] referred us, that that is an error which the Court is in use to rectify, and our duty is to rectify it. The only point is how that is to be done.[112]

Some cases indicate that the court is dissatisfied with the precedential quality of a decision, but does not disclose concern about the concept of a decision having the potential to carry precedential quality. It was said that a particular case involving the *nobile officium* "was strongly pressed upon our consideration as a precedent" but that ultimately "that case is no precedent in

---

[109] *McLaughlin, Petr* 1965 SC 243 at 246 per Lord President Clyde.
[110] *Bradshaw, Petr* 1993 SCCR 94 at 96–97.
[111] *Snodgrass, Petr* 1922 SC 491 at 496 per Lord Hunter.
[112] 1924 SC 372 at 375 per Lord Anderson.

the present".[113] It was also stated that a particular case which involved an exercise of the *nobile officium* was "an exceptional one, which cannot be, and certainly was not intended to be, treated as a precedent".[114]

Other cases have gone further by suggesting that the absence of precedent may actually be problematic. It was said that "[i]f there had been any case approaching the present I should have been glad to apply its principle so as to facilitate what the applicant here has in view".[115] Whilst it was also stated in the same case that "in spite of the absence of authority, still, if there were no way out of the difficulty but that [of the *nobile officium*], we should perhaps be obliged to accede to that suggestion",[116] indicating that the absence of authority was not fatal for the prospects of a petition to the *nobile officium*,[117] the court clearly signalled that, had there been authority, the outcome would have been different. This implies that the absence of authority was in fact decisive. In this vein, it was stated elsewhere that:

> If it had not been for the decision of the Court in *Sinclair's Trs* and the cases therein referred to, I should have doubted whether the Court, in the exercise of its *nobile officium*, ought to grant an application which so manifestly interferes with the express directions of the testator.[118]

It has also been stated that the court is "very desirous to guard against undue extension",[119] that the jurisdiction "has always been scrupulously guarded, and rarely carried beyond precedent",[120]

---

[113] *Mundell, Petrs* (1862) 24 D 327 at 329 per Lord Cowan.

[114] *Anderson's Trs, Petrs* 1921 SC 315 at 322 per Lord Justice-Clerk Scott Dickson. Near identical wording had been used with regard to the same case in *Hall's Trs v McArthur* 1918 SC 646 at 651 per Lord Johnston.

[115] *Anderson, Petrs* (1884) 11 R 405 at 407 per Lord Craighill.

[116] *Anderson, Petrs* at 407 per Lord Craighill.

[117] For another indication that a lack of precedent was not fatal to a petition to the *nobile officium*, see *Thomson's Trs, Petrs* 1930 SC 767 at 769–70 per Lord President Clyde.

[118] *Frew's Trs, Petrs* 1932 SC 501 at 504 per Lord Blackburn.

[119] *Stewart v Brown's Trs* 1941 SC 300 at 307 per Lord Mackay.

[120] *Hall's Trs v McArthur* 1918 SC 646 at 650 per Lord Johnston.

and more recently that "the court will not readily exercise the *nobile officium* in cases where there is no precedent".[121]

Another dimension from which to view the question has been one not of a search for precedent, but a consideration of an instant case as *setting* a precedent.[122] This view has variously been taken by several judges, including those at a senior level. Lord President Robertson made two statements to this effect. In one case he said that "[i]t appears to me that it would be a bad precedent were we to grant this application",[123] whilst in another:

> If we were to grant the authority for which he asks *we should be laying it down that our authority is necessary* whenever one voluntary association desired to amalgamate with another voluntary society in order to further the common purposes of both. That is a *rule* which we cannot adopt, and I am therefore for refusing this application.[124]

It was stated that "there is no justification, but the reverse, for the Court here making a new precedent in the exercise of its *nobile officium*",[125] and elsewhere that "[i]t must not be thought that we set a tempting precedent for every stranger to the truster ... to rush into Court for powers".[126] Lord President Cooper stated that "[t]o use the *nobile officium* in such circumstances and for such an object would create a dangerous precedent with alarming possibilities",[127] and Lord President Clyde that:

> No considerations of expediency or convenience can entitle the Court to authorise trustees operating under an existing scheme to invest

---

[121] *Anderson v Shetland Islands Council* [2014] CSIH 73 at para [12] per Lord Brodie.

[122] The source should be treated cautiously, but it may be noted that a late 18th-century writer regarded the *nobile officium* as a source of precedent: Stuart, *Observations concerning the Public Law* at 269; on which, see p 11.

[123] *Bowers v Pringle Pattison's Curator Bonis* (1892) 19 R 941 at 942 per Lord President Robertson.

[124] *Edinburgh Young Women's Christian Institute, Petrs* (1893) 20 R 894 at 896 per Lord President Robertson. Emphasis added.

[125] *Hall's Trs v McArthur* 1918 SC 646 at 651 per Lord Johnston.

[126] *Stewart v Brown's Trs* 1941 SC 300 at 308 per Lord Mackay.

[127] *Horne's Trs, Petrs* 1952 SC 70 at 72 per Lord President Cooper.

their funds in securities which Parliament has impliedly prohibited them from holding. For, were the Court to do so in one case, it would *inevitably follow* that the Court would *require to do so for all*, and the Act of Parliament would cease to be effective.[128]

The precedential quality of applications of the *nobile officium* was also cited with regard to their reception in the Outer House:

[A]lthough judgments of the Court pronounced in the exercise of what is called their *nobile officium*, are to be more cautiously adopted as precedents than their other judgments, the Lord Ordinary would certainly hold himself bound by them, if the precedent clearly applied.[129]

Further still in this direction are cases in which the court even refers to what is "binding". This featured in *Macfarlane v Macfarlane's Trs*, in which it was said that, with regard to an alternative appeal to the *nobile officium*, there were "decisions *pro* and *con*", and that in "the cases of *Robertson's Trs, Milne's Trs*, and *Sinclair's Trs*, the petitioner had in his favour the latest authorities and those which are most binding on this Court".[130]

It also occurred in the more recent case of *Harris v HM Advocate*,[131] which exposes a fundamental tension in attributing precedential quality to decisions made in exercise of the *nobile officium*. The Court described its decision in *Cochrane v HM Advocate*[132] – a petition to the *nobile officium* – as "binding on this court".[133] When the petitioner submitted that *Cochrane* (and *McIntyre v HM Advocate*,[134] which was not itself a petition to the *nobile officium*) had been wrongly decided and should not be followed, the Court, in its opinion delivered by Lord Carloway, stated:

---

[128] *Mitchell Bequest Trs, Petrs* 1959 SC 395 at 398–99 per Lord President Clyde. Emphasis added.

[129] *Allan v Glasgow's Trs* (1842) 4 D 494 at 499 (note) per the Lord Ordinary.

[130] *Macfarlane v Macfarlane's Trs* 1931 SC 95 at 100 per Lord Anderson.

[131] 2010 SCL 241.

[132] 2006 JC 135.

[133] *Harris v HM Advocate* at 245.

[134] [2009] HCJAC 63.

That is not a good argument in law. The principle of *stare decisis* applies. Such submissions as have been presented to the court are a negation of that principle and essentially just ignore what the law is in favour of an argument about what, in the petitioner's view, the law ought to be. In that sense, what were presented to the court were not legal submissions at all.[135]

This raises a very interesting question (so far as *Cochrane* is concerned), which is whether the principle of *stare decisis* does or should, as a matter of legal principle, apply in the ordinary way to the *nobile officium*.[136] The question raised is not whether prior decisions on petitions to the *nobile officium* should bind later courts as a matter of desirability, such as by reference to principles of legal certainty and fairness, although those are important considerations. The question is rather whether, logically, the application of *stare decisis* to decisions taken in exercise of the *nobile officium* can be conciliated with the fact that the *nobile officium* cannot be petitioned as a matter of right. It seems doubtful that if a petition was granted this year, and the court regards the principle of *stare decisis* to apply in the ordinary way, that it could be maintained that the *nobile officium* is a discretionary jurisdiction when it comes to dealing with an analogous petition next year. Indeed, if the court lacked discretion in its exercise, and was "bound" to follow previous decisions, then exercises of the *nobile officium* must surely be regarded as generating rights.[137] The jurisdiction has not been so regarded,

---

[135] *Harris v HM Advocate* at 245.

[136] It has been written that *stare decisis* tended not to feature in decisions of the Scots Privy Council: McNeill, *Jurisdiction of the Scottish Privy Council* at 37.

[137] An interesting context in which to consider this point is with regard to the European Convention on Human Rights. Article 13 requires an effective remedy before a national authority, and as noted at p 190, the European Court of Human Rights has indicated that the availability of the *nobile officium* could be an effective remedy (see *Mackay v United Kingdom* (2011) 53 EHRR 19 at paras 34–35). If, however, the *nobile officium* is as exceptional, discretionary and cautiously applied as the judicial narrative has portrayed, is it sufficiently certain and predictable to be properly classed as a remedy for the purposes of Article 13 of the Convention? If the *nobile officium* cannot be petitioned as of right, but only as a matter of equitable supplication, does it have the necessary regularity associated with a "remedy" in the human rights context?

however, as also indicated when Lord President Inglis said that a particular question was one "for the Court in exercise of its *nobile officium*, and is not a question of legal right".[138]

The imposition of precedential standards on the *nobile officium* is problematic for its being considered an equitable jurisdiction. The very idea of invoking an equitable jurisdiction is that it is not appropriate or possible to invoke an ordinary, "legal" jurisdiction. In other words, the court's original, appellate and even supervisory jurisdiction is not invoked because of some exceptional circumstances which cannot appropriately or at all be addressed via those jurisdictions. The petitioner resorts to the *nobile officium* precisely because there is no regular way of dealing with the circumstances of the case. The imposition of precedential requirements may erode the more freestanding equitable nature of the *nobile officium*, for the question is no longer about what is just or fair in the circumstances, and whether the court can intervene without contradicting statute, but also about whether there is prior authority for the court acting in the manner prayed.

It may of course be that practical considerations play a role in the courts' predilection for precedent. A restrained and cautious use of the *nobile officium*, and the expression of a desire not to expand its scope beyond existing parameters, assist in protecting the jurisdiction against speculative and adventurous applications. A rough, precedential framework may be a useful way of maintaining the scope of the jurisdiction and guarding against its undue expansion.

Precedent has by no means been an ubiquitous issue in cases on the *nobile officium*. First, there are cases in which the court seems fairly relaxed about precedent. In a case which appeared to be a petition to the *nobile officium*, Lord President Dunedin stated that counsel for the respondent "has said that there is no precedent for such a petition, but I do not think that any precedent is needed, only a little common sense".[139] In a case concerning the removal of a volume of public records from the jurisdiction,

---

[138] *Campbell v Grant* (1870) 8 M 988 at 988 per Lord President Inglis.
[139] *Cherry v Patrick* 1910 SC 32 at 33 per Lord President Dunedin.

Lord McLaren stated that the question was one not of law, but of administration, and that "in each case the Court must judge of questions of this kind upon the facts before it and independently of authority".[140] Furthermore, there is in many cases no mention of precedent at all. It is not in every case that the court has felt inclined to search for authority, or has been discouraged by the unprecedented nature of a petition.

It is clear, however, that where precedent for a particular application of the *nobile officium* can be found, the court takes encouragement. It can also be seen that a lack of precedent has sometimes been a cause for hesitation. To the extent that precedent features in the *nobile officium* jurisprudence, even to the extent driven by practical considerations, a circular dilemma is encountered: if the *nobile officium* was a response to the inadequacy of regular jurisdiction to deal with exceptional cases, how can prior authority be treated as a precondition for exercising the *nobile officium*? In other words, the *nobile officium* grew out of something; there must have been a putative first case. It cannot have depended on precedent from its inception, otherwise it would never have come to exist. Its *raison d'être* is precisely to deal with marginal cases which are not accommodated by regular jurisdiction, and as regular jurisdiction develops and evolves, so too does the *nobile officium* as a mechanism which is a response to regular jurisdiction. Its scope and parameters are inherently conditioned by those of regular jurisdiction, for its very essence is to account for those cases which are not adequately captured by ordinary adjudication. The imposition of precedential requirements therefore chafes against the very conceptual foundation of the *nobile officium*.

Finally, the capacity for equitable norms to crystallise or metamorphose into common law norms[141] complicates the issue of precedent. In concept, equitable norms should operate outside

---

[140] *King's Remembrancer, Petr* (1902) 4 F 559 at 561 per Lord McLaren. Notwithstanding this view, precedents were routinely cited in cases of this kind. For further discussion of cases concerning public records, see Section 8.9.

[141] See pp 23–24.

the normal parameters of precedent, whereas common law norms are substantially defined by precedent. If there is the potential for equitable norms to undergo a transitionary journey to common law norms, whether and to what extent precedent is relevant must also shift. This confounds the role of precedent as norms invoked in the context of the *nobile officium* do not necessarily have a fixed status as equitable norms.

CHAPTER 11

CONCLUSION

The *nobile officium* is an extraordinary jurisdiction allowing the Court of Session and the High Court of Justiciary to perform certain equitable actions which cannot be undertaken by inferior courts. This includes the supply of omissions, the amelioration of existing legal norms and the alleviation of procedural difficulties. The jurisdiction has received more historical remark in the civil context, where it grew out of a broad fund of equitable powers vested in the Court of Session. However, its acknowledged principles have largely been replicated in the criminal context, where the *nobile officium* of the High Court is now in receipt of a greater number of petitions annually than the Court of Session, albeit with a lower rate of success.

Although the very concept of equitable jurisdiction requires that many of the normative and systematic features of "legal" jurisdiction should not apply, the reality is that various principles have grown around the *nobile officium*. It is almost universally confined to cases in which it offers a remedy of last resort, with an intending petitioner almost always being required to utilise other procedural channels before petitioning the *nobile officium*. It is, with a notable exception in the criminal context, not a final mode of appeal and should not be treated as such. The jurisdiction is generally exercised in a way which will not override or conflict with the express or implied provisions of statute, nor to circumvent, extend or direct a person to act contrary to a statutory provision. There is also a loose precedential framework discernible in the *nobile officium* jurisprudence, and whilst a lack of prior authority will in itself seldom prove fatal to an application, the substantive prospects of an application will in many cases be enhanced if authority can be furnished.

The *nobile officium* is usually reserved for application where exceptional, unforeseen, unusual or otherwise special circumstances have arisen, and the petitioner would benefit from making a case as to the actual or potential injustice, oppression or excessiveness that would result were the court not to intervene. The jurisdiction is not a means of addressing general deficiencies in the law, nor of imploring the court to assume a legislative function. The courts will tend only to supply a statutory omission where it is apparent that a provision has been omitted by oversight of the legislature – omissions regarded as intentionally omitted by the legislature will fall beyond the scope of the jurisdiction.

There is no question that the reach of the *nobile officium* is narrower than it once was, particularly in the civil sphere. Whereas the jurisdiction gained much of its traction in trusts and bankruptcy cases, for example, many of the statutory gaps, mechanical flaws and procedural cul-de-sacs have since been remedied. Areas once considered the province of the *nobile officium* have arguably either been accounted for by statute, or have passed into the common law with a crystallisation of equitable into legal norms. The avenue for the *nobile officium* to be used as a final mode of appeal in summary criminal proceedings may soon be closed off. The *nobile officium* has resumed its more natural role as a residual jurisdiction for use in marginal cases.

There are several reasons, however, why the *nobile officium* remains relevant and important. First, the enactment of new statutes provides a continuing source of potential omissions. Whilst a statute may offset the need for the *nobile officium* to be invoked in a particular area, it also provides a source of new material for equitable intervention when the statutory machinery breaks down. In other words, there is a continuing potential for omissions to manifest in statutes. Unless the *nobile officium* was to be statutorily abolished, the jurisdiction may be displaced rather than replaced by statute. The Scottish Law Commission stated with regard to judicial factors, for example, that the enactment of legislation would not necessarily supersede the powers of the court under the common law and the *nobile officium*. The court would retain a "residual ability" to "appoint judicial factors under the *nobile officium* where circumstances arose which had not been foreseen by legislation".[1] The jurisdiction therefore has an enduring supplementary role in marginal cases where the statutory machinery is deficient.

Second, although it has been argued that equitable norms may crystallise or metamorphose into common law norms, thus gradually moving cases out of the *nobile officium* and into the common law, this does not lead to a full depletion of the *nobile officium* caseload. The shift from a sense of equitable supplication to vindication of a common law right would be more likely to occur in recurring cases, such as in the area of trusts or bankruptcy. The miscellaneous cases, of which there are many, would be less likely to cultivate a sense that the *nobile officium* is a generator of enduring legal rights on which future parties can rely. This is particularly apposite because the natural caseload of the *nobile officium* is one of miscellaneous cases, and its historical role in particular areas of law where it served a recurring function is not necessarily true to the basic principles of the jurisdiction. The *nobile officium* should never have been routinely invoked in any area of law, and it is largely because of the less developed state of the law in prior times that it acquired such a function. Instead, the jurisdiction is most appropriately invoked with regard to the miscellaneous case, and that is surely an inexhaustible supply of material.

A third reason why the *nobile officium* remains relevant and important is that caution should be urged in assuming too readily that the jurisdiction is in terminal decline. The trend is not uniformly downward. It was written in 1856 that the *nobile officium* was, even then, "seldom mentioned now except with a sneer",[2] yet many cases of successful invocation followed and continue to the present day. The jurisdiction has seen periods of increased activity including in the twentieth century, and the *nobile officium* of the High Court became much more active in the

---

[1] *Discussion Paper on Judicial Factors* (Scot Law Com DP No 146, 2010) at 4.

[2] Cockburn, *Memorials of his time* at 128.

late twentieth century, despite being described as rarely invoked between the time of the institutional writers and the late 1960s.[3]

There may be several reasons for these trends, but the activity of the *nobile officium* must surely be affected by the extent to which practitioners are conversant with the jurisdiction. The existing literature on the *nobile officium* is minimal, and the jurisdiction appears not to feature to any significant extent in the legal curriculum or professional legal training. One wonders how many clients have been informed by their solicitors that there was no way of proceeding in a given case, when a petition to the *nobile officium* might have offered a remedy. In short, there is an issue with knowledge and understanding of the *nobile officium*, and this may have impacted the extent to which the jurisdiction has been active. This may also account for some of the clusters of petitions in particular areas that are seen in the case reports.

The *nobile officium* is unlikely to return to the substantive role it once played in particular areas of law, but it retains importance and potential in both the civil and criminal context. It has often been said that human law will inevitably be imperfect, and that if the law is firmly applied to its unqualified extent, courts of justice will soon become courts of injustice. The *nobile officium* retains its core utility in those marginal cases which are not adequately captured by the corpus of existing law. It permits the supreme courts to deliver justice when the strict law would not adequately do so; to reconcile the articulated law with the exceptional and the unforeseen. It acts as an extraordinary safety valve where the strict application of law would be unduly oppressive or excessive. The value and utility of the *nobile officium* should be measured by the nature, rather than the number, of cases transacted thereunder.

To adapt a well-known passage from Aristotle,[4] the essence of the *nobile officium* is to look to justice rather than the law; to the spirit rather than the letter; to the whole rather than the part; to what is right rather than what is mandated; to fairness rather than formalism. It is directed at the integrity of a fair, rather than

---

[3] Stoddart, "The *nobile officium* of the High Court" 1974 SLT (News) 37.

[4] Aristotle, *Rhetoric*, I.13.1374b, 17–18.

an absolutist, construction of the law. The certainty, stability and predictability of law demand that this is not carried too far, but there is little justice in a system of law which stubbornly insists of these qualities to their maximal extent. The *nobile officium* is an appropriately residual mechanism for upholding the ethical standards of the law in those exceptional cases where the law falls short. It narrows, in its own modest way, the gap between the "is" and the "ought"; between law and justice.

APPENDIX A

PROCEDURAL RULES

A. THE *NOBILE OFFICIUM* OF THE COURT OF SESSION

Rules of the Court of Session
Chapter 14 – Petitions

Application of this Chapter

14.1 Subject to any other provisions in these Rules, this Chapter applies to a petition presented to the court.

Applications by petition in the Outer House

14.2 Subject to any other provision in these Rules, the following applications to the court shall be made by petition presented in the Outer House:-

- (a) an application for the appointment of a judicial factor, a factor *loco absentis*, a factor pending litigation or a curator *bonis*;
- (b) an application for the appointment of a judicial factor on the estate of a partnership or joint adventure;
- (c) an application to the *nobile officium* of the court which relates to-
  - (i) the administration of a trust;
  - (ii) the office of trustee; or
  - (iii) a public trust;
- (d) a petition and complaint for breach of interdict;
- (e) an application to the supervisory jurisdiction of the court;
- (f) an application for suspension, suspension and interdict, and suspension and liberation;
- (g) an application to recall an arrestment or inhibition other than in a cause depending before the court;
- (h) a petition or other application under these Rules or any other enactment or rule of law; and
- (i) an application to the court in exercise of its *parens patriae* jurisdiction.

Applications by petition in the Inner House

14.3 Any of the following applications shall be made by petition presented in the Inner House:-

(a) a petition and complaint other than for breach of interdict;

(b) an application under any enactment relating to solicitors or notaries public;

(c) an application which is, by virtue of these Rules or any other enactment, to be by petition and is incidental to a cause depending before the Inner House;

(d) an application to the *nobile officium* of the court other than an application mentioned in rule 14.2(c) (applications relating to the administration of a trust, the office of trustee or a public trust);

(e) a petition by trustees for directions under Part II of Chapter 63;

(f) an application under section 1 of the Evidence (Proceedings in Other Jurisdictions) Act 1975 (assistance in obtaining evidence for civil proceedings in another jurisdiction);

(g) an application under section 1 of the Trusts (Scotland) Act 1961 (variation or revocation of trusts);

(h) an application under section 17(6), 18(7), 20(7), 20(11)(b), 21(5), 21(7) or 21(10) of, or under paragraph 20 of Schedule 1 to, the Law Reform (Miscellaneous Provisions) (Scotland) Act 1990 (orders in relation to conveyancing or executry practitioners); and

(i) an application required to be made to the Inner House under any enactment.

Form of petitions

14.4(1) A petition shall be in Form 14.4.

(2) A petition shall include-

(a) a statement of facts in numbered paragraphs setting out the facts and circumstances on which the petition is founded;

(b) a prayer setting out the orders sought; and

(c) the name, designation and address of the petitioner and a statement of any special capacity in which the defender is being sued.

(3) In a petition presented under an enactment, the statement of facts shall expressly refer to the relevant provision under the authority of which the petition is presented.

(4) Where a petition is one to which the Civil Jurisdiction and Judgments Act 1982 applies, the statement of facts shall include averments stating-

    (a) the ground of jurisdiction of the court, unless jurisdiction would arise only if the respondent prorogated the jurisdiction of the court without contesting jurisdiction;

    (b) unless the court has exclusive jurisdiction, whether or not there is an agreement prorogating the jurisdiction of a court in another country; and

    (c) whether or not there are proceedings involving the same cause of action in subsistence between the parties in a country to which the convention in Schedule 1 or 3C to that Act[1] applies and the date any such proceedings commenced.

(5) The prayer of a petition shall crave warrant for such intimation, service and advertisement as may be necessary having regard to the nature of the petition, or as the petitioner may seek; and the name, address and capacity of each person on whom service of the petition is sought shall be set out in a schedule annexed to, and referred to in, the prayer of the petition.

(6) Where it is sought in a petition-

    (a) to dispense with intimation, service or advertisement, or

    (b) to shorten or extend the period of notice,

the appropriate order shall be craved in the prayer, and the grounds on which the order is sought shall be set out in the statement of facts.

First order in petitions

14.5(1) Subject to paragraph (2), on a petition on being lodged, the court shall, without a motion being enrolled for that purpose, pronounce an interlocutor for such intimation, service and advertisement as may be necessary.

(2) Where a petitioner seeks-

---

[1] Schedule 1 to the Civil Jurisdiction and Judgments Act 1982 was substituted by SI 1990/2591 and Schedule 3C was inserted by the Civil Jurisdiction and Judgments Act 1991, s 1(3).

(a) to dispense with intimation, service or advertisement on any person, or

(b) any interim order,

he shall apply by motion for such order as appears appropriate.

(3) On disposing of a motion under paragraph (2), the court shall make such order as it thinks fit.

Period of notice for lodging answers

14.6(1) Subject to any other provision in these Rules, the period of notice for lodging answers to a petition shall be-

(a) in the case of service, intimation or advertisement within Europe, 21 days from whichever is the later of the date of execution of service, the giving of intimation or the publication of the advertisement;

(b) in the case of service or intimation furth of Europe under rule 16.2(2)(d) or (e) (service by an *huissier* etc or personally), 21 days from whichever is the later of the date of execution of service or the giving of intimation;

(c) in the case of service or intimation furth of Europe other than under sub-paragraph (b), or advertisement furth of Europe, 42 days from whichever is the later of the date of execution of service, the giving of intimation or the publication of the advertisement;

(d) in the case of service by advertisement under rule 16.5 (service where address of person is not known), 6 months from the date of publication of the advertisement.

(2) An application may be made by motion to shorten or extend the period of notice.

(3) Where a motion under paragraph (2) is made in a petition at the time that an order for intimation, service or advertisement is made under rule 14.5 (first order in petitions), the decision of the court on the motion shall be final and not subject to review.

Intimation and service of petitions

14.7(1) A petition shall be intimated-

(a) on the walls of the court; and

(b) in such other manner as the court thinks fit.

(2) A copy of the petition shall be served on every person, specified in the petition or by the court as a person on whom the petition is to be served, with a citation in Form 14.7 attached to it.

(3) A petition to the court in exercise of its *parens patriae* jurisdiction shall not be intimated on the walls of the court.

Procedure where answers lodged

14.8 Where answers to a petition have been lodged, the petitioner shall, within 28 days after the expiry of the period of notice, apply by motion for such further procedure as he seeks, and the court shall make such order for further procedure as it thinks fit.

Unopposed petitions

14.9(1) Subject to paragraph (2), where the period of notice has expired without answers being lodged, the court shall, on the motion of the petitioner, after such further procedure and inquiry into the grounds of the petition, if any, as it thinks fit, dispose of the petition.

(2) Where-

- (a) the prayer of the petition seeks an order directed against a person,
- (b) service of the petition has been made on that person furth of the United Kingdom under rule 16.2, and
- (c) such order has been granted without that person having lodged answers,

a certified copy of the interlocutor granting the order shall be served forthwith by the petitioner on that person.

(3) The court may, on the motion of a person to whom paragraph (2) applies, recall the interlocutor and allow answers to be lodged if-

- (a) that person-
  - (i) without any fault on his part, did not have knowledge of the petition in sufficient time to lodge answers;
  - (ii) has disclosed a prima facie answer to the petition on the merits; and
  - (iii) has enrolled the motion for recall within a reasonable time after he had knowledge of the petition; and
- (b) the motion is enrolled before the expiry of one year from the date of the interlocutor sought to be recalled.

(4) The recall of an interlocutor under paragraph (3) shall be without prejudice to the validity of anything already done or transacted, of any contract made or obligation incurred, or of any appointment made or power granted, in or by virtue of that interlocutor.

(5) The provisions of this rule are without prejudice to the power of the court to make any interim appointment or order at any stage of the cause.

Disposals in petitions

14.10(1) The court may make such order to dispose of a petition as it thinks fit, whether or not such order was sought in the petition.

(2) An order referred to in paragraph (1) is any order that could be made if sought in any action or petition.

Form 14.4

Form of petition

UNTO THE RIGHT HONOURABLE THE LORDS OF COUNCIL AND SESSION

The petition of [A.B.] (*name, designation and address of petitioner and statement of any special capacity in which the petitioner is presenting the petition*)

HUMBLY SHEWETH:-

1. That (*here set out in this and following numbered paragraphs the facts and circumstances which form the grounds of petition*).

MAY IT THEREFORE please your Lordships to (insert prayer)

According to Justice, etc.

(*Signed*)

(*Backing of petition*)

THE COURT OF SESSION

The Petition

of

[A.B.]

for

(*here describe shortly the nature or object of the petition*).

(*Name of firm of agent for petitioner*)

Form 14.7

Form of citation in petition

CITATION

Date: (*date of posting or other method of service*)

To: (*name and address of person on whom petition served*)

IN HER MAJESTY's NAME AND AUTHORITY, and in the name and authority of Lord (*name*), I (*name of agent*), solicitor [*or* person having a right to conduct the litigation], for (*name of pursuer*) [*or* (*name of messenger-at-arms*), messenger-at-arms] serve the attached petition and interlocutor of the court on you.

The interlocutor requires you, if so advised, to lodge answers to the petition.

If you intend to lodge answers to the petition you must lodge them at the Office of Court, Court of Session, 2 Parliament Square, Edinburgh, EH1 1RQ within [21] days after the date of service on you of the petition. The date of service is the date stated at the top of this citation unless service has been by post in which case the date of service is the day after that date.

IF YOU ARE UNCERTAIN ABOUT THE EFFECT OF THIS CITATION, you should consult a solicitor, Citizens Advice Bureau or other local advice agency or adviser immediately.

(*Signed*)

Messenger-at-arms
[*or* Solicitor [*or* Agent] for petitioner]
 (*Address*)

B. THE *NOBILE OFFICIUM* OF THE HIGH COURT OF JUSTICIARY

Criminal Procedure (Scotland) Act 1995

298A Intimation of bills and of petitions to the *nobile officium*[2]

(1) This subsection applies where the prosecutor requires to intimate to the respondent—

(a) a bill of advocation;

(b) a petition to the *nobile officium*; or

(c) an order of the High Court relating to such a bill or (as the case may be) petition.

(2) Where subsection (1) above applies, the requirement may be met by serving on the respondent or the respondent's solicitor a copy of the bill, petition or (as the case may be) order.

(3) Service under subsection (2) above may (in relation to any proceedings) be effected—

(a) on the respondent, in the same manner as citation under section 141 of this Act;

(b) on the respondent's solicitor, by post.

(4) This subsection applies where a person requires to intimate to the prosecutor—

(a) a bill of suspension or advocation;

(b) a petition to the *nobile officium*; or

(c) an order of the High Court relating to such a bill or (as the case may be) petition.

(5) Where subsection (4) above applies, the requirement may be met by serving on the prosecutor a copy of the bill, petition or (as the case may be) order.

(6) Service under subsection (5) above may (in relation to any proceedings) be effected by post.

(7) It is sufficient evidence that service has been effected under subsection (3) or (6) above if there is produced a written execution—

---

[2] As amended by the Criminal Proceedings etc (Reform) (Scotland) Act 2007, and the Criminal Proceedings etc (Reform) (Scotland) Act 2007 (Commencement No 2 and Transitional Provisions and Savings) Order 2007 (as amended).

(a) in the form prescribed by Act of Adjournal or as nearly as may be in such form; and

(b) signed by the person who effected service.

(8) In relation to service effected by means of registered post or the recorded delivery service, the relevant post office receipt requires to be produced along with the execution mentioned in subsection (7) above.

(9) A party who has service effected under subsection (3) or (6) above must, as soon as practicable thereafter, lodge with the Clerk of Justiciary a copy of the execution mentioned in subsection (7) above.

(10) For the purpose of subsection (3)(a) above, section 141 of this Act is to be read with such modifications as are necessary for its application in the circumstances.

(11) This section is without prejudice to any rule of law or practice by virtue of which things of the kinds mentioned in subsections (1) and (4) above (including copies) may be intimated or served.

Act of Adjournal (Criminal Procedure Rules) 1996 (SI 1996/513) Schedule 2

Chapter 29A – Service of Bills of Advocation and Suspension and Petitions to the *Nobile Officium*

Service of bill or petition

29A (1) Where a first order for service is sought in relation to—

(a) a bill of advocation;

(b) a bill of suspension; or

(c) a petition to the *nobile officium*,

the complainer or petitioner shall provide two copies of the bill or petition when presenting it to the Clerk of Justiciary for registration.

(2) Where a first order for service is granted, the Clerk of Justiciary shall provide the complainer or petitioner with a certified copy of—

(a) the bill or petition; and

(b) the interlocutor granting first order for service.

(3) The complainer or petitioner shall serve the certified copy of the bill or petition and interlocutor on the respondent.

(4) Where a bill or petition arises from proceedings in a lower court, the Clerk of Justiciary shall intimate a copy to that court.

Chapter 31 – References to the European Court of Justice

Proceedings on appeal etc

31.4 (1) Where a question is raised in the High Court in any proceedings on appeal or on a petition for the exercise of the *nobile officium*, the court shall proceed to make a reference.

(2) In paragraph (1), the reference to proceedings on appeal is a reference to proceedings on appeal under the Act of 1995 or on appeal by bill of suspension, bill of advocation or otherwise.

Appeals against references

31.7[3] (1) Subject to paragraph (2), where an order making a reference is made under rule 31.4 (proceedings on appeal etc.), any party to the proceedings who is aggrieved by the order may, within 14 days after the date of the order, appeal against the order to the High Court sitting as a court of appeal.

(2) Paragraph (1) shall not apply to such an order made in proceedings in the High Court sitting as a court of appeal or in proceedings on petition to that court for the exercise of its *nobile officium*.

---

[3] See *Renton and Brown's Criminal Procedure* at paras 37-08 and 37-08.1.

APPENDIX B

STATISTICS

Figures on the *nobile officium* were obtained from the Scottish Court Service. These were available from 2000 for the Court of Session, and from 2004 for the High Court of Justiciary.[1] They give a contemporary overview of the extent of the activity of the *nobile officium*, and the extent to which petitions are successful.[2]

The figures indicate that the *nobile officium* of the High Court is now more active than that of the Court of Session, but that the number of petitions presented to the *nobile officium* of the High Court has almost halved over the past decade. From 2004 (the first year from which figures are available for both courts) to 2013 inclusive, 21 petitions were presented to the Court of Session, in contrast to 252 petitions presented to the High Court. The Court of Session granted 14 petitions from 2004 to 2013 inclusive, whilst the High Court granted 70 petitions across the same period.

However, it is worth noting that in every year since 2004, less than half the petitions presented to the *nobile officium* of the High Court have been successful. From 2004, from which figures are available for both courts, 27.7% of petitions presented to the High Court were successful, whilst 66.7% of petitions presented to the Court of Session were successful.

---

[1] The figures for 2014 are omitted as they were available for only part of the year.

[2] It was reported in *The Scotsman* on 20 January 1903 (p 6) that during the year ending 31 December 1901, there were 35 petitions to the *nobile officium* of the Court of Session, 26 of which were presented to the First Division, and nine to the Second Division

1. *Nobile officium* of the Court of Session

Year	Petitions presented	Petitions granted	Percentage of petitions successful
2000	5	2	40.00%
2001	3	0	0.00%
2002	5	2	40.00%
2003	4	1	25.00%
2004	0	0	N/A
2005	3	2	66.67%
2006	1	0	0.00%
2007	6	5	83.33%
2008	1	1	100.00%
2009	3	1	33.33%
2010	0	0	N/A
2011	3	2	66.67%
2012	1	1	100.00%
2013	3	2	66.67%

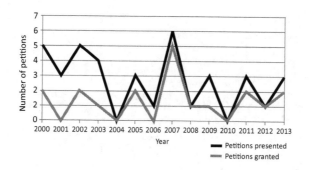

2. *Nobile officium* of the High Court of Justiciary

Year	Petitions presented	Petitions granted	Percentage of petitions successful
2004	44	16	36.36%
2005	36	12	33.33%
2006	27	13	48.15%
2007	11	5	45.45%
2008	34	8	23.53%
2009	29	5	17.24%
2010	20	3	15.00%
2011	24	5	20.83%
2012	10	1	10.00%
2013	17	2	11.76%

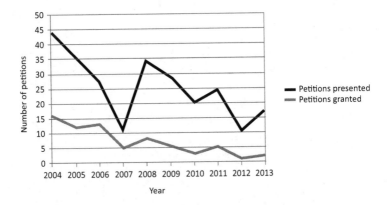

Notes provided by Scottish Court Service:

- Records from 2004 to 2006 are not computerised; data obtained from examining paper records.
- Paper records for 2007 disclosed that a number of petitions were incorporated into the computerised Case Management System (CMS) and are therefore included in the 2008 figures.[3]
- Records from 2008 are held on the CMS and data was established from Miscellaneous Appeal type filtered by Petition to the *Nobile Officium*.

---

[3] The figures for 2008 may therefore be overstated.

INDEX